ANGELA CARTER: WRITING FROM THE FRONT LINE

Sarah Gamble

EDINBURGH UNIVERSITY PRESS

In memory of Mark

© Sarah Gamble, 1997

Edinburgh University Press
22 George Square, Edinburgh

Typeset in Caslon
by Pioneer Associates, Perthshire, and
printed and bound in Great Britain
by The Cromwell Press

A CIP record for this book is available from
the British Library

ISBN 0 7486 0851 6

CONTENTS

ACKNOWLEDGEMENTS

The stereotype of the solitary scholar is all very well, but I now know from experience that it is impossible to write a book on your own. So thanks are therefore due to many people, including Jackie Jones of Edinburgh University Press, for all her help, and the University of Sunderland for allowing me sabbatical time in which to write. Thanks also to my colleagues at the Department of English Studies, especially Professor Stuart Sim, who gave me advice on how to prepare my original proposal for the consideration of Edinburgh University Press. My gratitude to Dr David Amigoni of the University of Keele, for reading much of the original manuscript, and to Dr Bryan Burns of the University of Sheffield, for introducing me to Carter's work in the first place, and for providing me both with ideas and material for this book. Very special thanks indeed to my mother, for her invaluable help with childcare and housework. And lastly, but by no means least, to Tabitha, for putting up with a parent who has spent most of the last few months either reading, writing or lost in thought.

INTRODUCTION

Since her death in 1992, Angela Carter's reputation has passed into academic urban legend. The story goes that, among the requests for grants for doctoral study received by the British Academy in the academic year 1992–3, there were 40 proposals to study Carter's work: more – and this is the punch-line – than the Academy received for the entire eighteenth century. Although I retrieved the above facts and figures from Paul Barker's 1995 article on Carter, 'The Return of the Magic Story-Teller', the story itself had already assumed quasi-folkloric status in the English Literature departments of university campuses long before he reproduced it in *The Independent on Sunday*.[1] But what moves this anecdote into the realm of folklore is the way in which, even while its overall message remains the same, the exact details of the story vary depending on the teller. A few months after Barker's piece, *Observer Life* magazine also published an article on Carter, in which Nicci Gerrard repeats Barker's assertion of her celebrity status, although this time she is reported as having overtaken Virginia Woolf in the student popularity stakes.

Indeed, the very fact that such stories are related in the context of an article in a Sunday supplement (albeit a 'quality' Sunday supplement) rather than the academic press in itself indicates Angela Carter's growing popularity among general readers. While both articles cover more or less the same ground, both are accessible assessments of Carter's career which, unhampered by academic jargon, have doubtless been instrumental in furthering the process of Carter's posthumous (re)discovery.

It is tragic that Carter died before attaining her present level of fame, and it is a tragic irony that it was probably the one that, at least partly, made the other possible. As Nicci Gerrard observes, the death of any author transforms her body of work into an '*oeuvre*, ready for academic

1

discussion and instant reappraisal',[2] and this general truism is particularly apposite when applied to Carter. Formidably well-read in literature and theory, she tended to anticipate critical responses to her work in a way that is distinctly disconcerting to the critic; Harriet Gilbert, in a review of a collection of essays on Carter, summed it up when she wrote that 'the problem facing anyone who attempts to assess Carter's *oeuvre* is that she has usually got there first'.[3] She certainly took a lot of keeping up with, for her body of work was consistently increasing and ever-varying. In the course of her career, Angela Carter wrote novels, short stories, plays, academic articles and pieces of cultural commentary. She loved to upset expectations, outrage convention and challenge preconceptions, which meant that the only thing she could be relied upon to do was the unexpected.

It would be inaccurate, however, to suggest that Carter was wholly ignored in her lifetime, because she wasn't. Furthermore, more often than not, the fluctuations in the progress of her career were at least partially self-induced. She certainly enjoyed her popularity when it came, and steadfastly maintained that there was no point in writing unless one made money out of it, but she was not the kind of writer who developed a winning formula and stuck with it. When she began writing in the 1960s she looked set for early success, winning two major literary prizes in as many years. In 1967, she won the John Llewellyn Rhys prize with only her second novel, *The Magic Toyshop*, and her third, *Several Perceptions*, won the Somerset Maugham Award in 1968. However, instead of capitalising on her burgeoning reputation, Carter then took herself off to Japan from 1969 to 1972. Her geographical distance from the British literary scene was only compounded by what she chose to write: her novels written over this period, including *The Infernal Desire Machines of Doctor Hoffman* and *The Passion of New Eve*, remain among her most shocking and experimental, and received a very lukewarm reception on their publication.

It was not until the late 1970s and early 1980s that Angela Carter's reputation began to extend much beyond a small circle of *cognoscenti*. Her collection of subversively rewritten fairy tales, *The Bloody Chamber*, gained widespread attention, all the more so when one story, 'The Company of Wolves', was made into a film in 1984 directed by Neil Jordan. There was much controversy when Carter's penultimate novel, *Nights at the Circus*, was not placed on the Booker Prize shortlist in the same year, indicating how far she had progressed from the days when her work was virtually ignored by a wider reading public.

Academic critiques of Carter's writing also began to appear during this time, both capitalising on her ever-growing popularity and furthering it. Carter, through her work teaching creative writing in universities both at home and abroad, made many friends in academia, as well as in the publishing world, and it is these who have led the way in developing a substantial body of criticism on her work. The pre-eminent critic in this area of literary research at the time of writing is Lorna Sage, whose first interview with Carter, published in 1977, probably constitutes the first published academic assessment of her work. Sage is also the author of a study of Carter's writing published in the Northcote House 'Writers and Their Work' series, and the editor of a volume of essays, *Flesh and the Mirror: Essays on the Art of Angela Carter*. However, criticism on Carter's work is widespread and ever-growing, although with the exception of Sage's study, it has taken the form of essays, reviews and conference papers rather than book-length studies.

The growing interest in Angela Carter's writing within the academy has led to the inclusion of her work on various courses, not only to do with literature but also with cultural studies and women's studies, which is where this particular book comes in. Although I would hope that it does not exclude the well-informed general reader, it is aimed primarily at a student audience who wish to gain some knowledge of Carter's career and the dominant themes and concerns within her work as a whole. As such, my discussion is general rather than specific, wide-ranging rather than narrowly focused. I have included analysis of all of Carter's published books, both novels and collections of short stories, as well as a substantial amount of her non-fiction, including her most controversial piece of feminist polemic, *The Sadeian Woman*. I have also attempted to give the reader some indication of the current state of criticism on Carter's work.

However, any critical study, no matter how broad, must have a specific agenda. My main area of concern in this discussion, in accordance with Edward Said's contention that 'every literary text is in some way burdened with its occasion, with the plain empirical realities from which it emerged',[4] is with charting the way in which Carter was constantly interacting with the cultural environment within which she wrote. I intend to argue that she did not do so in such a way as to integrate herself and her writing into the mainstream: on the contrary, she was primarily concerned with maintaining a sceptical, interrogatory position on the periphery of dominant cultural attitudes and conventions.

I think there is a wealth of evidence to suggest that Carter regarded such a position as an extremely empowering one, and her construction of both herself as writing subject and what she wrote as 'marginal' was crucial to the progression of her career. By 'marginal' in this context, I mean that she regarded herself as operating from the edge of consensus views of any kind; specifically, the conception of history as 'grand' or 'master' narrative,[5] conventional social codes regulating propriety and 'women's place', and the categorisation of any cultural product, especially literature, into 'high' and 'low' forms.

Carter linked this cultivation of the sceptical, marginal view to feminism and socialism, both doctrines she espoused, but even there she avoided integration into the mainstream of these movements. Her relationship with feminist critics and women's studies departments, for example, was an extremely ambivalent one. One of the most controversial areas of her work as far as feminists are concerned is both her apparent support for pornography, and her graphic depictions of violence against women in her writing, which have led some critics to conclude that, in spite of the feminist opinions she began expressing from the late 1960s onwards, she actually only furthers reactionary portrayals of women as nothing more than the objects of male desire.

Carter, however, took nothing, not even feminism, at face value. Instead, both her fiction and non-fiction writing showed her constantly pushing at, testing, the boundaries of any received belief system. 'I'm all for putting new wine in old bottles', she famously proclaimed in 1983, 'especially if the pressure of the new wine makes the old bottle explode'.[6] The kind of insouciant anarchism implicit in such statements shows Carter in her favourite role; as a kind of cultural saboteur, using her writing to blow up comfortable assumptions and habitual patterns of thought. Her fictions act as shattered mirrors through which her readers can still see themselves, but fragmented, refracted, multiple and startlingly defamiliarised.

It was this impulse that remained constant throughout her career, and which motivated the many changes in the way she wrote and in what she wrote about. To quote Carter again,

> once you become conscious, your position – however many there are of you – isn't the standard one . . . you have to keep on defining the ground on which you're standing, because you are in fact setting yourself up in opposition to the generality.[7]

Angela Carter's career as a whole can be viewed as an extended exercise in conscious redefinition, not only of her own cultural environment, but also of her own response to it. Setting yourself against convention is all very well, but Carter was also not unaware of the dangers inherent in the cultivation of a marginalised position or perspective. The trouble is, of course, that existing on the peripheries of anything involves performing an extremely delicate balancing act between inclusion and exclusion, and this is echoed in the way Carter's fiction persistently concerns itself with the evocation of boundaries and borderlines, precariously suspending itself at the very point at which one state, condition, place or mode merges into another.

In terms of form, her fiction resists the way in which postmodernism renders reality itself just another meta-narrative; but it isn't quite realism either. Categorising Carter's chosen mode of writing is made additionally difficult because of the fact that throughout her career, her narratives constantly negotiate and adjust their position on the margins of a variety of literary genres and forms. In his discussion of Carter's work in *Post-War British Fiction: Realism and After*, Andrzej Gąsiorek describes Carter's fiction as oscillating

> betwixt and between fantasy and analysis, allegory and rationalism. Her texts are deliberately aporetic, not only because they refuse decisive forms of closure, but also because they refuse to opt finally for one of these two discourses, thereby repressing the other. Carter's form neither implies that carnival and fantasy can suffice nor suggests that rationalism and critique be eschewed; rather, it urges a view of the novel as a composite form in which both kinds of discourse supplement one another, allowing the writer a fuller apprehension of reality.[8]

Gąsiorek, note, does not doubt Carter's belief in a reality capable of being apprehended, and neither do I. It is, however, sometimes difficult in her writing to pinpoint the moment where her narrative games end and an engagement with reality begins. In the context of this discussion, however, I find Linda Hutcheon's conception of 'historiographic metafiction' particularly useful, which she describes as 'always assert[ing] that the world is resolutely fictive and yet undeniably historical'.[9] While it problematises the nature of the real, therefore, historiographic metafiction does not discount the importance of the historical process, and thus it is a mode in which two 'views of history – as intertextual and as extratextual – appear to co-exist and operate in tension'.[10]

The content of Angela Carter's fiction, too, tends to be similarly predicated on tension, for she consistently uses it to celebrate borderline states and conditions of being. She is fascinated, for example, by the blurring of gender boundaries; by adolescence, that brief period when the subject is not quite a child, but also not yet adult; with the period of suspension between departure and destination which constitutes a journey; with the moment when the season or the millennium is caught at the instant of change. The settings of her fiction are also characteristically liminal, the dance-halls and toyshops of her early fiction giving way to the cinema and the fairground, the music-hall and the theatre. All are places of display and artifice, in which the extravagance of the illusion disguises the very hard work that goes into its maintenance.

In her essay 'Framing Marginality: Distinguishing the Textual Politics of the Marginal Voice', Sneja Gunew discusses the possibilities and limitations inherent in the act of speaking from the margins; issues Carter was constantly working through in her writing. Although Gunew agrees that 'the margin constitutes the place of transgression, which in turn subverts hegemonic discourses',[11] she is also concerned with problematising the kind of view, expressed by such theorists as Bakhtin and Kristeva, that the margin is a kind of utopian space of ultimate possibility. She claims that the dominant centre 'desires the existence of the marginal'[12] because

> The textual productions of marginal minorities exist to confirm hegemonic textualities. And these minority writings have been in general homogenised as the area of plurality, disruption, closure, deferred meaning and process; in other words, as affirming the dynamism of the centre and its ability to accommodate change – change which is safely contained.[13]

For Gunew, the problem intrinsic to writing from the margins is that it is almost impossible to do so without initiating a simplistic process of reversing binary oppositions, a reversal which can only ever be temporarily satisfying, since it lasts only as long as the moment of reading: 'There is a moment of ambivalent satisfaction in recognising their own marginality reconstructed as the dominant term . . . But the moment is fleeting, because neither for women nor migrants is there any lasting political advantage in merely reversing the old oppositions.'[14] What Angela Carter shares with Gunew is the realisation that such a process of simple reversal isn't enough, and this is what motivates her attempts to maintain a balance between the 'fantastic' and the 'real' in her work; a narrative strategy described by Andrzej Gąsiorek as walking 'the tightrope between carnivalesque fantasy and rational critique'.[15] Too close to the centre, and one runs the danger of being claimed by it: too far away, and one runs the risk of becoming an unheard voice crying in the metaphorical wilderness. Indeed, Carter's fictions are haunted by this fear, which is the fear of going too far, of losing touch with reality and disappearing completely into the world of the text or of performance. Deeper than that, it flirts with the fear of the loss of the independent, autonomous self who is capable of acting as historical or political agent within the empirical realm.

That such uncertainty extends even to the writing self is my major preoccupation in the first section of this book, which examines that writing of Carter's which could be termed 'autobiographical'. Essays by Carter covering a variety of topics are to be found in numerous books and journals, and amongst these articles, essays and reviews, which demonstrate the eclecticism which is so striking a characteristic of her fiction, are some references to her own family history and to important events in her life which shaped her as a writer. Carter's study of family photographs and family history, however, is diametrically opposed to the notion of autobiography as self-disclosure. Like Annette Kuhn, Carter obviously believed that identity is to a great extent mediated through the construction of narrative, to the extent that 'Telling stories about the past . . . is a key moment in the making of our selves';[16] however, she is not engaged in the kind of revelatory process implicit in what Kuhn terms 'memory work'.[17] The boundaries between 'fact' and 'fiction' blur in Carter's autobiographical writings, causing a rupture in the seamless relationship between real and implied author. The personal history Carter constructs through such texts is tenuous – in her words, 'true, but not strictly accurate'[18] – and they thus become the means by which she dramatises the constructed nature of subjectivity.

Angela Carter's exploration of subjectivity is one of the major strands in the discussion which follows the first section, which I break down into three subsequent parts. Each section examines Carter's work in relationship to the decade in which it was written, and the differing ways in which she configures the fact/fiction interface in a way that consistently keeps her at a tangential relationship with the 'real'.

I begin by looking at her writing of the 1960s, in accordance with my belief that a consideration of the cultural environment of this decade must act as a basis for any examination of Carter's work. With their persistent references to music, fashion and lifestyle, her early novels are very obviously products of the sixties, a period in which the concept of the counterculture was in the ascendant. As I will discuss, this was a movement which Carter later claimed to have espoused enthusiastically, and in spite of her subsequent disillusionment, the notion of acting against the dominant culture was one which stayed with her.

The counterculture, which offered the seductive chance of a completely new start unencumbered by the burden of history, is recreated in her novels through constant references to a camp aesthetic, in which everything – including, perhaps, the self – is made, rather than accepted as either natural or inevitable. In this context, the past is no more than debris to be picked over and eclectically reassembled according to the whim of the individual. The texts themselves conform to this pattern, built out of references to a variety of other texts, drawn from both 'high' and 'low' literary forms. This kind of breezy disrespect towards the concept of cultural value is personified in the dandy, the recurring dominant, or emblematic, subject in Carter's writing at this time. While his is not the controlling point of view in the text, for he never assumes the role of narrator, he nevertheless dominates it by functioning as the object of its compulsive fascination. Always male, he is the self-created being who exists for nothing but display, and in whom all the paradoxes of a constructed subjectivity are incarnated. In playing games with the state of being itself, the dandy raises the spectre of the empty self whose gaudy façade is no eccentric decoration, but perhaps a practice which is vital to his very existence in the world.

I then proceed to discuss Carter's retreat in the seventies, not only from the optimism of the sixties, but also from European culture itself. This is the period in which she claimed that her time in Japan was paradoxically responsible for both stimulating her fascination with the graphic extremism of pornographic forms and awakening her feminist consciousness. Over this decade, her fiction was increasingly self-reflexive and experimental, and also deliberately courted controversy. The dandy modulates into a new, far darker, emblematic subject, a creature who possesses the dandy's compulsion for display, but combines it with a soul-destroying self-centredness which negates the possibility of any other way of being. The utter egocentricity possessed by such figures gives them the potential to suck reality itself into their orbit, enabling them to rearrange it according to their own design.

However, the fictions which Carter wrote over this period, in spite of their extreme self-reflexiveness, engage with the world of the 'real' more radically than before. The picaresque is Carter's favoured form in her writing of the seventies, in which the narrative action takes the form of a kaleidoscopic process of endless change and repatterning, and the conclusive act of arrival is postponed for as long as possible. Weighing up the relative merits of fantasy and reality, the figures within these fictions eventually either reluctantly opt for reality, history and a life beyond the text, or pass beyond the scope of the author's imagination into a future incapable of being represented within the boundaries of discourse.

The final section is concerned with Carter's writing of the eighties and early nineties, in which her fiction became much more accessible, gentler and more humorous. For the first time, the emblematic subject not only assumes the role of narrator, but is also emphatically female. These are texts in which the heroines, now fully-rounded distinctive characters, write their own autobiographies, taking as many liberties with the notion of reality as their author.

The concept of 'story', particularly of the autobiographical story, gains a new importance in these later texts, where it is envisaged as a way in which both the world and the subject's place within it can be ordered. One of the things Carter emphasises in her writing about her own family is the inherent unknowablity of people, even those closest to you. Story, therefore, becomes a way to close the gap, and the exercise of the imagination a means by which bonds between individuals can be forged. But there's a paradox here, for although such a view suggests that our views of the world are textually-mediated, in Carter's case that isn't the same as saying there is no world outside of the text. On the contrary, her characteristically metafictional approach is muted by sincere appeals to an extra-textual world in which love is possible, and death is a certainty. Consequently, these texts anatomise the nature of the illusion and of story even while they celebrate them; addicted to performance, they nevertheless also know exactly where all the ropes and pulleys are.

In a study such as this, which assesses a writer's career in relation to both personal and cultural events, the inclusion of biographical detail is inevitable. However, it is important to stress that this book in no way sets out to become a biography. Unlike many academics now writing on Carter, such as Lorna Sage and Marina Warner, who knew her personally, I have no personal insights to offer. Although I have talked with friends of hers in the course of my research, my own contact with Carter herself is limited to one brief meeting in the mid-1980s, while studying for my doctorate. Instead, I would echo Sage's statement that

'Taking into account the writer's life doesn't mean that you have to reinvent your subject as a "real" person',[19] and maintain that what I am attempting to do is to examine Carter's life and career through a study of her own writing in which, ever the slippery subject, Carter creates an authorial persona for herself which does not necessarily have to correspond with actuality in every particular.

Notes

1. Paul Barker, 'The Return of the Magic Story-Teller', *The Independent on Sunday* (8 January 1995), pp. 14, 16.
2. Nicci Gerrard, 'Angela Carter Is Now More Popular than Virginia Woolf . . .', *Observer Life* (9 July 1995), pp. 20, 22–3 (p. 20).
3. Harriet Gilbert, 'Gothic Novelty', *The Guardian* (13 September 1994), p. 14.
4. Edward W. Said, *The World, The Text and The Critic* (London: Faber & Faber, 1984), p. 35.
5. These terms are drawn from Jean-François Lyotard, *The Postmodern Condition: A Report on Knowledge* (Manchester: Manchester University Press, 1984).
6. Angela Carter, 'Notes from the Front Line', in Michelene Wandor (ed.), *On Gender and Writing* (London: Pandora Press, 1983), pp. 69–77 (p. 69).
7. John Haffenden, 'Magical Mannerist', *The Literary Review* (November 1984), pp. 34–8 (p. 38).
8. Andrzej Gąsiorek, *Post-War British Fiction: Realism and After* (London: Edward Arnold, 1995), p. 135.
9. Linda Hutcheon, *A Poetics of Postmodernism: History, Theory, Fiction* (London: Routledge, 1988), p. 142.
10. ibid., p. 143.
11. Sneja Gunew, 'Framing Marginality: Distinguishing the Textual Politics of the Marginal Voice', *Southern Review* 18 (July 1985), pp. 142–56 (p. 144).
12. ibid., p. 143.
13. ibid., pp. 142–3.
14. ibid., p. 155.
15. Gąsiorek, p. 126.
16. Annette Kuhn, *Family Secrets: Acts of Memory and Imagination* (London: Verso, 1995), p. 2.
17. ibid., p. 3.
18. Angela Carter, 'The Mother Lode', in *Nothing Sacred: Selected Writings* (London: Virago Press, 1982), pp. 3–19 (p. 4).
19. Lorna Sage, *Angela Carter* (Plymouth: Northcote House, 1994), p. 4.

I
Autobiography and Anonymity

CHAPTER 1

The chatty, colloquial tone which Carter employs in most of her auto-biographical writings is deceptive, conning you into thinking that you're getting to know her. In fact, it is unclear as to how far such pieces can be used as a way of learning about the facts of their author's life, for her apparent disingenuousness functions as a strategy which allows for concealment and evasion. Carter chose to elaborate in detail only on certain episodes in her life: her childhood and her time in Japan – and those only to a certain extent. It is striking that, when questioned about her life, Carter tended to repeat almost word for word the content of the essays discussed here. Proclaiming, as she did in interview in 1984, that 'all attempts at autobiography are fraught with self-deceit and narcissism',[1] it appears that she chose what she wished to make public with care, creating a carefully contrived story to which she did not add spontaneously, in interview or anywhere else.

I would therefore argue that Carter is no more and no less definitively 'present' in her supposedly 'autobiographical' writings than she is any-where else in her fiction. Far from telling a straightforward account of her origins, these essays correspond to her authorial agenda as a whole; the creation of open-ended texts accessible to a multiplicity of readings within which the author no longer occupies a central position. Lorna Sage argues that the Barthesean concept of the 'Death of the Author' was very attractive to Carter for the precise reason that it renders the writer anonymous. 'Meaning' in the literary text is no longer tied down to the intentions of an implied author; it becomes 'an action in language, not an act of intended meaning . . . Its resources are a per-petual motion of signifying possibilities.'[2]

However, while Carter's autobiographical essays do not give us a great deal of reliable information about her life, they do relate directly to an understanding of her fiction. She herself maintained the existence

13

of a connection between life and art was obvious – in an interview published in *The Literary Review* in 1984, for example, she claimed to 'write about the conditions of my life, as everyone does. You write from your own history'.[3]

The key term here is 'history'. Although her work is distinguished by its rejection of naturalism, Carter nevertheless staunchly upholds history as a concept, which necessarily includes a commitment to the notion of a material reality which exists beyond the text. The conditions of that reality influence the actions and the beliefs of the individual, whose decisions in turn affect historical causation. Carter claimed to write from the perspective of 'an absolute and committed materialism – i.e., that this world is all that there is, and in order to question the nature of reality one must move from a strongly grounded base in what constitutes reality'.[4]

Carter's autobiographical writings, however, might seem to contradict such a statement for, far from 'mov[ing] from a strongly grounded base in what constitutes reality', they appear dedicated to destabilising both authorial identity and her place within a stable, discernible, reality. In one of Carter's last novels, *Nights at the Circus*, the question which reverberates through the text in relation to its central character is 'Is she fact or is she fiction?'. One might well ask the same question about the first-person narrator of Carter's autobiographical essays, all of which, to a greater or lesser extent, consciously foreground the contradiction between the 'real' and the 'imagined' inherent in all autobiography. As Shari Benstock, for example, points out in her essay 'Authorizing the Autobiographical',

> [autobiography] reveals gaps, and not only gaps in time and space or between the individual and the social, but also a widening divergence between the manner and matter of its discourse. That is, autobiography reveals the impossibility of its own dream: what begins on the presumption of self-knowledge ends in the creation of a fiction that covers over the premises of its construction.[5]

As a result, 'history', rather than being a monolithic process, is rendered mutable and polysemous, and thus is opened out to allow the expression of multiple, even contradictory, perspectives. In Carter's words, 'everything is relative – you see the world differently from different places. . . . Everything is determined by different circumstances.'[6]

Rita Felski sees the kind of 'blurring of the distinction between autobiography and fiction' in which Carter is engaged as specifically characteristic of feminist literature, which 'exemplifies the intersection between the autobiographical imperative to communicate the truth of unique individuality, and the feminist concern with the representative and intersubjective elements of women's experience'.[7] This statement both is and is not applicable to Carter's work. In her most well-known feminist apologia, 'Notes from the Front Line', Carter unequivocally asserted the importance of feminism to both her life and her work: 'The Woman's Movement has been of immense importance to me personally, and I would regard myself as a feminist writer, because I'm a feminist in everything else and one can't compartmentalise these things in one's life'.[8]

However, she was suspicious of the concept of an undifferentiated, collective, female identity. While 'the notion of a universality of human experience is a confidence trick', she wrote in her ironically entitled 'Polemical Preface' to *The Sadeian Woman*, 'the notion of a universality of female experience is a clever confidence trick'.[9] As these essays demonstrate, she was no radical separatist, but a firm believer that the oppressive myths which freeze women into the passive representatives of what, in *The Sadeian Woman*, she termed 'false universals',[10] affect 'men much more than women, because women know in their hearts that they're not true'.[11]

In a perverse way, therefore, women become privileged through the very experience of oppression, for it inspires them to question, in Carter's words, 'how that social fiction of my "femininity" was created, by means outside my control, and palmed off on me as the real thing'.[12] In other words, the very experience of marginalisation in itself challenges the centre's claim to possess ultimate truth. In all her autobiographical writings, whether they were about her experiences in Japan or her childhood, Carter consistently represents herself as existing on the cultural margins, not only because of her gender, but also her cultural inheritance and, in the case of Japan, her race.

Carter's preoccupation with both marginal identity and marginal forms is nowhere more evident than in her writings which came out of her two years in Japan. The very fact that she went at all showed her unwillingness to become part of the 'establishment'. By then she had worked as a journalist (where her career was somewhat hampered by 'a demonic inaccuracy as regards fact'),[13] married, gained a degree in English from the University of Bristol, and written three novels in three years: *Shadow Dance* (1966), *The Magic Toyshop* (1967) and *Several Perceptions* (1968).

Instead of capitalising on her burgeoning reputation, however, she did the unexpected – she removed herself from both a failing marriage and the British literary scene. The Somerset Maugham Award for *Several Perceptions* gave her the money to travel, so, believing that a writer should get 'out and about and around',[14] she went to Japan and remained there for two years. Although she continued to publish novels – *Heroes and Villains* was published in 1969, *Love* in 1971, and *The Infernal Desire Machines of Doctor Hoffman*, which was written while in Japan, in 1972 – she also ventured into the field of non-fiction, publishing articles about Japan in *New Society*. Consequently, says Paul Barker, 'after her pyrotechnic start, she didn't get much notice. She was probably known to more readers through her essays than through her novels'.[15]

In the long term, though, her years in Japan provided Carter with new insights which energised her writing for years afterwards: Lorna Sage, indeed, categorises it as 'the place where she lost and found herself'.[16] At the very moment when, through marriage, education, and career, she could have been assimilated into the mainstream, she chose to resituate herself on the periphery of another, overwhelmingly alien, culture, and the essays she wrote while in Japan show her actively celebrating the possibilities of marginalisation in both form and subject-matter.

An Oriental culture offered Carter the experience of alienation writ large. According to her, one of the valuable lessons she learned while in Japan was 'an involuntary apprenticeship in the interpretation of signs'. '[S]ince I kept on trying to learn Japanese, and kept on failing to do so, I started trying to understand things by simply looking at them very, very carefully.'[17]

Although in Japan her very difference from the norm rendered her an absolute spectacle, it also guaranteed her absolute anonymity. As she wrote in 'A Souvenir of Japan': 'I had never been so absolutely the mysterious other. I had become a kind of phoenix, a fabulous beast; I was an outlandish jewel'.[18] In one of her *New Society* articles, 'Poor Butterfly', she tells the story of how she and an American friend were recruited to work as hostesses in a bar, 'exotic extras, like a kind of cabaret' (p. 48). They are not desired as individuals, though, in an environment in which 'Both customers and hostesses are interchangeable commodities' (p. 47).

Carter's sense of alienation went beyond mere differences in appearance and customs, however. Later on, in interviews, she described Japan as 'a country that is absolutely superficial, in the sense that they have no metaphors, the action is the man'.[19] Japan, as she portrays it, inverts the Western habit of thought which treats symbols and signs as pointers to a deeper 'truth'. Instead, what you see is what you get.

In this, her attitude is strikingly similar to that of the French theorist Roland Barthes, whose book on Japan, *Empire of Signs,* makes many of the same observations. For Barthes, Japan is a country characterised by 'the precise, mobile, empty' sign, which is manifested at every level of Japanese culture. Even the body is pure spectacle, which 'exists, acts, shows itself, gives itself ... according to a pure – though subtly discontinuous – erotic project'.[20] Tokyo itself is a city of 'precious paradox: it does possess a center, but this center is empty'.[21]

Carter's article on the art of *irezumi,* or tattooing, 'People as Pictures', comes to the similar conclusion that 'In Japan, the essence is often the appearance' (p. 36).

> *Irezumi* is tattooing *in toto.* It transforms its victim into a genre masterpiece. He suffers the rigorous and ineradicable cosmetology of the awl and gouge (for the masters of the art do not use the needle) until, unique and glorious in his mutilations, he becomes a work of art as preposterous as it is magnificent. (p. 33)

However, this essay shows a social and humanistic concern which is not present in Barthes's analysis of the culture. In his hands, Japan becomes a pure theoretical abstract populated not by people, but by signs to be decoded, while Carter's approach is a great deal more involved.

'People as Pictures' provides a striking example of both the differences and similarities between Barthes's and Carter's attitudes towards Japan. Referring to it in her study of Carter, Lorna Sage points out that 'despite the cultural common ground she shares with Barthes, her understanding of all this lets in (as his does not) pain, and the drama of sado-masochism'.[22] Unlike Barthes, Carter moves away from a contemplation of *irezumi* as sign, and towards an analysis of its social significance, finding it has sinister implications, especially for women. *Irezumi,* she says, is 'a recurring motif' in popular art, especially 'involuntary tattooing, for both men and women. . . . Women are also stripped and lengthily tattooed in certain kinds of blue movie' (pp. 37–8).

In his analysis of Barthes, Rick Rylance describes Barthes's Japan as 'knowingly unreal'.[23] While Carter's Japan, too, hovers on the verge of unreality, it is in a different sense. Carter's writings show a fascination with the surreal perspectives of alienation, and unlike Barthes, who always maintains a proper academic distance from his subject, she experiences Japan as a real place to be lived in. In her writings it is an environment at once pragmatic and fantastic, a country which the author strives to understand yet also marvels at. In other words, it embodies her continuing fascination with the tension between the two opposing modes of 'fantasy' and 'fact'.

'Once More into the Mangle' (1971)

An aspect of Japanese society explored by Carter which particularly inspired this tension in her work was its obsession with sadomasochistic pornography. Indeed, the interest in pornography she developed in Japan resulted in her 1979 analysis of the work of the Marquis de Sade, *The Sadeian Woman*. 'Once More into the Mangle' is a study of Japanese comic books, and, emphasising the dual nature of its author's response, it hovers between detachment and involvement.

Carter's attitude towards 'the heightened emotional intensity and stylised violence' (p. 41) in these comic books is interesting, divided as it clearly is between repulsion and fascination. She always spoke of Japan as providing her with experiences which heightened her feminist awareness. In the introduction to the essays reprinted in *Nothing Sacred*, for example, she stated 'In Japan, I learnt what it is to be a woman and became radicalised' (p. 28). What these comic books, 'obtainable at any book stall' (p. 44) offer is a disturbing blend 'of . . . blatant eroticism and perverse sophistication', in which 'Woman' functions only as 'masochistic object' (p. 42). Referring to the work of an artist named Hachiro Tanaka, Carter succinctly describes the role he routinely assigns to female figures in his comic strip:

> Formed only to suffer, she is subjected to every indignity. Forced to take part in group sex where it is hard to tell whose breast belongs to whom, her lush body unwillingly hired out to reptilian and obese old men, the eyes of a Tanaka woman leak tears, and her swollen lips perpetually shape a round '0' of woe, until the inevitable denouement, where she is emphatically stuck through with a sword, or her decapitated but still weeping head occupies one of his favourite freeze-frames. (p. 42)

'Woman' becomes nothing more than the static, hapless object of male sadism, for no individuality can emerge through the tidal wave of suffering to which she is subjected for the gratification of others. Carter's objection to pornography, implied here and stated explicitly in *The Sadeian Woman*, was not based on moral grounds. Instead, she regards it as another way in which patriarchal society can perpetuate a process of 'false universalising'[24] which diminishes women, in all their infinite variety, to the irreducible singular 'Woman':[25]

> In the face of this symbolism, my pretensions to any kind of social existence go for nothing; graffiti directs me back to my mythic generation as a woman and, as a woman, my symbolic value is primarily that of a myth of patience and receptivity, a dumb mouth from which the teeth have been pulled.[26]

Even in this context, however, Carter evades a simplistic 'all men are bastards' analysis. Deciding that 'Woman in the strips is nevertheless a subtly ambiguous figure' (p. 42), she regards their comic-strip mistreatment as more expressive of male fears and repressions than of active misogyny, for 'A culture that prefers to keep its women at home is extremely hard on the men' (p. 43). Instead, frozen by the nature of the comic-strip form, which 'is essentially a series of stills', the effect 'of continuous static convulsion' (p. 40) is indicative of the nature of modern Japanese society as a whole. What the comic books contain are the 'uncensored, raw subject-matter of dream' (pp. 43–4) which exist as the necessary underside to the extreme restraint demanded of the Japanese by their society.

> They are read at idle moments by the people whose daily life is one of perfect gentleness, reticence and kindliness, who speak a language without oaths. . . . Few societies lay such stress on public decency and private decorum. Few offer such structured escape valves. (p. 44)

It is this paradox which delights Carter, for, while as a feminist she finds such images of erotic violence disturbing, as a fantasist she is fascinated by their fabulous surrealism. Alongside 'ferocious imagery of desire, violence and terror' (p. 39), she proclaims, 'One also finds the marvellous' (p. 41). The marvellous, as Carter presents it here, is predicated on paradox, the creative energies unleashed by the tension generated between irreconcilable polarities – restraint and excess, decorum and violence, romance and sadism. And, of course, such images become

doubly marvellous when viewed from an alien perspective, which is
always tempted to construct the unknown as 'fantastic'.

'Flesh and the Mirror' (1974)

The same fascination with the possibilities offered by the distorting
perspectives of alienation can be seen in 'Flesh and the Mirror', a short
story written sometime between 1970 and 1973, and published in
Carter's 1974 collection, *Fireworks*. It is a piece in which her usual
autobiographical game-playing is taken to extremes, for it is not possible
to ascertain how much is fact, and thus autobiographical, and how
much is fiction, and therefore fantasy. Written in the first person, the
narrative's intimate and confiding tone initially invites the reader to
approach it as autobiography in the confessional mode. However, this
persona differs dramatically from the authorial 'I' on show in the *New
Society* essays, which thrives on a tone of wry detachment. In fact,
Carter refers to herself in the first person surprisingly rarely in these
pieces, where she shows a marked preference for submerging her individual 'I' within the plural or impersonal. 'Poor Butterfly' is a typical
example of this tendency. It begins in the first person, with Carter and
her friend accepting temporary employment as hostesses in a bar, but
as the narrative continues, Carter retreats from the proceedings until
she becomes nothing more than the detached transcriber of what could
very possibly be her own words and actions in a conversation between
an unnamed hostess and a customer.

The authorial persona in 'Flesh and the Mirror', who, in the throes
of hopeless love-inspired *ennui*, is eager to analyse her most personal
desires and motivations, is therefore not the Carter we are familiar with
from her other writings on Japan, with the result that the narrator's
seeming sincerity is thus called into question. And once we are introduced to the controlling symbol in this piece, the mirror, the prospect
of distinguishing 'fact' from 'fantasy' becomes even more distant, for the
authorial 'I' becomes impossibly refracted in its distorting perspectives.

Placed almost literally at the centre of the story, the mirror functions
as the focal point for the narrator's metaphysical speculations, in which
Carter seems to be sending up the foreigner's tendency to perceive the
unfamiliar as fantastic. Wandering the streets of a foreign city in search
of her absent lover, the narrator/author begins to question the validity
of her emotions, suspecting herself of having staged the whole thing,
so perfectly does it reproduce the iconography of tragedy. 'I moved

through these expressionist perspectives in my black dress as though I was the creator of all and of myself, in the third person singular, my own heroine' (p. 62).

When the narrator encounters a stranger who takes her to a hotel room for a brief, anonymous sexual encounter, the 'I' of the text, its authenticity already in question, makes a brief, abrupt, leap into the third person: 'However hard I looked for the one *I* loved, *she* could not find him anywhere and the city delivered her into the hands of a perfect stranger' (p. 63, my italics). It is only in the mirror that the authorial subject appears to acquire some kind of stable identity within the 'real', yet, paradoxically, that stability is conveyed through a distorting confusion of authorial perspective, where the narrator is both watching and watched, yet also in a state where she is neither:

> The magic mirror presented me with a hitherto unconsidered notion of myself as I. Without any intention of mine, I had been defined by the action reflected in the mirror. I beset me. I was the subject of the sentence written on the mirror. I was not watching it. There was nothing whatsoever beyond the surface of the glass. Nothing kept me from the fact, the act; I had been precipitated into knowledge of the real conditions of living. (pp. 64–5)

So is the vision the mirror offers authentic, or is it only another illusion? Underneath the linguistic contortions of the narrative, the lesson of the mirror appears simple: for a split second, it has allowed the narrator/ author to see herself stripped of fiction and artifice. Her lurid imagination 'pre-empted' (p. 64), she exists purely within the act and the moment. Although she flees into the 'banal morning' from the 'objective lesson in the nature of things' (p. 66) offered to her in the mirror, it is a lesson she cannot evade.

Initially, then, the story attempts to replay its opening, with the author, again seeking her lover, recasting herself as heroine in her own tragic drama: 'I thought I was the most romantic spectacle imaginable as I wandered weeping down the alleys' (p. 66). But once she finds her lover, she sees only 'an object created in the mode of fantasy . . . I created him solely in relation to myself, like a work of romantic art' (p. 67). Unable to bear very much reality, the relationship soon ends; simultaneously, the author finds that the city has become 'home', and so has 'ceased, almost immediately, to be a magic and appalling place' (p. 70).

But is the lesson of the mirror really concerned with the establishment of authenticity? It seems to me that any assertions concerning reality within the context of a narrative which plays so many games with the concept of identity and experience must necessarily be questionable. The authorial 'I' is rendered so unstable that by the end, it is almost impossible to accept the authority of any of its assertions, and even the narrator's final disillusionment is yet another pose. The introduction of the mirror, ironically, only adds to this confusion for, as Rosemary Jackson argues, it is a staple motif in fantasy literature for the precise reason that it 'employs distance and difference to suggest the instability of the 'real' . . . and it offers unpredictable (apparently impossible) metamorphoses of self into other'.[27] So, rather than the narrator/author gaining some kind of objective view of her behaviour, the narrative can be viewed as the kind of 'empty' sign which Barthes claims is typical of Japanese culture:

> It is in the envelope that the labor of the confection (of the making) seems to be invested, but thereby the object loses its existence, becomes a mirage: from envelope to envelope, the signified flees, and when you finally have it (there is always a little something in the package), it appears insignificant, laughable, vile . . . to find the object which is in the package or the signified is to discard it.[28]

What the narrator of 'Flesh and the Mirror' discovers from the mirror is not necessarily herself as she 'really' is, therefore, since the narrative is such a dense palimpsest of constructed selves as to be impenetrable. What she does do, however, is recognise the process by which such a constructed identity is achieved, and learns that she cannot evade it, as the throwaway final line of the story implies: 'The most difficult performance in the world is acting naturally isn't it? Everything else is artful.' (p. 70). Especially this story – as Lorna Sage says, 'it looks like an "exercise" in literary gymnastics'.[29]

Sage reads 'Flesh and the Mirror' as an expression of Carter's obsession 'with the notion that what we accept as natural is the product of a particular history. Art's purpose on this view is to help us recognise our own artificiality . . . and to estrange us from our own selves'.[30] This neatly encapsulates the paradox on which Carter's work is based, since it bases the practice of fabulation within a historical context. In 'Flesh and the Mirror' the two opposing concepts of 'fact' and 'fantasy' become firmly yoked together within Carter's fiction. Moreover, the revelation is achieved on the margins of a culture, for the alien perspective, although not always enviable, is both creative and critical. It is this belief which motivates the second autobiographical 'cluster' in Carter's writing – the essays dealing with her family background, which show that you don't necessarily have to go all the way to Japan to experience alienation. You can find it on your own doorstep.

Outside of interviews, Carter described her childhood in two essays written in 1976.[31] In 'The Mother Lode' she relates the story of her birth and upbringing during and after the Second World War. 'My Father's House' explores her father's Scottish heritage. In both of them, she looks back beyond her experiences in Japan in order to create a persona for herself who has experienced alienation and displacement as her birthright. The content of 'My Father's House' was also largely reiterated in a later piece, 'Sugar Daddy', published in 1983.[32]

'The Mother Lode', in particular, can as easily be read as a short story as a piece of autobiography: as if intent on revealing the problematic nature of its chosen form, ambiguity is a self-consciously recurring trope within this essay. From the opening sentence: 'The first house in which I remember living gives a false impression of our circumstances' (p. 3), Carter's maternal family history, as well as the narrative which 'tells' it, is defined through paradox, embodying, in the words of Barthes, 'the ambiguity of a double object, at once believable and false'.[33]

Through these essays, Carter dramatises these two distinct polarities in her work – the pull towards fabulation and the push towards concrete social action – by linking them to specific figures within her family history. Moreover, by making a distinction between matriarchal and patriarchal inheritance, to a certain extent she attaches gender distinctions to the opposing concepts of 'fantasy' and 'fact'.

Although originally published separately, 'The Mother Lode' and 'My Father's House' work well when set side by side, as they are in *Nothing Sacred*. Read this way, the explicit contrasts Carter draws between the matriarchal and the patriarchal become evident. 'The Mother Lode', as its title suggests, is about the maternal side of Carter's family – her mother, and, most importantly, her maternal grandmother. It is a long piece of anecdotage whose whimsical tone and linguistic liveliness bears an obvious comparison with her fiction. 'My Father's House', while open to readings which are no less complex, is a much briefer piece, and although, ostensibly, the central figure within it is that of Carter's father, he remains a half-realised, shadowy figure. While 'The Mother Lode' abounds with colourful characters and fanciful anecdotes, 'My Father's House' focuses much more starkly on the experience of alienation, exploring a part of Carter's family history which, she says, 'remains, in some ways, inaccessibly foreign' (p. 23).

This stress on the 'foreigness', or inaccessibility, of the past is a recurring trope in Carter's writings on family. In 'Sugar Daddy', for example, she writes of her father in a passage which evokes a relationship built on a paradoxical combination of intimacy and distance:

> I know so little of him, although I know so much. Much of his life was conducted in my absence, on terms of which I am necessarily ignorant, for he was older than I am now when I was born, although his life has shaped my life. This is the curious abyss that divides the closest kin, that the tender curiosity appropriate to lovers is inappropriate, here, where the bond is involuntary, so that the most important things stay undiscovered. (p. 30)

These exercises in autobiography, whether they deal in facts or imaginative reconstruction, are therefore a way to develop a history through which the past can be known and also shared. Biological consanguinity isn't enough: a true family is founded on a sense of shared history and familiar stories.

'The Mother Lode' (1976)

'The Mother Lode' tells the story of Angela Carter's birth in Eastbourne in 1940, which was where her family – her grandmother, her mother, her eleven-year-old brother, as well as her 'embryonic self' (p. 5) – had moved to from London following the outbreak of war. In her account, significant stress is laid on the absence of her father, who stayed in London to work in his reserved occupation, although he visited his family 'whenever he could manage it and that was very often because he and my mother were very attached to each other' (p. 5).

In spite of this attachment, however, soon after Carter's birth the space between this matriarchal group and the figure of the father was increased when they moved to join her grandmother's brother and sister in the mining village of Wath-upon-Dearne in South Yorkshire. This was, says Carter, at the direct instigation of her grandmother, who vowed that 'there was *one* place in the world the Germans would not dare to bomb' (p. 5). In this, Carter's 'Gran' displays an uncanny prescience, for 'though the Germans bombed hell out of the South Coast and also bombed the heart out of Sheffield, twenty odd miles away from where we had removed, not one bomb fell on us, just as she had predicted' (p. 5).

Gran, therefore, establishes her absolute dominance over both family and text from the very beginning of 'The Mother Lode', becoming a figure who embodies the paradox which lies at the heart of the 'Carteresque' narrative. Described by her granddaughter as 'an old woman, squat, fierce and black-clad like the granny in the Giles' cartoons in the Sunday Express' (p. 4), she is, on the one hand, an incontestable part of history, both in the private (family) sphere, and the public (socio-political) arena. But on the other, for anyone who has already read some of Carter's fiction written either before or after the publication of this essay, Gran must be strangely familiar. As Lorna Sage has observed, she bears a close resemblance to the figure of 'Grandma who presides over the matriarchal space of the Carter house of fiction'.[34] Like Lizzie in *Nights at the Circus*, or Grandma Chance in *Wise Children*, Carter's grandmother is described in terms which lend her a slightly fantastic aura. Through the transformative power of Carter's narrative, she becomes a figure who exists on the very verge of credibility. She is the means by which the 'story-telling' function of autobiography is again exposed, and its claim to be a transparent form rendered questionable.

As the title, 'The Mother Lode', makes immediately clear, Carter is engaged in an exercise in genealogical archaeology, digging up the past in the same way as her mining forebears dug for coal in the Yorkshire mines. Gran is simultaneously the object of that search and its agent. She is the object because it is she whom Carter's narrative is seeking to find. She is the 'mother lode' – the original source of the author's story and her story-telling abilities. But Gran is also the agent by which the quest is carried out, because she, as well as her granddaughter, excavates the rich veins of the past. In so doing, she becomes the representative of a hidden history of female strength and ingenuity.

In the first paragraph of the essay, Carter describes how her grand-mother 'dug . . . up' the house which 'was part of the archaeology of my mother's life' and 'dived back within it when times became precarious . . . and she took me with her, for safety's sake' (p. 3). Gran mines, not through earth, but history, removing her family not only from Eastbourne, but from time altogether. Living in her cottage in the 'mucky pastoral' (p. 6) of a South Yorkshire mining village, Gran takes on, for Carter, an archetypal, fairytale significance, associated with the power to generate a protective space which it is beyond even the power of German bombers to penetrate. Defiantly anachronistic, and fiercely protective, she can be easily associated with a mythic, prehistoric past in which both time and history are mutable.

However, in spite of the formidable nature of Carter's grandmother, possessor of an 'architectonic' personality (p. 11), Carter's mother is an equally important figure in this essay. Lorna Sage has argued that in Carter's narratives 'mother is almost a missing person', and sees Carter's feminism as arising out of the desire to react against what her mother represented.

> The women who really nailed patriarchy were not on the whole the ones with authoritarian fathers, but the ones with troubled, contradictory mothers: you aim your feminism less against men, than against the picture of the woman you don't want to be, the enemy within. In this case, the girl-wife.[35]

While I agree that a certain ambivalence of attitude can be found in Carter's representation of mothers in her fiction, I would maintain that 'The Mother Lode' also creates explicit links between the three generations of women, even though they are in many cases links maintained through opposition. And, as Carter makes clear, Gran is a hard act for any daughter to follow.

Although completely opposed to Carter's grandmother in many ways – she speaks standard English, not broad Yorkshire, and strives to separate herself from her working-class roots – Carter's mother nevertheless possesses her own eccentric, and slightly fantastic, attributes. She inherited, says Carter, 'the family talent for magic realism'; for example, telling her daughter that her pregnancy was confirmed 'on the very day' war was declared (p. 4), and through her love of jokes and puns giving her daughter 'my first introduction to a wonderful world of verbal transformations' (p. 3). ('My family have always behaved anecdotally,' Carter said in a later interview.)[36] Like Gran, Carter's mother is a figure with fairytale potential, the beautiful possessor of 'a talent for histrionics' (p. 13), who married 'young to an adoring husband' (p. 12).

When, at the end of the war, both mother and grandmother return to their separate houses in London, Carter goes back to live with her mother and father, leaving behind her grandmother's cottage for 'a

curious kind of deviant middle-class life' (p. 15) in a house where 'a
curious kind of dream-time operated; life passed at a languorous pace,
everything was gently untidy, and none of the clocks ever told the right
time, although they ticked away busily' (p. 14). As in Wath-upon-
Dearne, therefore, Carter again represents herself as living in a tangential relationship to history. During that time of deepening political crisis,
the Cold War, she lives within a 'recreate[d] snug, privileged, thirties
childhood. . . . a perpetual Sunday afternoon in which you could never
trust the clocks' (p. 18). Typically, even Carter's mother's 'passion for
respectability' becomes 'in itself a source of deviance', resulting in 'a
curious, self-crafted lifestyle . . . that flourished on its own terms but
was increasingly at variance with the changes going on around it'
(p. 15).

Through such statements, the links between the female members of
Carter's family are reinforced. The legacy of both mother and grandmother is defined through reference to a cyclical, mythic, timescale
rather than a linear and historical chronological progression, and their
linguistic and imaginative creativity, which Carter by the very act of
writing shows she also shares, are directly attributed to that. Such a view,
however, can justifiably be regarded as being dangerously essentialist,
'femininity' becoming defined as mystic, intuitive, ahistorical – the
passive 'Other' against which man defines himself as an active, dominant being. Simone de Beauvoir sums up the problems inherent in this
view in *The Second Sex*:

> Thus, as against the dispersed, contingent, and multiple existences
> of actual women, mythical thought opposes the Eternal Feminine,
> unique and changeless. . . . To pose Woman is to pose the absolute
> Other, without reciprocity, denying against all experience that she
> is a subject, a fellow human being.[37]

However, it is obvious from the rest of the essay that Carter has no
intention of positing woman as changeless 'Other'. Although 'The
Mother Lode' is about family, it is also clearly about the larger environment within which the family structure is constituted; the world of
class and political concerns. That Carter's family live slightly out of step
with the world around them is due to the fact that they are being
recorded in the process of shifting classes, and the female figures in 'The
Mother Lode' participate in this theme. Carter tells, for example, how
her mother was a scholarship girl, going from a Battersea elementary

school to a ladies' grammar school, a feat which set her at odds with her own defiantly working-class mother. As Carter recalls:

> My gran attended prize-days to watch my mother score her loot with a huge Votes For Women badge pinned to her lapel and my mother, my poor mother, was ashamed because my gran was zapping the option her daughter had been given to be lady just by standing up for her own rights not to be. (p. 11)

Although it may lay her open to charges of essentialism, in this essay, however, it is primarily through the male members of her family that Carter establishes the importance of political and historical agency in the world of lived experience. Her grandfather, although dead before she was born, is especially important in this role. Whereas Gran is portrayed as aggressively 'present' throughout Carter's childhood, her grandfather must be imaginatively reconstructed from the few fragments of memorabilia that Gran has left intact. When sorting through her grandmother's possessions after her death, Carter finds 'a little stack of certificates for exams my grandfather had passed in the army' (p. 9). It is these qualifications, gained while serving with the British army in India, which are her grandfather's passport out of the coal fields of South Yorkshire, able to use 'his literacy to be shot of manual labour, first rung up the ladder of social mobility' (p. 10). Working in London, he becomes 'radicalised' (p. 9) as well as educated, joining the Independent Labour Party and, on one occasion, shaking Lenin's hand. If, for Carter, her grandmother's legacy is one of subversive creativity and wilful perversity enacted within a fantastic, fairytale landscape, her grandfather's is equally important, anchoring her in the world of social and political concerns. 'Of all the dead in my family', she writes, 'he is the one I would most like to have talked to. He had the widest experience and perhaps the greatest capacity for interpreting it' (p. 9).

The need for some kind of political action (specifically *socialist* political action) is rendered explicit in 'The Mother Lode' through Carter's descriptions of Wath-upon-Dearne, in which fantasy and social realism combine. In places, Carter's narrative evokes an atmosphere suitable as a setting for the archetypal grandmother and her cottage: 'The canal was fringed with willows, cruelly lopped, and their branches were always hung with rags tied in knots. I don't know why. It was a witchy, unpremeditated sight' (p. 4). More than that, the landscape is also described as incipiently romantic, rural as well as industrial, with sheep grazing 'right up to the pit-heads' – even if they are 'all black with soot' (p. 6).

However, Carter writes into the text her unease at her tendency towards romanticism within a working-class environment – 'Of course I romanticise it. Why the hell not' (p. 8). The stagy rhetoric of such a statement, while it registers defiance, also indicates resistance to the kind of mythologising process in which, at times, she appears to be engaged. It is a resistance Carter made explicit in *The Sadeian Woman*, where she argues that 'the notion of a universality of human experience is a confidence trick', and that all aspects of that experience, even 'Birth and death, the only absolute inescapables, are . . . absolutely determined by the social context in which they occur'.[38] In 'The Mother Lode', therefore, the 'witchy' landscape of the eccentric grandmother from fairytale is represented directly alongside Carter's depiction of the stark realities of life in the northern coalfields during the Second World War. It is an environment where 'Death was a part of daily life . . . scarcely a family had not its fatality, its mutilated, its grey-faced old man coughing his lungs out in the chair by the range', and where life is a daily struggle to make ends meet, for it 'wasn't until the 1960s that miners were earning anything like a reasonable living wage' (p. 8).

Although the two strands of the narrative exist in sometimes uneasy juxtaposition, 'The Mother Lode' is nevertheless an excellent example of Carter's approach in her fiction generally, within which an astute social awareness is mingled with the urge towards imaginative and linguistic excess which is so characteristic of her fantasy. Thus this essay, while ostensibly autobiographical, is not so much concerned with describing the actual circumstances of its author's life as with mapping the fault line between the actual and the imagined from which all of Carter's stories spring. Her grandmother functions as the text's matri-archal origin, for like the fairy and folk-tales to which all of Carter's narratives are, to a greater or lesser extent, indebted, this is a narrative which has women at its centre and as its source. Her grandfather's inheritance of social displacement and political activism is equally important, however, since it is through him that Carter turns her vision outward into the realm of actual experience and social concern.

'My Father's House' (1976)

So although 'The Mother Lode' is a piece of writing dominated by the female members of Carter's family, it is not exclusively matriarchal in its focus, nor does it strive to be so. It also enunciates a desire to know the father and in that respect, Gran's role is not wholly admirable, for her dominant place within the narrative allows her to overshadow the male figures within it. Carter's father is even more of a cipher in 'The Mother Lode' than is her grandfather. Although Carter was reunited with him at the end of the war, at the end of 'The Mother Lode' she records how she was separated from him again after her mother's death. In a neat reversal, however, it is he, not she, who moves away this time, back to his childhood home in Scotland. If her grandfather symbolises Carter's feelings of class alienation, carried by her family from one class to the fringes of another, then her father, through his return to his native home, emphasises her cultural alienation, for his return to 'his granite village beside its granite sea' enables Carter 'to understand better how it was we were always somehow askew. I felt like a foreigner because my mother had married a foreigner' (p. 15).

While 'The Mother Lode', therefore, is primarily about presence, community and historical agency, in many ways 'My Father's House' evokes the opposite of all these things – absence, alienation and solitude. In this essay, it is a *female* history and presence for which the author is nostalgic. Contemplating a photograph of her paternal great-grandmother, of whom she knows almost nothing, she sees a woman 'with the stern face of a kirk-goer' who is, puzzlingly, dressed in an outfit appropriate to a witch: 'a long cloak, wimple, and modified steeple hat' (p. 20). Conformity and subversion, puritanism and the tantalising possibility of excess combine to make this woman a paradox forever incapable of solution, like all the other family photographs 'no longer identifiable' (p. 20) which hang on the walls of Carter's father's house.

This gallery of images without a history is an apt metaphor for the essay's preoccupation with alienation and separation, which problematises Carter's father's attempt to return to his roots. Not only has he returned to a house full of echoes of an unrecoverable family history, but to a country which does not, and cannot ever, know itself. Alienation in both the private and the public spheres are literally placed side by side in this essay, for alongside the anonymous family photographs hang pictures of 'stags in depopulated Highland glens', representative of 'a purely emblematic Scottishness' (p. 21) which bears absolutely no relationship to either the actual landscape of north Aberdeenshire or to the day-to-day experience of those who live there. Here, Carter demonstrates to her readers another function of 'story-telling'; the rewriting of history in order to cover up the record of oppression, for these romanticised landscapes are 'untenanted except for deer ... in which man is most present in his resonating absences' (p. 21). Viewed through a subversive eye, this is the landscape of Scotland after the clearances; the manufactured and sanitised environment of the alien English invader.

Carter's consciousness of being, at least partially, the product of a colonised culture is not shared by her father. In her 1977 interview with Lorna Sage, Carter said: 'I always felt foreign in England, and I realised the reason I'd always felt foreign was that I was. My father's not into Scottishness at all . . . He never perceived himself as Scottish, as being different, but it *is* different, I think'. Carter's father, the product of 'classic English colonial Scotland' is not concerned with decoding the myth, refusing to read the books Carter sends him on Scottish history with the claim that they are '"too bloody depressing", which is his attitude to the history of his people.'[39]

His attitude, however, is characteristic of his home town, where pragmatic concerns have always taken precedence over larger political issues. According to Carter, this is a town whose people 'were too busy putting in the harbour to even notice the Jacobite rebellion' (p. 22). It is only the author herself, viewing this culture from the margins, and existing in an uneasy relationship with it, who sees a necessity to recover its lost history.

Her father's heritage, therefore, is represented in this essay as a double cultural estrangement, for even were Carter to miraculously gain a coherent 'Scottish' identity it would remain one only capable of definition in negative terms. Carter communicates a convincing sense of displacement throughout the essay, claiming both a sense of identification with the town of her father's birth through her use of the possessive pronoun 'my', while the simultaneous usage of the more impersonal third person 'they' implies detachment. This linguistic vacillation can be seen in a passage where she describes how her resemblance to her paternal grandmother only accentuates this sense of alienation:

> Everybody says I look just like my paternal grandmother, further-more, I can't go out to buy morning rolls without somebody who remembers the old lady grappling with me on the pavement and stressing the resemblance.
>
> They're still a bit bewildered by my accent. My Aunt Katie used to explain, almost apologetically: 'Hugh marrit an English girl, ye ken.' And I'd stand there, smiling, feeling terribly, terribly foreign

in that clean white town, under that clean, white, un-English light
which is nevertheless, in some dislocated way, home – which is
where my ain folk are from. (p. 24)

Scotland is at once 'foreign', but it is also 'where my ain folk are from'
– family relationships are asserted ('*my* paternal grandmother'; '*my* Aunt
Katie'), yet also undermined through references to dialectical difference.

However, although Carter's paternal ancestry is expressed in terms of
almost schizophrenic confusion, that is not to say that it is all negative.
On the contrary, this essay recalls the Japan pieces in its reiteration that
the experience of not belonging brings with it mixed blessings, especially for the writer. An episode in 'My Father's House' demonstrates
this, where an old 'triple-masted schooner' sails into Macduff Harbour,
reminding the old people of the town of a long-ago period of maritime
prosperity. As far as most of those who watch it sailing down the
Moray Firth are concerned, however, the schooner is a glamorous and
romantic image which is, quite literally, floating free of any historical
context. Instead, it represents the return of a past which has become
foreign because forgotten, and can therefore function as the focus of
imaginative speculation. This episode achieves prominence within the
essay through Carter's use of exaggeratedly stylised language: 'It came
floating like a tethered cloud past the little white toy-like lighthouse
at the pierhead. It floated, it materialised, out of yet another vulgar,
Technicolour, Cinerama sunset' (p. 22). The ship represents a gap in
history which can be filled by the imagination, through which an
imaginary past can be (re)constructed.

However, Carter also stresses that such story-making is no substitute
for the reality which has been lost beyond all hope of retrieval. While
her description of the ship is self-consciously poetic, crammed as it is
with figurative language, the passage is typical of Carter in that it also
consciously debases its own romantic imagery. The ironic reference to
the 'vulgar, Technicolour, Cinerama sunset' which forms the climax of
the passage takes it beyond any claim to 'reality', emphasising that the
event is one that has become only capable of being authenticated
through references to other fictions.

Like the ship in 'My Father's House' or the foreigner in Japan, therefore, the writer who is divorced from class and culture can 'float' in a
sea of self-referential fictions precisely because, 'peculiar rootless,
upward, downward, sideways socially mobile ... living in twilight
zones',[40] she exists on the fringes of the dominant hegemonic discourse.

... position, she can weave a web of stories which do not point
... controvertible 'truth', and yet which, paradoxically,
... by which she establishes her authenticity as writing
..., the establishment of such an authenticity is vital, as
... de' and 'My Father's House' demonstrate. In these
... represented for herself a past which both gives her
... talent to tell stories, and a firm belief in the existence
... of political concern and social agency.

... biographical essays thus represent a dual experience of
... one willed and the other involuntary. Her tendency,
... throughout her fiction, to mix the opposing modes of
... fact' is foregrounded in her use of the autobiographical
... ch it is never certain whether what takes place is an
... rtrayal of the author's experience, or pure invention. But
... ious intentions at work here too, for the games Carter's
... lay aim to make the reader aware that the self and the his-
... familial environment within which it is constituted is not
... d thus immutable, but *constructed*, and thus able to be
... Constructing and reconstructing herself as marginal, on both
... and artistic level, Carter used her carefully cultivated out-
... spective to both entertain and to communicate, in the words
of Rita Felski, 'a new sense of autonomy which makes possible political awareness and activity'.[41]

Notes

1. John Haffenden, 'Magical Mannerist', *The Literary Review* (November 1984), pp. 34–8 (p. 34). Reprinted in Haffenden, *Novelists in Interview* (London: Methuen, 1985).
2. Rick Rylance, *Roland Barthes* (Hemel Hempstead: Harvester Wheatsheaf, 1994), p. 80.
3. Haffenden, p. 38.
4. Angela Carter, 'Notes from the Front Line', in Michelene Wandor (ed.), *On Gender and Writing* (London: Pandora Press, 1983), pp. 69–77 (p. 70).
5. Shari Benstock, 'Authorizing the Autobiographical', in Shari Benstock (ed.), *The Private Self: Theory and Practice of Women's Autobiographical Writings* (London: Routledge, 1988), p. 11.
6. Haffenden, p. 38.
7. Rita Felski, *Beyond Feminist Aesthetics: Feminist Literature and Social Change* (Cambridge, Mass.: Harvard University Press, 1989), p. 93.
8. Angela Carter, 'Notes from the Front Line', p. 69.

9.   Angela Carter, *The Sadeian Woman: An Exercise in Cultural History* (London: Virago Press, 1979), p. 12.

10. ibid., p. 5.

11. Haffenden, p. 38.

12. Carter, 'Notes from the Front Line', p. 70.

13. Peter Kemp, 'Magical History Tour', *The Sunday Times* (9 June 1991), p. 6.

14. Olga Kenyon, *The Writer's Imagination* (University of Bradford Print Unit, 1992), p. 24.

15. Paul Barker, 'The Return of the Magic Story-Teller', *The Independent on Sunday* (8 January 1995), p. 16.

16. Lorna Sage, *Angela Carter* (Plymouth: Northcote House, 1994), p. 24. An earlier, shorter version of this study, entitled 'Death of the Author', can be found in *Granta* 41 (1992), pp. 235–54.

17. Angela Carter, introduction to her essays on Japan in *Nothing Sacred*, p. 28.

18. *Fireworks* (London: Virago Press, 1974), p. 7. All further references in the text are from this edition.

19. Lorna Sage, 'The Savage Sideshow: A Profile of Angela Carter', *New Review* 4/39–40 (July 1977), pp. 51–7 (p. 56).

20. Roland Barthes, *Empire of Signs*, trans. Richard Howard (London: Jonathan Cape, 1983), p. 10.

21. ibid., p. 30.

22. Sage, *Angela Carter*, p. 28.

23. Rylance, p. 127.

24. Carter, *The Sadeian Woman*, p. 12.

25. Barthes, it is worth noting, praised the tendency of Japanese culture to reduce gender difference to universals. Writing on Japanese theatre, in which men play the female roles, he describes how they 'absorb and eliminate all feminine reality. . . . Woman is an idea, not nature; as such, she is restored to the classifying function and to the truth of her pure difference' (*Empire of Signs*, p. 91).

26. Carter, *The Sadeian Woman*, pp. 4–5.

27. Rosemary Jackson, *Fantasy: the Literature of Subversion* (London: Methuen, 1981), pp. 87–8.

28. Barthes, *Empire of Signs*, p. 46.

29. Sage, *Angela Carter*, p. 27.

30. ibid.

31. 'The Mother Lode' originally appeared in *The New Review*, and 'My Father's House' in *New Society*, where it was entitled 'Time to Tell the Time'. They were reprinted together in *Nothing Sacred* in 1982, and all references in the text are from this edition.

32. 'Sugar Daddy', in Ursula Owen (ed.), *Fathers: Reflections by Daughters* (London: Virago Press, 1983), pp. 20–30. All references in the text are from this edition.

33. Roland Barthes, *Writing Degree Zero*, trans. Annette Lavers and Colin Smith (New York: Hill and Wang, 1968), p. 33.
34. Sage, *Angela Carter*, p. 6.
35. ibid., p. 7.
36. Haffenden, p. 34.
37. Simone de Beauvoir, *The Second Sex*, trans. H. M. Parshley (London: Picador Classics, 1988), p. 283.
38. Carter, *The Sadeian Woman*, p. 12.
39. Sage, 'The Savage Sideshow', p. 53.
40. ibid., p. 53.
41. Felski, p. 118.

II
*Living on
a Demolition Site*

CHAPTER 2

In this chapter, I will begin to consider part of Angela Carter's literary output during the decade leading up to her departure for Japan in 1969; the period in which she published *Shadow Dance* (1966), *The Magic Toyshop* (1967), *Several Perceptions* (1968), and *Heroes and Villains* (1969). I am also including *Love* in my analysis of Carter's novels of the sixties, for although it was not published until 1971, Carter herself was explicit about the fact that it was written in 1969, and the characters in it 'the pure, perfect products of those days of social mobility and sexual licence'.[1] It certainly, as Marc O'Day has already observed, shares many similarities with the rest of Carter's output during this period.[2] However, while O'Day seems to have no difficulty linking *Love* to *Shadow Dance* and *Several Perceptions*, making it the third element in what he terms Carter's 'Bristol Trilogy', I wish to argue that it also has much in common, both thematically and stylistically, with *Heroes and Villains*.

The liberal and experimental atmosphere of the sixties undoubtedly suited Angela Carter. It was the decade in which she launched her writing career, and its mood and mores – as well as its contradictions – remained an indelible influence on her work. The fiction she wrote during this period is extremely varied, in terms of both tone and quality. Although she built up a repertoire of ideas and techniques which run throughout the novels she was writing at this time, it is difficult to analyse these texts in chronological order, as the greatest similarities appear between books which were not written sequentially. I have therefore chosen to begin with a discussion of *Shadow Dance* and *Several Perceptions*, both texts which draw overtly on the concept of a counterculture, and which celebrate the decade's devotion to narcissistic spectacle – a movement otherwise known as 'camp'. Camp had an undoubted appeal for Carter, as Lorna Sage says, 'because it represented a kind of fault-line running through contemporary culture, where the binary opposition of masculine and feminine broke down. Camp mocked at seriousness, sincerity, authenticity. . . . What existentialists labelled "bad faith" and deplored, camp taste enjoyed and admired'.[3]

I am well aware, however, that 'camp' is a loaded term, the implication of which has been the topic of fierce debate in the years since Susan Sontag published her 'Notes on "Camp"' in 1966. In its most popularly understood context, camp denotes an exaggerated, over-the-top effeminacy assumed by some gay men as a calculated outrage against prevailing codes of masculinity. But this isn't really the context in which I am using it here. Instead, I am interested in the concept of a camp aesthetic, which revolves around issues of taste. According to Susan Sontag,

> The experiences of Camp are based on the great discovery that the sensibility of high culture has no monopoly upon refinement. Camp asserts that good taste is not simply good taste; that there exists, indeed, a good taste of bad taste.[4]

Proclaiming that 'the essence of Camp is its love of the unnatural: of artifice and exaggeration',[5] Sontag's portrayal of camp as extravagant, parodic, ironic and excessively stylised could also function as a fair description of the novels discussed here.

But Sontag's definition of camp has come in for excessive criticism from those who argue that it is nowhere near as subversive a sensibility as it supposes itself to be. Andrew Britton, for example, claims that 'As a logic of "transgression", camp belongs to the second class. If the transgression of boundaries ever threatened to produce the redefinition of them, the *frisson* would be lost, the thrill of "something wrong" would disappear'.[6] George Melly dismisses it as 'hardly more than a sophisticated means of keeping any form of qualitative judgement at bay by agreeing enthusiastically with adverse criticism',[7] and makes more or less the same point as Britton when he states that 'Camp is an "in" idea, the property of a minority. Once public property, once everybody is in on the joke it stops being funny'.[8]

However, the study of camp I've found most useful in the context of my discussion of Carter is that contained in Andrew Ross's *No Respect: Intellectuals and Popular Culture*. Ross explores the concept of a camp aesthetic in far more detail than either Britton or Melly, and, while critical, his attitude is not dismissive or reductive. He reiterates Sontag's placing of the advent of camp within the cultural environment of the

1960s, during which, seduced by the notion of a revolutionary 'Year One', history and all its accompanying detritus was up for appropriation and redefinition, and his notion of an 'economy' of camp, which aims to 'liberate ... the objects and discourse of the past from disdain and neglect',[9] is very much in line with Carter's narrative intentions in the two books discussed here.

I would argue that *Shadow Dance* and *Several Perceptions* are linked by a similar camp sensibility, embodied most obviously in the iconic figure of the dandy. Dandyism, however, is an attribute also shared by Carter's narrative itself. According to Andrew Ross, in its ironic valorisation of the artefacts of consumer culture, camp 'represented a direct affront to those who governed the boundaries of official taste' by 'problematizing the question of *taste* itself'.[10] Put this statement in a literary context, and you have an apt summary of Carter's approach in both these narratives, which are an eccentric and eclectic assemblage of references and techniques drawn from a wide variety of 'high' and 'low' literary forms in which the likes of Shakespeare and Keats are placed on an equal level with references to Hammer Horror, folk-tale and the Marquis de Sade. In this way, the method by which mainstream culture allocates categories of value, taste and morality is systematically dismantled.

Both *Shadow Dance* and *Several Perceptions* received mixed reviews when they first appeared, and remained out of print until the resurgence of interest in Carter's work after her death. The fact that reviews on their reissue by Virago in 1994 were equally mixed indicates that they had not lost their ability to shock and disturb in the interim. In both novels, Carter tries quite deliberately to arouse the reader's distaste in order to use it as a starting point for the questioning of accepted categories of value and morality. However, she sometimes tends to work rather too hard at this, wandering over the fine line that divides deliberate artifice from mechanical posturing. A 1969 review of *Several Perceptions*, for example, regarded the novel as being 'marred by some unconvincing dialogue and a good deal of overwriting [which] ... easily becomes wearisome':[11] a verdict which was echoed in a 1994 review of *Shadow Dance*, which describes Carter's prose style as 'intensely histrionic'.[12] Amongst such histrionics, a sense of Carter's more subtle ideological aims can easily be lost.

Yet this very propensity towards grandiloquent exaggeration which became Carter's hallmark can be seen as being rooted in the kind of cultural changes that were taking place in the sixties. Taking 'mutability' as the keyword for describing Carter's writing during this period (borrowing it from her essay 'Notes For a Theory of Sixties Style'), Marc O'Day offers an interesting analysis of the link between the culture of the sixties and Carter's art. He argues that her 'consistent focus on the malleability, flexibility, mobility and turnover in ideas, images and language, selves and things, styles and lifestyles, reality itself' was inextricably linked to the time in which she was writing, as the sixties were 'arguably the crucial period in which this logic of change became fully institutionalised as an objective feature of economic and social life'.[13] It was a link which Carter herself was to make explicit in an essay published years later, which looked back at the decade with nostalgic, but also critical, eyes.

'Truly, It Felt Like Year One' (1988)

In 'Truly, It Felt Like Year One', Carter identified the sixties as a time which formed her ideas and her politics in profound ways, arguing that:

> The sixties were the first, and may well turn out to be the only, time, when we had an authentic intelligentsia in this country just like the ones in Europe and America – a full-blooded, enquiring rootless urban intelligentsia which didn't define itself as a class by what its parents had done for a living.[14]

If one takes her account of her awkward class and cultural history in her autobiographical essays at face value, perhaps it was not surprising that this was the aspect of the decade Carter seized upon: a chance to define yourself for who you were rather than where you did – or perhaps in Carter's case did not – come from.

'Truly, It Felt Like Year One' is also another of those exercises in semi-autobiography through which Carter periodically reinvented her authorial persona; it can, indeed, be read as a kind of sequel to such essays as 'The Mother Lode' and 'My Father's House'. While those pieces deal with Carter's childhood and parental relationships, this is an account of her period of coming-of-age. As in 'The Mother Lode', she represents the fifties as a period of restraint, both in English culture at large and as far as her own personal circumstances were concerned, growing up as she was in the genteel atmosphere of the lower-middle-class suburbs of London. The fifties, she mock-heroically declaims, were 'tough. . . . Girls wore white gloves' (p. 210).

For Carter, the sixties represented a relief from the restraints of feminine respectability. Not only did she remove herself from the parental home, but she did so at a time of change in society at large, when the children of the 1944 Education Act, grown 'big and strong and glossy-eyed' on 'All that free milk and orange juice and codliver oil', and educated into a new form of classlessness, were 'simply tak[ing] what was due to us whilst reserving the right to ask questions' (p. 210). As she portrays it, the decade was a euphoric time for members of this new youth culture, who enjoyed the benefits of new physical, social and intellectual mobility. The cost of living was cheap, all kinds of conventions were being questioned, and Britain was opening itself up to European cultural influences, as well as celebrating a new sense of political empowerment.

This, I think, is one of the most important attractions the concept of the counterculture held for Carter, because it represents a strategy by which she could renegotiate the boundaries between fantasy and concrete political action. The ending of the war in Vietnam, as 'the first war in the history of the world where the boys were brought back from the front due to popular demand from their own side' (p. 214), proves the ability of the counterculture to actually change things. So, while on the one hand it stands for the demolition of convention, on the other it is crucially concerned with the transformation of political process. In writing out of the countercultural environment, Carter can therefore have her cake and eat it too, gaining the licence to create fantastic narratives which nevertheless persistently refer back to the conditions of their own production.

Furthermore, Carter's writing during this decade shows that she viewed the counterculture as a phenomenon which, at least temporarily, solves the problem of writing from the margins that I have already discussed in the previous chapter. Because marginality is customarily associated with silence, the articulate marginalised subject is always at risk of becoming recruited into serving the interests of the centre of discourse, thus being deprived of the ability to genuinely disrupt that centre.

As Patricia Waugh points out, the counterculture of the sixties eventually acted as the agent of its own demise, for its 'wholesale rejection of rationality was always likely to play into the hands of the capitalist entrepreneurs and subsequently into those of the authoritarian right'.[15] For Carter, however, the sixties becomes transformed into an emblematic historical moment in which the counterculture is dynamically disruptive, refusing to stand still long enough to become codified as part of the discursive centre. And because it is a movement permanently in flux, it offers her the perfect standpoint from which mainstream culture can be interrogated.

Although written in the 1980s, Carter's essay can be read as a kind of retrospective countercultural manifesto. Patricia Waugh, describing the writing of such prominent figures within the intellectual counterculture as R. D. Laing, Timothy Leary and Jean Genet, says: 'Barriers, thresholds, and doorways, which must be blown up, or broken down, are pervasive metaphors throughout the countercultural manifestos of the time'.[16] 'Truly, It Felt Like Year One' conforms to Waugh's description almost too knowingly, organised as it is around recurrent images of demolition and upheaval. According to Carter's account, the cultural and social changes instigated during this period were so profound that by the end of the decade, 'it started to feel like living on a demolition site – one felt one was living on the edge of the unimaginable' (p. 211). Characteristically, Carter reveals little of her actual personal circumstances during this period apart to mention her first marriage in terms which tie her emotional life into the dominant mood of the time: 'I was married most of the sixties – the sense of living on a demolition site was perfectly real, in one way, because I stopped being married in 1969' (p. 213).

The picture Carter paints of her sixties self, therefore, is of someone perfectly in tune with her environment personally, politically and intellectually. It is a decade which nurtures her not only as an individual, but also, most importantly, as a writer; an element which is emphasised by the fact that this is a characteristically 'writerly' piece. Carter's style here is deliberately self-conscious, foregrounding attempts made by the fabulator to take over from the social commentator. At one point, for example, she figuratively represents class as a disfigurement on the face of Britain, and the new idea of education for all as offering 'some of the benefits of plastic surgery'. But then the fanciful analogy is abruptly terminated by an arch warning to the writing self to 'not get carried away by my own imagery' (p. 211).

Within the frame of reference Carter herself sets up, however, this period is one in which such an elaborate response is not unfitting, given her portrayal of it as a decade in which 'everyday life . . . took on the air of a continuous improvisation' (p. 212). After all, she concludes, this is 'the time of the loony' (p. 215), in which R. D. Laing's book *The Divided Self* – which argued that 'In the context of our present pervasive

madness that we call normality, sanity, freedom, all our frames of reference are ambiguous and equivocal'[17] – made insanity fashionable. Thus,
even while her belief that the sixties were a period of complete sexual
equality and classlessness turns out to be to some extent delusional, it
is at least a delusion appropriate to the time.

Although it approaches the subject from a totally opposite direction,
this aspect of Carter's portrayal of the sixties is worth comparing with
Christopher Booker's study, *The Neophiliacs*, as he describes the decade
in terms that are very much reminiscent of her approach. It was, he
argues, a time of consensual mass-hallucination, in which traditional
values were subsumed in sensation-seeking and theatricality, transforming Britain's cultural landscape into a kind of unreal city populated
only by 'the strangely garbed young'.[18] However, Booker arrives at quite
different conclusions from Carter, proclaiming that this 'path of illusion
leads inevitably to frustration ... and self destruction',[19] as humanity
loses touch with all the values, myths and social rituals which 'hold
together man's sense of unity'.[20]

But what has Booker reeling in horror is precisely what Carter was
celebrating in her fiction of the time – the defeat of sincere, reactionary
belief in the social and ideological status quo. As far as she was concerned all myth, far from representing 'that fundamental harmony
between this framework of myths [which] represents that fundamental
harmony between man's [*sic*] life and order instincts which shapes his
only true and healthy mode of existence',[21] was merely so much 'conso-
latory nonsense'.[22] And in the wreckage of old myths and moral values,
the subversive writer is free to play.

'The Man Who Loved a Double Bass' (1962)

'The Man Who Loved a Double Bass' is an accessible example of how
Carter explicitly linked both the form and the content of her fiction to
the countercultural environment from the beginning. It was one of
Carter's earliest published stories, appearing in *Storyteller Contest* in
July 1962.[23] The story is simple enough. It centres around Johnny
Jameson, who plays the double bass with a mildly successful band
called the West End Syncopators. An eccentric individual, Jameson
insists on treating his double bass as though it were alive, calling it
'Lola', and endowing it with a exaggeratedly genteel female personality.
The other players in the band go along with the joke, to the extent that
they almost come to believe it themselves. However, whilst playing an

engagement in an isolated part of the East Anglian Fens, a fight breaks out amongst different cliques in the audience and the double bass is smashed. Unable to live without his beloved instrument, Jameson hangs himself.

Measured by Carter's later standards, this story is only mildly weird, but it is an interesting indication of how her narrative technique was evolving, even as early as 1962. Although she later moved on to develop more unequivocal fantastic forms, much of her early fiction is based upon a subversion of realism. As Marc O'Day says,

> Several of the early novels actually invite readings in terms of quite traditional literary realism. True, it is a sixties realism saturated with domesticated gothic and psychological fantasy elements, but 'magic', in the sense of supernatural or fantastic violations of the laws of everyday life, hardly comes into it.[24]

This is an apt summary of Carter's approach in this early short story, in which nothing happens which cannot be explained away rationally, but which is nevertheless presented in such a way as to subvert rational explanation.

Carter achieves this by situating the point of view of a clearly unbalanced primary protagonist within a subculture in which standards of behaviour not usually thought of as 'normal' are condoned or even celebrated. In 'The Man Who Loved a Double Bass' this is the 'phenomenally close-knit creative community' in which 'the consciously eccentric are always respectful and admiring of those who have the courage to be genuinely a little mad' (p. 3). Within this environment, Jameson's fellow musicians are happy to treat Lola as if she were the woman of his fantasies. They always, for example, buy her drinks in cafes and pubs because it is an eccentric affectation that appeals to their sense of the bohemian. Because there are thus no characters who oppose the general fantasy, Carter can move smoothly into a mode of writing that allows for Lola's maximum personification: 'Jameson was very worried in case the damp should hurt Lola, warp her, rot her strings. He allowed one of the grammar school boys ... to buy her a rum and orange, for her health's sake' (p. 5). Although it is always perfectly obvious to the reader that Jameson is deluded, and probably at least a little deranged, Carter's treatment of Lola nevertheless makes the double bass a disquieting anomaly in the surface realism of the text.

The theme of derangement, however, is not permitted to remain

comfortably quarantined within either a subculture or the perspective
of a particular individual. Instead, as the story continues, it permeates
into the wider social order. The sixties are portrayed as an era of collective schizophrenia, in which the individual is presented with a number
of potential, often conflicting, identities. It is a theme which Carter
evokes primarily through her references to fashion, a phenomenon
which interested her throughout her career, believing as she did that
'everybody's appearance is their symbolic autobiography'.[25] In the setting of a remote jazz club in East Anglia, the different modes of dress
of the sixties are described and paraded: the mods, the rockers, the
beatniks and the pseudo-beatniks, all divided from one another by the
uniform of their chosen allegiance:

> Gradually the room began to fill. Art students from a nearby town,
> sniggering at the bourgeois who aped them; a party of crop-haired
> modernists, who had also travelled some distance. The modernists
> had sharp, pointed noses and Italian suits. Their girls dressed with
> studied formality, faces stylised, pale cheeks and lips, vividly
> painted eyes, hair immaculate, stiff with lacquer. (pp. 6–7)

This is no party, but a parade of antagonistic difference in which incipient violence is an integral element, and it is therefore no surprise when
the scene soon erupts into brawls among the different factions. The
whole unwieldy apparatus of the ghost story which Carter includes
here – the isolated fenland settlement, the fog, the 'slow creak, creak,
creak' (p. 10) of the rope by which Jameson's body hangs from the
rafters – is only so much window-dressing, stale from convention. What
is really disquieting in this narrative is the inversion of values taking
place within a public social setting. Here, what should be superficial
frivolity (fashion) becomes frighteningly serious, while violence is
treated as spectacle: 'The Young Conservatives came scurrying past
shepherding frightened Susans, Brendas, and Jennifers. But the art
students clustered safely at the door to giggle. The tight-skirted teddy
girls dropped their impassivity; like valkyries they rode the battle,
cheering the fighters on' (p. 8).

Short though it is, in this story Carter has created a sketch of sixties
culture which is celebratory and chilling at one and the same time.
Identities in this narrative are precarious and changeable, and not only
for the costumed youngsters on the jazz-hall dance floor. All the characters are to some extent playing games with who they are. On the

strength of a song which 'had penetrated to the lower reaches of the top twenty' (p. 4), the West End Syncopators are play-acting the role of stars, while their Jewish manager makes 'his race ... his gimmick', dressing 'like a stage Jew' and 'affect[ing] a strong Yiddish accent' (p. 5) in order to obscure his respectable bourgeois origins. In a more positive context, such adopting and dismantling of identities could seem to offer the freedom to experiment with different versions of the self; however, it is difficult to make a case for such an interpretation here. Instead, the world of the story collapses into a fragmented, irreconcilable collage of arbitrary difference, literally embodied in the 'heap of chestnut-coloured firewood' that is Lola's 'pathetic fragmented corpse' (p. 9).

Furthermore, there is no stable identity on which a resistance to such a conclusion could be built, for the only figure in the story who deserves the epithet 'sincere' is Jameson, whose fixation on Lola is such that it leads to his suicide. Consequently, the narrative presents the reader with two, equally problematic, extremes: the insane obsession of Jameson versus the frenetic theatrical flaunting of alternative identities engaged in by everyone else. The problem inherent in this tactic is, however, that Carter's narrative can itself be viewed merely as an artefact of sixties cultural style, all fragmented superficiality and no substance, rather than as a critique which is rooted in an effective political sensibility.

Shadow Dance (1966)

What 'The Man Who Loved a Double Bass' therefore sets up – and purposely conspicuously fails to resolve – is a tension between excess and restraint, through which the freedom the decade offered for playing with new images and versions of the self is simultaneously configured as both desirable and dangerous. In claiming the freedom to construct identity as multiple and mutable, Carter's narratives also flirt with the risk of the obliteration of an independent subjectivity altogether. However, in Shadow Dance, and later on in Several Perceptions, Carter demonstrates her awareness of this risk by dramatising it within her narrative structures. Both novels are littered with imagery suggestive of borderlines and liminal spaces, which are no sooner evoked than transgressed. In their introductory scenes, the alienated individual whose narrative point of view pervades the action moves uneasily within a setting which is largely coloured by his own subliminal fears and fantasies, and which intentionally makes the line between subjectivity

and objectivity almost impossible to draw. Thus, reader as well as character is drawn into an environment within which the validity of everything
is open to question.

The opening of *Shadow Dance* is a case in point. It begins with a
meeting between Morris, the novel's main character and its controlling
narrative voice, and Ghislaine, a once beautiful girl, now horribly
scarred. Morris's unhealthy fascination with Ghislaine's mutilation
permeates and distorts the scene, transforming it into a surreal mixture
of Hieronymous Bosch nightmare and an over-the-top Hammer Horror
sensibility which verges on the risible. Ghislaine, whose 'long vowels
moan . . . like the wind in pines' (p. 1)[26] is 'the bride of Frankenstein' (p.
4); a 'witch-woman' (p. 6), disfigured by a scar which is 'like a big, red
crack across ice and might suddenly open up and swallow her into herself, screaming, herself into herself' (p. 10). The scar, a quite literal
boundary-line which divides Ghislaine's face into two halves, is
described in detail later on in the book:

> The whole cheek was a mass of corrugated white flesh, like a bowl
> of blancmange a child has played with and not eaten. Through
> this devastation ran a deep central trough that went right down
> her throat under the collar of her coat. . . . But the other half of
> the face was fresh and warm as fruit in the sunlight. (pp. 152–3)

For Morris, paralysed by his guilty feelings of complicity in Ghislaine's
wounding, the scar comes to represent a conceptual break between the
past and the present; what Ghislaine was and what she is: 'a beautiful
girl, a white and golden girl, like moon-light on daisies, a month ago. So
he stared at her shattered beauty' (p. 3). He finds this rift in normality
horrific, terrified that her face 'might suddenly – at too large a mouthful
of drink or a smile too unwisely wide or a face-splitting request for
"bread and cheeeeeeese" – leak gallons of blood and drown them all,
and herself, too' (p. 3).

As Morris's fixation on blood in the above quotation suggests, the
disruption of his world (as in 'The Man Who Loves a Double Bass') is
represented primarily through violence. In the bar which is a glorious
testament to sixties kitsch, 'a mock-up, a forgery, a fake; an ad-man's
crazy dream' (p. 1), Ghislaine's presence arouses an anticipatory tension
among the crowd of regular drinkers. Like emotional vampires, they
gather to witness 'an orgy of emotion, with blows and tears and violence'
(p. 8). While a fight does not actually break out, Morris has a bottle

thrown at him as he leaves the bar. Unable to believe that he is unhurt, his shock at the aggressive act throws him into 'a metaphysical hinterland between intention and execution . . . there was a dimension, surely, in the outer nebulae, maybe, where intentions were always executed, where even now he stumbled, bleeding, blinded . . .' (p. 11).

In a sense, Morris's worst fears have indeed been realised. He has stumbled into the crevice that has opened up between past and present, reality and fantasy, and precipitated into a world composed of, in the words of Lorna Sage, 'leftovers, quotes, copies, *déjà vu*', in which 'the borders between art and trash, life and death, are busily dissolving'.[27] One could add another disintegrating binary opposition here – thought and action. In this moral and cultural wasteland (and the echo of T. S. Eliot is entirely intentional), the thought *is* the act; not in the sense of being able to control one's environment through the exercise of the intellect, but in terms of hidden, guilty desires freed of the prison of their originator's mind, and thus enabled to wreak havoc in the realm of the 'real'.

Although Morris's world is largely constructed through his own neuroses, the novel gains its Gothic impetus from implying that it is as actually bereft of value and meaning as he supposes it to be. In an echo of 'The Man Who Loved a Double Bass', his larger environment loses none of its sense of historical specificity. Instead, his private derangements both feed into and are fed by the public cultural turmoil of the period, with the result that no standards of 'normality' can be employed by which to judge his thoughts or actions. In *Shadow Dance*, this dilemma is foregrounded in the figure of the dandy, whom Carter configures as the primary representative of this moral crisis.

For Carter, the dandy is not just someone who likes dressing up, even though he does indeed tend to possess that characteristic. More than that, he is the representative of 'modernity' according to Baudelaire's definition of the term. In his essay 'What is Enlightenment?', Foucault argues that Baudelaire characterised modernity 'in terms of consciousness of the discontinuity of time: a break with tradition, a feeling of novelty, of vertigo in the face of the passing moment'.[28] The dandy is the man who responds to modernity's demand that he 'face the task of producing himself',[29] as opposed to the concept of *discovering* 'himself, his secrets and his hidden truth'.[30] An entirely self-created being who is the possessor of neither past or a future, only an ever-changing yet also curiously static present, he is therefore the embodiment of a particular cultural moment, itself dandified and inherently superficial.

George Melly describes sixties pop culture as promoting 'the idea of instant success based on the promotion of a personal style rather than a search for content or meaning',[31] which is effectively Baudelaire's definition of the dandy rendered in twentieth-century terms.

But although the dandy is born of a particular response to the modern condition, he also embodies the eternal nightmare of non-being, for behind his seductive mask may lie, quite literally, nothing. In this sense, he is capable of being read through Bakhtin's theory of the Romantic grotesque.[32] According to Bakhtin, although the concept of carnival and its humorous references to the grotesque originated out of medieval festivals, Romanticism 'radically transformed' the meaning of the grotesque genre by making it 'the expression of subjective, individualistic world outlook very different from the carnival folk concept of previous ages, although still containing some carnival elements'.[33] The Romantic grotesque embraces a frightening solipsism, in which the isolated, alienated subject can no longer draw on a comforting tradition of community and laughter:

> The world of Romantic grotesque is to a certain extent a terrifying world, alien to man. All that is ordinary, commonplace, belonging to everyday life, and recognized by all suddenly becomes meaningless, dubious and hostile. Our own world becomes an alien world. Something frightening is revealed in that which was habitual and secure.[34]

This is an apt description of the dilemma faced by Morris, of which his business associate Honeybuzzard becomes the personification. Honeybuzzard, a fallen angel with dirty fingernails and greasy shirt-collar, is an ambiguous character who is the embodiment of transgressed categories and boundaries, as Lorna Sage describes:

> To understand Honeybuzzard's dubious charm for his creator, as well as for characters in the book, you have to recognise that he alone belongs to two words, in gender terms, and, in terms just as vital to Carter the writer, the real (life) and the shadow (art). He is on that fault-line, an early embodiment of her conviction that the fantastical and the actual can exist in the same plane.[35]

Honeybuzzard is a creature of the sixties cultural hinterland, and thus inherently problematic: a 'mobile, empty'[36] sign in the Barthesean sense, who stands for nothing but the negation of meaning. As his name implies, he is an irreconcilable combination of the sweet and the predatory – 'beautiful', but also 'indefinably sinister' (p. 56); a compulsive liar who, because he believes his own stories, is perversely sincere. His games and affectations are inventive and entertaining at the same time as being exploitative and, eventually, murderous.

He is also definitively camp, both in his mode of dress and his cultural attitudes. His 'flamboyant and ambiguous beauty' (p. 55) is androgynous, thus posing an implicit challenge to dualistic categories of gender, and his love of flashy, outrageous costume renders notional any concept of a fixed and stable identity. Indeed, it is an idea which is totally alien to Honeybuzzard, whose wish is 'to have a cupboard bulging with all different bodies and faces and choose a fresh one every morning' (p. 78). Elizabeth Wilson defines camp fashion as an 'aesthetic of the banal in which everything is surface':[37] a neat description of Honeybuzzard, for he is so dedicated to making a spectacle of himself that it is impossible to ascertain the underlying motives behind his increasingly irrational actions. In his very being, he represents Bakhtin's idea of the grotesque mask of Romanticism, which 'hides something, keeps a secret, deceives'.[38] It is no accident, after all, that he is the person responsible for the horrific scarring of Ghislaine.

Within his setting, however, Honeybuzzard is no anomaly, but an expression – as well as an exploiter – of the larger camp culture within which he moves. According to Andrew Ross, an inherent characteristic of camp is its 'rediscovery of history's waste. . . . [which] retrieves not only that which had been initially excluded from the serious high cultural tradition, but also the more unsalvageable material that had been picked over and left wanting by purveyors of the "antique"'.[39] This is an apt summary of the situation evoked by Carter in *Shadow Dance*, for as well as *being* camp, Honeybuzzard is also a knowing purveyor of sixties camp taste. Together with Morris he deals in junk, plundered from the debris of the past in nocturnal excursions to abandoned houses that are on the point of demolition. Here they find the personal flotsam and jetsam of long-gone people's lives, which they clean, polish and sell for a profit to Americans 'as conversation pieces' (p. 90).

Floating free of any historical or aesthetic value system which might give them meaning, scruffy artefacts can be turned into profit by such cultural scavengers, giving an added ingenuousness to Carter's statement in 'Truly, It Felt Like Year One' that the people of the sixties were 'early into recycling'.[40] Morris frequently feels a certain nostalgia for the past, often trying to decipher clues about the lifestyle of the original owners from the items they find. No such emotions bother Honeybuzzard, however, for centred as he is around the self and the moment, such relics can have only two possible uses: either to make money, or to act as props in his ever-changing production of himself.

In this novel, therefore, there comes a moment when this production fails, for Honeybuzzard, in his excesses, finally steps too definitively over the boundary dividing camp from tragedy. Susan Sontag argues that camp must never get too serious, for while 'There is a seriousness in camp . . . there is never, never tragedy',[41] and *Shadow Dance* quite deliberately transgresses this divide. Honeybuzzard's final theatrical presentation is the murder of Ghislaine in an abandoned house, laying her out on a trestle table in a makeshift chapel 'illuminated by innumerable candles stuck with their own grease to every horizontal surface' (p. 176). What he has set up is another over-the-top scene from a Hammer Horror film, or perhaps a piece of avant-garde performance art. The trouble is, however, that Ghislaine is really dead, and with this action, Honey has broken through the boundaries of camp. In abandoning the space between art and life, fantasy and reality, he has 'fallen through a hole in time into a dimension of pure horror' (p. 178). His final appearance reinforces this impression, with all the layers of artifice and costume 'pared away'. For the first time in the book he is not conscious of being watched, and so does not perform, appearing 'naked and elementary and unknowable in the integrity of his own skeleton' (p. 179).

Carter said later that she had drawn the ending of this book directly from Dostoyevsky's *The Idiot*.[42] Nevertheless, Honey ends the book still a figure defined by references to theatre as much as to literature, although tellingly he has passed into a different genre. Dancing a cakewalk in his 'happy hat' (p. 89) for Morris, he is a character from burlesque or music-hall. Jumping out at an unsuspecting old lady like 'a spectre, a madman, a vampire' (p. 136), he participates in the Hammer Horror mode already evoked through Ghislaine. Underneath it all, however, as has actually been apparent to us from the beginning of the novel, is a far darker and more destructive persona which deals in authentic horror and real death. With the 'angles and planes of the skull . . . showing through the flesh' (p. 179), his role is now that of a murderer from a Jacobean tragedy, whose savage excesses put him beyond the reach of the redeeming, and comforting, exercise of irony.

Essentially, therefore, where the camp burlesque of *Shadow Dance*

falters badly is over its treatment of women, which could come as a
nasty shock to any reader accustomed to thinking of Carter as a feminist writer. Although Carter appears to be trying to create a world in
which you make your own rules unfettered by the traditions or moral
assumptions of an outmoded past, it is a freedom that the text often
seems only to extend to men. Furthermore, the treatment meted out to
Ghislaine makes some kind of moral response to the text on the part of
the reader unavoidable.

To be fair, it would be incorrect to try to force this narrative to
conform to contemporary feminist views that were not in the author's
mind when she wrote it, for at this period in her career Carter 'didn't
see the point of feminism'.[43] One should also take into account her
tendency towards wilful perversity, which delighted in toppling belief
systems of any kind; an iconoclastic process from which nothing was
exempt.

It is also possible to argue, as Lorna Sage does, that Honeybuzzard
is an early example of Carter's 'radical pornographer', who 'strips away
the mystifications of sex and sentiment to reveal the working of power
underneath'.[44] In this context, his violent treatment of Ghislaine – and
thus by implication the violent treatment meted out to many of Carter's
female characters in her early fiction – can be justified as a kind of
(anti)morality play which aims to undermine through exaggeration.

It was nevertheless an element in her writing for which Carter later
apologised, claiming in 1992, for example, that 'It took me a long time
to identify patriarchal bias in my discourse'.[45] It is in *Shadow Dance* that
this bias is most disturbingly obvious, for this is a text in which women
are resolutely denied the privilege of a narrative voice. By excluding
them from the formation of discourse, they are rendered figments of a
fevered male imagination, and become the targets of a disturbing blend
of violence and eroticism. Like Lola in 'The Man Who Loved a Double
Bass', women become silent receptacles for male desires, yet from a
male point of view their very passivity renders them dangerously
destructive. Even Lola, it can be argued, becomes a kind of monster at
the end, for Jameson's desire for her, magnified and reflected through
the medium of her acquiescent receptivity, rebounds upon him with
fatal consequences.

Ghislaine, of course, is the most extreme example of this process.
When Morris meets her in the bar at the beginning of the book, his
extreme reaction to her is partly revulsion at her ugliness, combined

with guilt at 'the memory of her naked, threshing about beneath him' (p. 5). He is also patently annoyed at her 'unfeminine' display of economic independence: 'Shall I buy a drink for you, Morris? Have you no money? Always penniless, poor Morris' (p. 1). Yet he can transfer his guilt for both emotions onto Ghislaine herself by classifying her as the monstrous representative of a voracious, predatory, female sexuality. Infinitely malleable to any number of interpretations, Ghislaine's scar again becomes the focus of this symbolism, where it is transformed into a grotesque image of the female genitalia; open, grinning and never satisfied. Later on in the book, for example, Morris dreams of Ghislaine as 'a vampire woman, walking the streets on the continual qui vive, her enormous brown eyes alert and ever-watchful, and the moment she saw him she would snatch him up and absorb him, threshing, into the chasm in her face' (p. 39). This description of himself as 'threshing' chimes yet contrasts with his earlier use of the verb. Then, it was applied to Ghislaine, but now its transferral to himself signals her transformation from sexual prey to street-walking predator.

Although Honeybuzzard is the person who finally kills Ghislaine, Morris recognises his own complicity in the crime, for all Honey has done is to dare to act out what Morris 'had always wanted but never defined. . . . choking out of Ghislaine her little-girl giggle . . . filling up her voracity once and for all by cramming with death the hungry mouth between her thighs' (pp. 178–9). As a statement of murderous misogyny, this could hardly be bettered, but the elaborate mythology which is built up around Ghislaine tends to obscure the fact that she has done very little, if anything at all, to deserve it, apart from becoming the repository of the guilty secret of Morris's own adultery. And as Mary Russo has noted, misogyny and the grotesque spectacle have always had a certain affinity, enabling woman to be 'cruelly observed in intricate detail, but never allowed to make words'.[46] In later books, Carter will give her female characters the power to appropriate and subvert that process, but it is not a power shared by poor Ghislaine.

Morris's attitude towards women is also evident in his treatment of his wife, Edna. Mousey and meek, Edna bears very little relation to the glamorous and predatory Ghislaine, but she is no less a product of the male imagination. Whereas it is a process which renders Ghislaine monstrously larger-than-life, in Edna's case it works to reduce her, viewed as she is by Morris as 'a Victorian girl' who thinks 'marriage . . . [is] for submission and procreation' (p. 45). If he had not married her, he thinks self-righteously at one point, 'she would have aged into a cat-spinster in a bed-sitter' (p. 23). Honey's reaction to her is characteristic: he regards her as an example of the type of woman 'you can only vivisect . . . the pink-eyed, laboratory-rat sort of woman' (p. 62).

Incongruously, however, it is through Edna that the possibility of female empowerment can be glimpsed, however faintly, for at the end of the book she demonstrates a sexual independence that Morris, and hence the reader, has never suspected her of being capable. Presumably tired of bearing the weight of Morris's constant self-castigation, she finds happiness with another man. All unsuspecting, Morris comes upon them asleep in bed, like babes-in-the-wood, 'their two soft mouths curved flower-like in tranquillity, their tender eyelids waxen petals of repose' (p. 156). In freeing Morris from their sterile union, she also frees herself – a feat which Ghislaine, abasing herself before Honeybuzzard's sadism, proves unable to achieve.

Edna is not the only female in *Shadow Dance*, either, who resists the male impulse to reduce, belittle or damage women, for this text also contains characters who can be seen as the forerunners of the kind of subversive female figures who will assume increasing importance in Carter's later fiction. Honeybuzzard's girlfriend Emily and the enigmatic, ever-cheerful cafe waitress known only as the Struldbrug are seen by Lorna Sage as 'spell[ing] hope in the midst of the underworld of gloom'[47] which *Shadow Dance* otherwise evokes.

When she makes her first appearance in the narrative, complete with silver enamel fingernails, eclectic dress-sense and drugged white cat, Emily appears to be wholly part of Honeybuzzard's world. She also shares Honey's attribute of gender ambiguity, for

> With her height and her strong face and her heavy tread, one might almost have taken her for a boy dressed up as a girl in the Elizabethan theatre, when transvestism was an art form; what a foil she made for Honey's golden softness. (pp. 66–7)

However, while Honey might have chosen her for precisely that reason, there is far more to Emily than the role of supporting actor in his surreal personal drama. The epitome of solid, commonsense values – as Sage observes, Emily is a matriarch-in-the-making – she sets about getting Honeybuzzard's life organised according to her own rigorous standards of cleanliness and order. Although she is momentarily transfigured by her love for him, it does not affect her basic down-to-earth realism, for unlike Morris, who remains dazzled by Honeybuzzard's potent combination of glamour and menace to the end, Emily does not hesitate to turn him over to the police when they discover Ghislaine's body.

Emily's matriarchal proclivities are echoed in the text by the figure of the Struldbrug; a name which evokes the immortal beings in Swift's *Gulliver's Travels*, who grow old, ugly and senile, but are denied the release of death – but on a positive note, a term which signifies, perhaps, that one of the benefits of age is no longer being subject to the male habit of categorising women according to their perceived desirability. For Morris, whose mother died in an air-raid during the War, the Struldbrug signifies 'protective and benevolent' (p. 38) maternity, and he is shocked when Honey maliciously renders her prostrate with fear when they come across her squat in the basement of the ruined house which is to become the scene of Honeybuzzard's final descent into murderous insanity. The Struldbrug, however, proves to be beyond his power, resurfacing alive and singing in the morning.

It is the women in *Shadow Dance*, therefore, who become the means by which the text's camp façade is ruptured. They are not participants in the narcissistic spectacle, but its victims, and when they resist the role forced upon them, they reveal the true horror of a cultural environment in which ethical and evaluative concepts have become wholly relative. So although this text portrays the seductive glamour of the world of the spectacle, it is through its female characters that the necessity of an exterior reality is, however unwillingly, asserted.

Several Perceptions (1968)

Although written two years after *Shadow Dance*, and with *The Magic Toyshop* lying between, *Several Perceptions* bears a remarkable similarity to Carter's first novel. Its chief protagonist, Joseph, plays almost exactly the same role in the text as that allocated to Morris, and it also features a dandy figure, Kay Kyte, who possesses many of Honeybuzzard's attributes. However, although it shares many of the same narrative elements as *Shadow Dance*, and some of its horrific spirit, in the final analysis it is a much more optimistic novel, ending with reconciliation and renewal rather than murder and madness.

Madness, nevertheless, is a pervasive theme within the text; but perhaps this is part of the reason why *Several Perceptions* is not as horrific as *Shadow Dance*. While Honey's insanity, although hinted at, is never

examined, and thus seems to stem from a kind of inexplicable malig-
nancy, *Several Perceptions* is more explicit in its exploration of the
contradictions of madness. According to Carter, madness was 'one of
the sixties' preoccupations', and the novel's narrator 'is, in a very
Laingian and sixties fashion, responding to an insane world by becoming
insane'.[48]

The novel's opening directly recalls *Shadow Dance*, and Morris's confusion between reality and nightmare. Here, the protagonist is Joseph,
whose perspective, 'now and then glimpsing immense cracks in the
structure of the real world' (pp. 2–3),[49] renders it consistently strange.
Just as Morris is fixated on the line of Ghislaine's scar to the point that
it becomes indicative of any number of hidden meanings, so Joseph
becomes obsessed with the line which divides truth from lies. This
notion is initially embodied in the figure of Sunny, an old man who
plays an imaginary fiddle on the Down near Joseph's home. Sunny is
full of stories concerning his 'fascinating experiences as a professional
musician and man of the world'; however, Joseph reflects, 'he lied all
the time; it was hard to tell where the lies ended and the truth began'
(p. 2).

This existential uncertainty comes to extend to Joseph's perception
of himself. He becomes the quintessentially alienated subject, unable
to trust the validity of his own reflection in mirrors because when he
looks into them, he sees 'some other person and not himself at all, some
comparative stranger from whom he had rented this secret face out of
Jacobean drama' (p. 5). But although Joseph here takes on Honey's role
as Jacobean malcontent, incarnated in him it loses many of its dark
connotations. In *Radical Tragedy*, Jonathan Dollimore argues that the
malcontent can 'be seen as a prototype of the modern decentred subject, the bearer of a subjectivity which is . . . the focus of political, social,
and ideological contradiction',[50] and it is in this sense, I think, that the
allusion is being used here. Unable to grasp any sense of himself as
occupying a secure place within a stable reality, Joseph's response is to
become much obsessed by death, consumed by feelings of guilt and an
unconsummated desire for expiation in a world he reconfigures in
nightmare terms. Bereft of meaning or value, it is 'a world of paralogic
and irrationality' populated by 'strange flora and fauna of the antipodes
of the mind, where concepts stood on their heads' (p. 20).

In self-defence, Joseph develops a fascination with facts, in the hope
that 'they might help to shore up the crumbling dome of the world'
(p. 3). When he decides to escape 'the banal apparatus of despair' (p. 16)

with which he feels himself surrounded, he seizes on the one fact he thinks he knows to be true – his own mortality. When even this lets him down, however, and he survives his dramatic attempt to kill himself, he believes he has gained a position on the far side of catastrophe where 'even the idea of meaning was abandoned; nothing was sacred and, since there was no reason for his arbitrary resurrection, there was no significance in anything he would do again' (p. 30).

Yet, as in *Shadow Dance*, Carter ultimately refuses to confirm this sense of nihilistic alienation as the delusion of one man. Instead, she reinforces Joseph's phobias in a scene which signals that sixties culture as a whole is precariously balanced on the edge of breakdown and fragmentation. A fight breaks out between Joseph's friend Kay and an anonymous young man, maliciously engineered by a girl with 'extraordinary flashing black eyes and a backcombed beehive of black hair' (p. 51) for seemingly no particular reason other than to make herself the leading character in her own private 'Jacobean tragedy' (p. 51). When the unwilling antagonists square off against each other, Joseph senses 'a jagged atmosphere in the bar; things were happening without a sequence, there was no flow or pattern to events. Causation was still awry' (p. 52). The scene is described by means of a series of disjointed tableaux, and the whole surreal episode ends suitably inconclusively, motivation and meaning – if they were ever there at all – undisclosed. However, its larger purpose – to confirm Joseph's paranoid irrationality as the only rational response within an irrational environment – has been achieved.

But while *Shadow Dance* makes the dandy the representative of this essentially meaningless and incipiently violent world, *Several Perceptions* allocates him a far more redemptive role. Kay Kyte, who conveys little of Honeybuzzard's implicit menace, is a much more straightforward embodiment of the creative aspect of the carnivalesque in a narrative that lacks the dark nihilism of *Shadow Dance*, and which defines the characteristics and aims of camp slightly differently. Whereas Honey revels in iconoclastic destruction, Kay ends the book as the master of ceremonies of a riotous Christmas party which signifies renewal, and an escape (although maybe only a temporary one) from the incoherence of everyday existence.

Nevertheless, the two characters are closely, consciously, linked. Kay's surname alone is enough to link him to Honeybuzzard, for it contains similar predatory allusions; in fact, Joseph can never see him without thinking 'with distress of the habits of kytes, fierce birds of

prey' (p. 11). And, like Honeybuzzard, Kay always gives 'the appearance of being in costume' (p. 10), his dress a flamboyant and colourful
assemblage of disparate parts described by Carter in loving detail:

> He wore Levi jeans and jacket. . . . On his head he wore a khaki
> forage cap and golden ear-rings glinted in his ears. The rest of his
> outfit comprised: a flannel shirt, lacking a collar, probably bought
> at or stolen from a jumble sale then dyed a cheerful orange in the
> communal spaghetti saucepan; green round wire-rimmed sun-
> glasses; dirty white plimsolls; and a blue enamel St Christopher
> medallion round his neck, together with a doorkey on a bit of
> string and an iron cross. (p. 10)

Kay, even more than Honeybuzzard, conveys the love of dress-up and
disguise which for Carter was one of the most potent symbols of the
sixties cultural revolution. In her essay 'Notes for a Theory of Sixties
Style', she argues:

> The inscrutable but imperative logic of change has forced fashion
> in the sixties through the barriers of space and time. Clothes today
> sometimes seem arbitrary and bizarre; nevertheless, the startling
> dandyism of the newly emancipated young reveals a kind of logic
> of whizzing entropy.

Sixties style, she says, is eminently individual, composed of 'eclectic
fragments, robbed of their symbolic content, [which] fall together to
form a new whole'.[51]

Kay's environment, though, is one which Honeybuzzard would
recognise; a huge, crumbling mansion owned by Kay's mother, who has
made it a shrine to her semi-mythical theatrical past. But the novel ends
with it becoming the scene of a party, not a murder, where Kay and his
'floating world' of followers celebrate amongst 'antic surroundings of
faked luxury and rampant neglect' (p. 128). In an indiscriminate jumble
of junk and art, Woolworth paper-chains are hung around the marble
fireplace which is 'carved with a chastely sumptuous design of urns and
garlands' (p. 128); and a light fitting which is 'the relic of an abandoned
super-cinema' (p. 129) is 'wreathed with plastic roses' (p. 130). In addition, every wall is hung with mirrors, with the result that 'normal'
spatial perspective becomes completely distorted, making the party-
goers 'in their gipsyish clothes of so many colours . . . seem . . . fragments

in a giant kaleidoscope kept continually on the turn by a child's restless hand or pieces of disintegrated rainbow' (p. 126).

However, this episode is more than just a celebration of the sixties' talent for recycling; it is a quasi-fantastic environment within which Kay is transformed into a carnivalesque figure full of hidden significance. Unlike Honeybuzzard who, however actively he may assert it, still stands for nothing but meaninglessness, Kay becomes indicative of a new kind of cultural rebirth based on the courage to reject, rather than be reconciled with, the past. Under his auspices, marvellous things happen. Sunny regains his fiddle, which, it turns out, he really can play. Joseph's limping neighbour, Annie Blossom, is persuaded to walk properly again, throwing off, by implication, her belief that her lameness was a punishment for past misdeeds. Joseph, too, is finally restored, vowing to 'throw away my book of facts' (p. 140) and reject the 'rational' perspective his psychiatrist keeps trying to foist upon him. This momentarily resembles the Bakhtinian concept of the medieval carnival, which represents 'temporary liberation from the prevailing truth and from the established order. . . . the feast of becoming, change and renewal'.[52]

It is also, however, pure camp, for according to Susan Sontag, while camp 'is playful, anti-serious', it also 'involves a new, more complex relation to "the serious"'.[53] This is precisely the final assertion of *Several Perceptions*, and what sharply differentiates it from *Shadow Dance*. Momentary though its usurpation of the 'real' might be, Kay's party symbolises a brief period in which the camp flaunting of artifice and the breakdown of categories of value might actually work a change on people's lives.

It is perhaps unsurprising that a text which avoids the Gothic excesses of *Shadow Dance* should lack a figure analogous to that of Ghislaine. Nevertheless, Carter briefly allocates a kind of watered-down Ghislaine role to Annie Blossom, Joseph's fellow lodger. When Joseph first meets her he has developed a jaundiced view of womankind after the failure of his relationship with Charlotte, a woman he recreates in his imagination in Ghislaine-like terms:

That face, reincarnated in fantasy after fantasy, recreated nightly in dreams for months after she left, had become transformed in his mind to a Gothic mask, huge eyeballs hooded with lids of stone, cheekbones sharp as steel, lips of treacherous vampire redness and a wet red mouth which was a mantrap of ivory fangs.

Witchwoman. Incubus. Haunter of battlefields after the carnage
in the image of a crow. . . . His Madonna of the abattoir'. (p. 15)

Although Joseph has a certain self-awareness that is lacking in Morris,
appearing to be aware that the image he is constructing of the departed
Charlotte does not correspond to reality, he preserves Morris's tendency
to see sexually desirable women as dangerous, whilst disregarding and
belittling those he classifies as unattractive. When he first meets Annie,
for example, he sees 'a plain brick in the wall of the world . . . shy and
ungracious', possessing the 'anonymous face . . . of a girl with a paper
carrier bag of groceries waiting at a rainy bus stop or the blurred news-
paper face of a girl raped and murdered by a perfect stranger while
walking by herself in a wood' (p. 37). Again, there's a sinister undercurrent of incipient violence underlying these reflections, and a sense in
which, at this point, he resembles Honeybuzzard in regarding the
anonymous woman as fair game for vivisection, rape or murder.

However, Annie also recalls Edna's apparent colourlessness and hidden
drive for independence, demonstrating the capacity to step outside the
confines of Joseph's preconceptions by revealing herself possessed of a
history and a strength for survival which he has never suspected. In this
text, though, Carter gives the reader a hint by surrounding Annie with
incongruously extravagant Keatsian imagery from early on in the text.
Joseph comes upon her, for example, 'alone and palely loitering' in the
garden one morning, 'a mystery, she in her secretary suit among the
withered flowers' (p. 43). Annie, though, is no 'la belle dame sans
merci', but victim of a heartless seduction, left pregnant with a child she
was forced to give up in 'an act of savage love' (p. 100). And she, like
Morris, is liberated from her sense of guilt at Kay's Christmas baccha-
nal, an experience which, quite literally, grants her physical freedom by
curing her of her lameness.

In a further parallel with *Shadow Dance*, *Several Perceptions* also
features an indestructible older woman who is an object of fascination
for Joseph, another motherless boy. Mrs Boulder embodies the contradictory combination of matriarch and whore (paint and power on top,
'gentle, withered skin' [p. 50] underneath); a dichotomy which echoes
her narrative role. Like the Struldbrug, Mrs Boulder is both real
woman and a representative of the fantastic. In one dimension she is a
pathetic woman desperately afraid of growing old, but in the other, she
is a powerful embodiment of the female principle who is wholly in
control of the hold she has over Joseph's imagination. And, like the

majority of Carter's other strong female characters (Fevvers comes to mind), Mrs Boulder is also the possessor of a sound economic sense. As she says of her career in prostitution:

'For years I felt degraded, I felt I was such a sinner I'd never be washed clean. But if death is the wages of sin, it's the wages of virtue, too. And I was making such a lot of money, you'd never believe it'. (p. 117)

Along with Annie, Mrs Boulder participates in the text's festive resolution, playing the white queen to a magnificent African king at Kay's fancy-dress party, and it is this integration of women into the carnivalesque that signifies a distinctive point of departure from *Shadow Dance*. While in the earlier book, the concept of the empowered woman is antithetical to the camp aesthetic, here they are allowed a participatory role. Their power to change things within their narrative world is not limited to strategies of stubborn resistance, and they appear to have the power to redeem others as well as themselves. However, they are still to a certain extent marginalised in a text which is narrated from a male point of view, as their portrayal is always mediated through Joseph's undoubtedly warped perception of them.

Carter later criticised her own initial preference for such a male perspective, claiming in 'Notes from the Front Line' that in her writing of the sixties 'I'd – quite unconsciously – posit a male point of view as a general one. So there was an element of the male impersonator about this young person as she was finding herself'.[54] She is, however, being slightly hard on herself here, for this was also the period in which she began experimenting with female points of view, creating, in *The Magic Toyshop* and *Heroes and Villains*, heroines who are well able to withstand the seductive blandishments and murderous desires of the dandy.

Notes

1. Angela Carter, 'Afterword', in *Love* (London: Picador, 1988) [rev. edn], p. 113.
2. Marc O'Day, '"Mutability is Having a Field Day": The Sixties Aura of Angela Carter's Bristol Trilogy', in Lorna Sage (ed.), *Flesh and the Mirror: Essays on the Art of Angela Carter* (London: Virago Press, 1994), pp. 24–58.
3. Lorna Sage, *Angela Carter* (Plymouth: Northcote House, 1994), p. 9.

4. Susan Sontag, 'Notes on "Camp"', in *Against Interpretation* (New York: Dell Publishing, 1966), pp. 275–92 (p. 291).
5. ibid., p. 275.
6. Andrew Britton, 'For Interpretation: Notes Against Camp', in *Gay Left*, issue details unavailable.
7. George Melly, *Revolt into Style: The Pop Arts in the 50s and 60s* (Oxford: Oxford University Press, 1989), p. 18.
8. ibid., p. 192.
9. Andrew Ross, *No Respect: Intellectuals and Popular Culture* (London: Routledge, 1989), p. 151.
10. ibid., p. 149.
11. Richard Boston, 'Logic in a Schizophrenic's World', *New York Times Book Review* (2 March 1969), p. 42.
12. James Wood, 'Bewitchment', *London Review of Books* (8 December 1994), pp. 20–1 (p. 20).
13. O'Day, p. 30.
14. Angela Carter, 'Truly, It Felt Like Year One', in Sara Maitland (ed.), *Very Heaven: Looking Back at the 1960s* (London: Virago, 1988), pp. 209–16 (p. 210). All further references in the text are from this edition.
15. Patricia Waugh, *Harvest of the Sixties: English Literature and its Background 1960–1990* (Oxford: Oxford University Press, 1995), p. 116.
16. ibid., p. 7.
17. R. D. Laing, *The Divided Self* (Harmondsworth: Penguin, 1965), p. 11.
18. Christopher Booker, *The Neophiliacs: A Study of the Revolution in English Life in the Fifties and Sixties* (London: Collins, 1969), p. 20.
19. ibid., p. 310.
20. ibid., p. 315.
21. ibid., p. 312.
22. Angela Carter, *The Sadeian Woman* (London: Virago Press, 1979), p. 5.
23. It has been recently republished in *Burning Your Boats: Collected Short Stories* (London: Chatto & Windus, 1995), pp. 3–10. All further references in the text are from this edition.
24. O'Day, p. 24.
25. Lorna Sage, 'The Savage Sideshow', *New Review*, 4/39–40 (July 1977), pp. 51–7 (p. 56).
26. Angela Carter, *Shadow Dance* (London: Virago Press, 1994). All references in the text are from this edition.
27. Sage, *Angela Carter*, p. 10.
28. Michel Foucault, 'What is Enlightenment?', trans. Catherine Porter, in Paul Rabinow (ed.), *The Foucault Reader* (Harmondsworth: Penguin, 1984), pp. 32–50, (p. 39).
29. ibid., p. 41.
30. ibid., p. 42.
31. Melly, p. 4.
32. Although all the early novels are extremely susceptible to such a reading,

for once the echoes of Bakhtin were not, it seems, the result of a conscious decision on Carter's part. In a late interview with Lorna Sage Carter claimed not to have read Bakhtin until after having written *Nights at the Circus*, which many readers assumed was clearly influenced by his theories of the carnivalesque: 'She eventually read him', says Sage, 'because he was so often evoked by readers'. Lorna Sage, 'Angela Carter', in Malcom Bradbury and Judy Cooke (eds), *New Writing* (London: Minerva Press, 1992), pp. 185–93 (p. 188).

33. Mikhail Bakhtin, trans. Hélène Iswolsky, *Rabelais and His World* (Bloomington: Indiana University Press, 1984), p. 36.
34. ibid., pp. 38–9.
35. Lorna Sage, *Angela Carter*, p. 12.
36. Roland Barthes, *Empire of Signs*, trans. Richard Howard (London: Jonathan Cape, 1983), p. 10.
37. Elizabeth Wilson, *Adorned in Dreams: Fashion and Modernity* (London: Virago Press, 1985), p. 177.
38. Bakhtin, *Rabelais and His World*, p. 40.
39. Ross, p. 151.
40. Carter, 'Truly, It Felt Like Year One', p. 215.
41. ibid., p. 287.
42. Les Bedford, 'Angela Carter: An Interview' (Sheffield: Sheffield University Television, February 1977).
43. Susannah Clapp, 'On Madness, Men and Fairy-Tales', *The Independent on Sunday* (9 June 1991), pp. 26–7 (p. 26).
44. Sage, *Angela Carter*, p. 12.
45. Olga Kenyon, *The Writer's Imagination* (University of Bradford Print Unit, 1992), p. 25.
46. Mary Russo, *The Female Grotesque: Risk, Excess and Modernity* (London: Routledge, 1994), p. 6.
47. Sage, *Angela Carter*, p. 13.
48. Bedford, 'Angela Carter: An Interview'.
49. Angela Carter, *Several Perceptions* (London: Virago Press, 1995). All references in the text are from this edition.
50. Jonathan Dollimore, *Radical Tragedy: Religion, Ideology and Power in the Drama of Shakespeare and his Contemporaries*, 2nd edn (Hemel Hempstead: Harvester Wheatsheaf, 1989), p. 50.
51. Angela Carter, 'Notes Towards A Theory of Sixties Style', in *Nothing Sacred: Selected Writings* (London: Virago Press, 1982), pp. 84–90 (p. 86).
52. Bakhtin, p. 10.
53. Sontag, p. 288.
54. Carter, 'Notes from the Front Line', p. 71.

CHAPTER 3

Thematically as well as chronologically, *The Magic Toyshop* stands in-between *Shadow Dance* and *Several Perceptions*, sharing elements of each, yet distinct from both, which is why I have not chosen to analyse these three novels in the order in which they were written. While *The Magic Toyshop* does not share the nihilism of *Shadow Dance*, its ending does not quite convey the carnivalesque exuberance of *Several Perceptions*. Moreover, while *Shadow Dance* and *Several Perceptions* are clearly expressions of sixties sensibility, in particular through their adoption of the aesthetics of camp, *The Magic Toyshop* is ostensibly less of a period piece. This is essentially due to the fact that Carter draws more overtly in this text on fairytale and folklore. Although faint echoes of fairytale motifs are to be found in *Shadow Dance* (in references to the story of Bluebeard, for example), in the main the texts to which both it and *Several Perceptions* refer most persistently are Romantic (Keats, Shelley and the eighteenth-century Gothic), nineteenth-century fantasy (Lewis Carroll and Edgar Allan Poe), or schlock (Hammer) horror. While *The Magic Toyshop* also alludes to such texts, certainly, its main inspiration lies in older, more ahistorical, traditions of story-telling.

Although I intend to go into Carter's views on fairytale in more detail in Chapter 5, it is worth introducing the issue here, particularly because her interest in this ancient narrative form stands as an interesting correlative to her fascination with camp. As her introduction to *The Virago Book of Fairy Tales* makes clear, Carter regarded the fairytale as a form eminently worth appropriating, not least because it undermines the faith modern Western culture has 'in the work of art as a unique one-off'. Of the typical fairy story, she says:

> [It] was put together in the form we have it, more or less, out of all sorts of bits of other stories long ago and far away, and has been

tinkered with, had bits added to it, lost other bits, got mixed up with other stories, until our informant herself has tailored the story personally, to suit an audience of, say, children, or drunks at a wedding, or bawdy old ladies, or mourners at a wake – or, simply, to suit herself.[1]

According to Carter's definition, therefore, appropriation and adaptation is really what the fairytale is all about. It is also dedicated to excess, to 'the pleasure principle',[2] and delights in the subversion of propriety and convention – just like Carter's own fiction.

While fairytale thus resembles camp in its narrative strategies, in that it is innately performative and deliciously aware of its own ficticiousness, it crucially differs from camp in that it avoids the elitism that Andrew Ross argues is inherent in that aesthetic. In his critique of Sontag's essay 'Notes on "Camp"', Ross claims that

[Sontag's argument] suggests that what is being threatened in an age of mass culture is precisely the power of tastemaking intellectuals to influence the canons of taste, and that the significance of the 'new sensibility' of camp in the sixties is that it presents a means of salvaging that privilege.[3]

In other words, camp, rather than dismantling the boundaries that purport to separate 'good' taste from 'bad', is instead only a strategy which allows 'low' culture to be awarded an acceptable place within the already existing hierarchy.

This is an accusation which could also be levelled at Carter's work, which contains a similar contradiction at its centre. While it sets out to debunk notions of literary value by mixing 'high' and 'low' forms, in order to get the joke Carter's audience has to be fairly well read to start with. While her politics were unequivocally socialist, she never made intellectual concessions – when asked by Olga Kenyon in 1992, for example, whether her readers ever complained 'about your erudition', she replied that because 'I went to grammar school at a time when we had a shared culture . . . I expect people to look things up'.[4] The trouble is that, although the grammar school system certainly democratised access to good-quality education, it didn't abolish elitism so much as merely extend it to more people; in the same way that camp, according to Andrew Ross, merely broadened the boundaries of a tastemaking system whose fundamental elitist tenets remained unchallenged.

Although Carter's appropriation of the fairytale form certainly doesn't solve this problem, it is nevertheless worth mentioning that the books which primarily draw on the familiar narrative patterns and motifs of fairytale remain amongst her most accessible, and hence most widely read.

There is another element to fairytale which is relevant in this context: that it has always been identified primarily with women. Indeed, as Marina Warner argues, its classification as a female form has frequently led to its denigration as 'old wive[s] tale', and thus no more than 'stuff and nonsense'.[5] Like Carter, however, Warner sees a subversive, proto-feminist undercurrent beneath these stories. Their 'greater purpose', she says, is 'to reveal possibilities, to map out a different way and a new perception of love, marriage, women's skills, thus advocating the means of escaping imposed limits and proscribed destiny'.[6] In the context of this argument, Warner's description can also stand as an apposite outline of the plot of both *The Magic Toyshop* and *Heroes and Villains*.

The Magic Toyshop (1967)

Given its firm roots in the subversive potentiality of a female art form, it is therefore not surprising that *The Magic Toyshop* is a far more obviously 'woman-centred' text than either of the other two books discussed in the previous chapter, which teeter on the very edge of being engulfed by the misogynistic attitudes of their principal narrative personae. Whether employed ironically or not, it is a risky strategy – as Elaine Jordan has so cogently put it, 'to be immediately specific, to query the political value of speaking as a victim can only be a hairs-breadth away from blaming the victim'.[7] In this novel, however, the narrative point of view is gendered female, and the system it is up against is much more specifically patriarchal.

Although her author described her rather acerbically as 'a good screamer . . . silly and overprivileged',[8] Melanie is nevertheless a heroine who is a more fully developed version of Emily in *Shadow Dance*, as well as an early intimation of the spiky and self-reliant heroines of future novels, such as Marianne in *Heroes and Villains*, Albertina in *The Infernal Desire Machines of Doctor Hoffman*, or the Red Riding Hood figure in 'The Company of Wolves'. Not so much actively heroic as simply bloody-minded, the stubborn refusal of these young women to be victims causes patriarchal structures to collapse under the weight of their own aggression.

This subversive element in the text ties it in with more specifically 'sixties' novels such as *Shadow Dance* and *Several Perceptions*, because it thus shares their preoccupation with 'recycling'; breaking down forms, conventions and cultural codes and reassembling them in new combinations. And although the figure of the dandy as embodied in Honeybuzzard and Kay is absent here, his attributes are still present in the text, shared out among various characters. Thus, although *The Magic Toyshop* lacks the references to fashion and environment which places *Shadow Dance* and *Several Perceptions* so firmly within a particular historical moment, it is nevertheless faithful to the spirit of the sixties as Carter herself defined it. And it also shares the same awareness of the dangers it runs in engaging in this process of deconstruction, for at the other end of change lies . . . what?

As in the other two novels, the narrative of *The Magic Toyshop* expresses awareness of the risks involved in this enterprise by dramatically suspending itself between diametrically opposed states and conditions. It opens with a description of Melanie's fifteenth summer, which represents a moment of hesitation between childhood and adulthood. This is the realm of narcissistic desire, in which Melanie, self-consciously posing in front of her bedroom mirror, can try out the feminine roles patriarchy assigns to women without having to specifically commit herself to any of them, since 'the slowly ripening embryo of Melanie grown-up' (p. 20)[9] she is gestating inside herself has not yet been born.

What is so interesting about this episode is that it simultaneously offers two equally valid interpretations. On the one hand, Melanie is already regarding herself from a male-identified perspective, envisaging her future adult female role as a man's bride or muse, which leads her to continually assess her body's worthiness as the object of male desire. She is, she thinks at one point, 'too thin', and the size of 'her small, hard breasts' (p. 2) is disappointing – yet she is also paradoxically afraid of growing too fat, because then 'nobody would ever love her and she would die virgin' (p. 3). So from this point of view Melanie's passage into the patriarchal system is inevitable. She may live under the aegis of an essentially benevolent father, but he's a patriarch nonetheless, and Melanie already sees herself through his eyes.

On the other hand, however, even while Melanie 'gift-wrap[s] herself for a phantom bridegroom' (p. 2), a wonderfully self-absorbed auto-eroticism keeps breaking through her reveries, showing that the real object of her desire is, in fact, herself: 'In readiness for him, she revealed a long, marbly white leg up to the thigh (forgetting the fantasy in sudden absorption in the mirror play of muscle as she flexed her leg again and again)' (p. 2). What goes on between the brackets here is significant, marking a moment when Melanie isn't that much different from the narcissistic Honeybuzzard with his ever-changing collection of costumes and attitudes. Femininity, in this context, is just another costume: cultural construct rather than natural condition, the self-centred, self-producing self remaining unchanged underneath. In Carter's own words, Melanie 'is very conscious of desire, she is filled with it. And that gives her power'.[10]

The opening of *The Magic Toyshop* therefore echoes both *Shadow Dance* and *Several Perceptions* in allocating the narrative point of view to someone whose tangential relationship to the world of the real renders it consistently strange. In the case of Morris and Joseph, this estrangement from the real stems from alienation and angst, while in Melanie's it is due to her adolescence, which Carter describes as both a biological and psychological condition. In all three books, the main characters' rather peculiar points of view gain some kind of objective confirmation in the wider world of the text: however, *The Magic Toyshop* transgresses the boundaries which divide fantasy from reality particularly blatantly.

When Melanie's mother and father die in an aeroplane crash, she, along with her younger brother Jonathon and sister Victoria, are sent to live with their Uncle Philip in London. The ensuing change of scene, however, has repercussions on just about every level of the text, situating it even more firmly in the realm of the marginal, where anything and everything is possible. Instead of proceeding in a logically straightforward manner from point of departure to destination, at some point on the train journey to London Melanie's adolescent state becomes the blueprint for the ordering of her world. Like Alice falling down the rabbit hole, she is precipitated into a world which, in a number of different ways, is essentially transitional, something which is echoed in her inability throughout the text to distinguish between waking life and dreams, the original and the copy, the authentic and reflected self. Most obviously, the text moves, not exactly into a realm of fantasy, but into a dimension where the real and the fantastic mix and mingle. It is, as Lorna Sage says, a world 'which works according to the laws of dream, fairytales, folktales, myths and magic',[11] in which, as Melanie finds, 'nothing was ordinary, nothing was expected' (p. 60).

However, this is no escapist fantasy, but one which, like fairytale, is continually referring back to the social conditions out of which it is produced. *The Magic Toyshop* is also a novel about class, moving Melanie from a comfortable middle-class life 'in a house in the country, with a bedroom each and several to spare, and a Shetland pony in a field' (p. 7), to a seedy, cluttered urban environment which is not so much classless as situated in the gap between class divides. The landscape within which Melanie finds herself is distinctly reminiscent of the distinctively sixties landscape Carter has already evoked in *Shadow Dance*, situated at the point at which history has run out, leaving nothing but the wreckage of past glories. It differs from *Shadow Dance*, though, in also being a novel about growing up female within a patriarchal order, and thus inherently concerned with sexual politics. Although the feminist perspective expressed in *The Magic Toyshop* is still rather tentative, it is here that Carter begins to explore the cracks, contradictions and fissures in the dominant discourse.

In what she herself described as a 'malign fairy tale',[12] Carter creates a grotesquely exaggerated form of the patriarchal structure. 'Hewn out of thunder itself' and full of 'irrational violence' (p. 92), Uncle Philip is patriarchy incarnate, less a character than barely embodied principle. (Lest the reader miss the point, Carter has him drink his morning tea from 'his own, special, pint-size mug which had the word "Father" executed upon it in rosebuds', p. 73). Uncle Philip shares Honeybuzzard's compulsion to manipulate, which in both characters is expressed through a love of puppetry. But while Honey whips up his jumping jacks on a whim at his kitchen table, toymaking is Uncle Philip's profession. While his artificial marionettes are life-size, his family are reduced to the status of playthings, tied to his whims by strings of fear, obligation and economic dependence. In this respect, Uncle Philip functions as an exemplar of another element of the Romantic grotesque; what Bakhtin calls 'the theme of the marionette', where 'the accent is placed on the puppet as the victim of alien inhuman force, which rules over men by turning them into marionettes'.[13] However, the extent of the elaborate ficticiousness in which he is enmeshed – Lorna Sage, for example, describes him as the possessor of 'grotesque, pantomimic maleness'[14] – renders Uncle Philip curiously one-dimensional, and hints at the possibility that his tyranny is only another role generated from within the narrative; a surface behind which there may be very little actual substance.

The culminating episode in the book in which, 'resenting her because she was not a puppet' (p. 144), he forces Melanie to play the part of Leda to his artificial swan, serves as an example of the intentionally contradictory way in which Carter treats the issue of patriarchal control in this text, representing it in threatening, monolithic terms and deflating it at one and the same time. As far as the former is concerned, the swan acts as the displaced representative of Uncle Philip's incestuous desires, enacting a virtual rape on Melanie, who is genuinely frightened:

> The swan made a lumpish jump forward and settled on her loins. She thrust with all her force to get rid of it but the wings came down all around her like a tent and its head fell forward and nestled in her neck. The gilded beak dug deeply into the soft flesh. She screamed, hardly realising she was screaming. She was covered completely by the swan but for her kicking feet and her screaming face. The obscene swan had mounted her. She screamed again. (p. 167)

But as Gina Wisker argues, 'while the full reality of the horror of this enacted power relationship is emphasised, it is also debunked, satirised, laughed at'.[15] While the swan becomes a thing of terror to Melanie, it is also terribly ridiculous; no more than 'an egg-shaped sphere of plywood painted white and coated with glued-on feathers. . . . dumpy and homely and eccentric' (p. 165). Indeed, Melanie's first impulse upon seeing it is to laugh. And herein perhaps lies Carter's clue to the deconstruction of patriarchy – its greatest horror and its greatest weakness is that it is sustained by the force of its subjects' belief. Cease to believe, and it becomes nothing more than a masquerade or a puppet show in the simplest, most obvious sense: theatrics.

This is certainly what happens in *The Magic Toyshop*; Uncle Philip's authority, which he himself believes is absolute, is actually being constantly challenged and undermined throughout the book by his wife, Margaret, and her brothers Finn and Frankie. Together, they are the 'red people' (p. 52), whose love of music, dancing and, indeed, of each other, cannot be stamped out through the imposition of patriarchal tyranny. Melanie comes to see them as helpers and guides out of the patriarchal maze, 'lighting a bonfire for her to brighten away the wolves and tigers of this dreadful forest in which she lived' (p. 122).

Finn, in particular, gains importance as the book's object of dubious desire, and Melanie's relationship with him is one in which fear, fascination and motherly sympathy are mixed in just about equal amounts. He is a disquieting mass of contradictions, and the path along which he guides Melanie is as 'disturbing and oblique' (p. 33) as his squint-eyed glance. For example, she finds he has been spying on her bedroom through a peephole concealed in the elaborate rose pattern of the wallpaper, and is angry to think that he may have been watching her 'without her knickers' (p. 109). But she's annoyed enough to turn tables and use the peephole to spy on him, catching him walking on his hands across the room; a grotesque spectacle that accurately encapsulates the topsy-turvy situation in which both protagonists find themselves. Melanie, who has already likened the wallpaper to a 'thick hedge of crimson roses', and herself, like Sleeping Beauty, 'imprisoned in a century's steadily burgeoning garden' (p. 53), therefore finds that, perversely, it is through the practice of Finn's voyeurism that she is enabled to see out.

In the end, though, it is Uncle Philip's discovery of Margaret and Frankie's incestuous relationship, carried out outside the bounds of patriarchal propriety, which brings about the destruction of his tyrannous toyshop. Enraged, he sets fire to the place, an action which also signals the collapse of the text under the strain of its self-generated and elaborately upheld contradictions. This is the point where both reality and fantasy unravel, with the result that all endings are rendered partial and uncertain. While Jonathon departs to a world of his own nautically inspired imagination, and is never seen again, Victoria is taken by Margaret and Frankie into the fire of patriarchy's self-inflicted destruction. In the end, only Melanie and Finn are left standing amongst the wreckage staring at one another 'in wild surmise' (p. 200), Adam and Eve at the beginning of a new world. Yet, strangely bereft in the absence of the patriarch, neither of them know where to go from here. Melanie's fairytale journey may have brought her her prince, but what exactly happens in their 'happily ever after' future – the point at which stories end and systems are overthrown?

Heroes and Villains (1969)

While Carter's next novel, *Several Perceptions*, does not really address that question, returning instead to the narrative patterns of *Shadow Dance* and reshaping them in a more carnivalesque form, the novel which followed in many ways begins at the point at which *The Magic Toyshop* ends. While *The Magic Toyshop* is unable to think beyond the breakdown of ideological structures which it itself has initiated, *Heroes and Villains*, Carter's first venture into science fiction, proceeds directly into that speculative future. To quote Lorna Sage, 'The vertiginous uncertainty of the earlier novel's ending, with girl and boy on the brink of an unknowable future, is the dominant feeling throughout the narrative'.[16]

There are indeed many resemblances to be found between *The Magic Toyshop* and *Heroes and Villains*. Both mix references to eighteenth-century Gothic with a post-Freudian sensibility and a substantial dash of fairytale. Both have adolescent heroines whose path to adulthood is metaphorically represented as a journey from her father's house to an encounter with a sexually predatory male through whom she must negotiate her future adult role. However, *Heroes and Villains* is in every way a more extreme reworking of these themes, in accordance with not only Carter's greater maturity as a writer, but also her changing relationship with her cultural setting. As all good science fiction should, this novel connects with the concerns of the time in which it was written; in this case, the growing fear throughout the sixties of the possibility of nuclear devastation. (This was after all, the decade which, much to its own surprise, survived the Cuban Missile Crisis.) In its turn, this becomes symbolic in this novel of the impending dissolution of sixties optimism.

Carter said to Les Bedford that *Heroes and Villains* was an attempt to break away from the kind of novels she'd been writing before. Irritated at being classified as a writer of Gothic fictions – 'I knew perfectly well what a Gothic novel was. I knew it was all owls and ivy and mad passions and Byronic heroes who were probably damned, and I knew I wasn't writing them' – she 'very consciously chose the Gothic mode' for her fourth book, with a kind of revenge in mind. Part of this endeavour involved striving 'to rid myself of the charm' she in retro-spect considered to be a hallmark of her early work, and which she considered to be 'a great handicap'. Wryly, she remarked that perhaps, however, in *Heroes and Villains*, she had 'over-succeeded' in the attempt. 'I remember that one of the reviewers likened the novel to a sanitary inspector's report of a particularly dilapidated premises. He [sic] makes one thank God for modern sewage disposal techniques, he said'.[17]

However, I don't find this break between *Heroes and Villains* and the novels that had gone before quite as definitive as Carter claimed. Lorna Sage, for example, points out that the novel's post-apocalyptic scenario links it to the bleak urban landscapes of *Shadow Dance* and *Several Perceptions*, whose narrative settings, populated by alienated men, vic-timised women and the gaudy, posturing figure of the dandy, are redrawn within a much more obviously fantastic, but no less 'sixties' context. In *Heroes and Villains*, Sage says, 'the cataclysm suspended over the city streets has happened. . . . The student drop-outs, King's road peacocks and junk-collectors of the earlier novels have inherited the earth'.[18] Or perhaps only a portion of it, for in an echo of the establishment/anti-establishment clashes of the period in which Carter was writing, humanity after the Bomb has divided itself up into three main groupings. The Professors, guarded – or possibly supervised – by the Soldiers, are dedicated to recovering the arts and technologies of civilisation before the holocaust, while the Barbarians are nomadic tribespeople motivated by only two imperatives; survival and display.

The Barbarians, at first glance at least, are pure incarnations of camp – to them, surface is all. If they lack the knowing self-awareness of Honeybuzzard, Finn or Kay Kyte, who are absorbed in the roles they play in the full knowledge that they *are* only roles, that is only because, in this post-apocalyptic future, there is no longer any standard of the 'real' or the 'acceptable' against which such a revolt can be measured, since everything, even language itself, is now up for grabs. Dressed 'in furs and brilliant rags' (p. 4),[19] the Barbarians are visually spectacular, and a clear contrast to the regimented and colourless lifestyle of the Professors, who are engaged in an interminable, and obviously hopeless, quest for an irrecoverable history.

Isolated like Rapunzel in her white tower in the Professors' settlement, Marianne regards the Barbarians as 'hobgoblins of nightmare' (p. 5), and objects of forbidden desire. Warned by her Professor father that, although he knows she isn't wholly content with her uneventful existence, 'chaos is the opposite pole of boredom' (p. 11), Marianne – like all good Carter heroines – opts for chaos. In the process, she becomes the willing hostage of the Barbarian youth Jewel, and, eventually, his wife. She also, inevitably, learns what lies beneath the Barbarian façade, and so begins what Lorna Sage describes as 'the novel's sceptical exploration of the whole mystique of Otherness'.[20]

This marks a new development in Carter's treatment of countercultural concerns in her fiction of the sixties, which so far has exploited, rather than explored, 'Otherness'. I have already argued that in novels such as *Shadow Dance* and *Several Perceptions* – and *The Magic Toyshop* too – Carter draws on references to the counterculture in order to create and maintain a particularly dynamic discourse of flux and marginality. In *Heroes and Villains*, however, I would argue that Carter is marking the end of the counterculture as an effective force. Heretofore, love them or hate them, her camp sixties dandies have always preserved their spectacular mystique one way or the other. As soon as Honey-buzzard's actions get too excessive, he is removed from the text; Kay survives the narrative with his carnivalesque identity intact; Finn's habitual costume of a second-hand fireman's jacket proves an ironic counterpoint to the fire which consumes patriarchy, stranding him and Melanie on the edge of the unknown.

This privilege isn't extended to Jewel, however, for the brutal glamour with which Marianne's point of view initially endows him is systematically deconstructed in the course of the text. Indeed, the narrative is largely devoted to charting Marianne's disillusionment, for as Roz Kaveney says, although she is at first irresistibly 'drawn to the glamour of Jewel and the lost, roaring boys of whom he is the leader . . . the glamour wears thin'.[21] Like Melanie in *The Magic Toyshop*, it is Marianne's perspective which shapes the narrative of *Heroes and Villains*, and, spiky and spiteful as she is, she is absolutely merciless in the thoroughness with which she engages in the process of demolition once she begins to see past outward appearances. The Barbarians as a whole, she finds, are dirty, smelly and riddled with disease, while Jewel himself falls short of the glamorous, murderous hero of Marianne's adolescent imagination – he's far too introspective, for a start. Falling into the pattern of Carter's previous novels, Marianne turns out to be another middle-class girl attracted by the allure of the rough working-class boy, only to find that he has been educated into a kind of ambiguous classlessness, and thus isn't as alien as she had hoped. By the time Marianne has finished with Jewel, he is 'far fallen from that magnificence bred of sophistication and lack of opportunity' (p. 148), and she has learnt how to manipulate the mystique of myth and spectacle for her own ends.

Within this framework, Carter inserts a discussion of gender relationships which renders in more explicit, and complicated, terms the kind of issues that have preoccupied her from *Shadow Dance* onwards, where the participation of women like Ghislaine in the process of their own, extreme, victimisation is a problematic aspect of the text. Here, although the same kind of scenario is played out, the altered perspective of the participants makes a significant difference. Describing the bare facts of the story, as Paulina Palmer does in her essay 'From "Coded Mannequin" to Bird Woman: Angela Carter's Magic Flight', it seems obvious who is victim, who aggressor:

Jewel's treatment of her [Marianne] quickly lapses into physical violence. Having persuaded her to steal a lorry and drive him to freedom, he hits her to make her drive faster. Subsequently, he introduces her into the tribe to which he belongs. When she tries to escape, he follows her to her hiding place in the forest, and rapes her.[22]

But Palmer goes on to argue, and I agree with her, that although Carter thus 'runs the risk of tainting her fiction with the attitudes associated with popular genres which exploit the topic of sex and violence for the purpose of titillation', it is a problem she 'succeeds in surmounting'.[23] Palmer justifies this statement by concentrating on a discussion of Carter's liberal humanistic tendencies, claiming that not only does she endow Marianne with a resourceful and defiant personality, but also invites compassion for Jewel who, 'trapped in codes of aggression and competition',[24] is motivated to dominate Marianne primarily through fear. However, while Palmer's interpretation is certainly valid, on the whole I think the issue is rather more complex, as well as more controversial. An American reviewer of the novel summed it up when she observed that *Heroes and Villains* shows that Carter's feminism 'is not rhetorical; she sees no reason to ignore women's complicity in their own victimisation'.[25]

Although no passive, suffering victim in the Ghislaine mould, it has to be said that Marianne nevertheless brings much of the violence she suffers at the hands of Jewel upon herself. This is at least partly because in many ways he is her own unconscious creation anyway, made up of everything she most fears and most desires. Indeed, Carter herself described Marianne as 'very much a stranger to her own desire, which is why her desire finds its embodiment as a stranger'.[26] When she leaves the white tower behind and enters the world of the Barbarians, like Melanie before her she is also entering the world of her own adolescent fantasies. Having been bitten on the leg by an adder, the journey to the Barbarian settlement passes for her literally in a fever-dream, emphasising that this is no straightforward geographical journey, but one which takes the protagonist into the realm of her own erotic imagination. The roles Jewel plays within that world are, to a great extent, the roles Marianne permits him – he is, throughout the novel, curiously insubstantial. However hard Marianne tries to discern a genuine self behind his extravagantly painted, tattooed and bedecked exterior, she never can, finding instead 'a fantastic dandy of the void whose true nature had been entirely subsumed into the alien and terrible beauty of a rhetorical gesture' (p. 72). 'Everywhere I go,' says Jewel himself at one point, 'I'm doomed to be nothing but an exhibit' (p. 124).

Even when Jewel's rape of Melanie occurs, therefore, the relative roles of terrorist and victim are difficult to ascertain. Certainly, Melanie is taken by force; an act which involves 'a great deal of blood' (p. 55). But, as David Punter claims, Jewel's acts of violence are 'never wholly convincing'.[27] Like Uncle Philip in *The Magic Toyshop*, one gets the sense that Jewel is sustained only by the force of others' belief. Although he genuinely wishes to hurt and humiliate Marianne (and certainly manages to do so), Carter nevertheless succeeds in undermining the overt allocation of power at this point in the text.

Marianne's first sight of Jewel is when he kills her brother during a raid on the Professor's compound, and the description of the encounter contains an unsettling mixture of the terminologies of death and desire. Marianne sees Jewel and her brother 'locked in an embrace to the kill' (p. 5), and when Jewel finally cuts her brother's throat, he 'hold[s] him with a strange, terrible tenderness until he was still and dead' (p. 6). This event is deliberately recalled during Marianne's rape, when she is reminded of 'the murder she had witnessed, how the savage boy stuck his knife into her brother's throat, and the blood gushed out' (p. 55). Not only does this bring to the surface the homoerotic undercurrent implicit in the earlier event, it also hints that for Marianne, sex and violence are not poles apart. It is this murderer, after all, whom she transforms into 'the furious invention of my virgin nights' (p. 137). Even after their marriage, when they negotiate an uneasy truce, their sexual encounters maintain a resemblance to rape, being acts of mutual antagonism and annihilation during which, Marianne feels, she is 'courting her own extinction as well as his' (p. 87).

In seeking the Other, therefore, Marianne only finds the Same, for beneath the superficial glamour of Jewel's exterior appearance, all she finds is the echoes of her own violent desire reflected back to her. The result is that this novel not only anticipates Carter's controversial deconstruction of female innocence and victimisation in *The Sadeian Woman*, but also finally strips the dandy of his theatrical façade. Marianne may be Jewel's victim at the beginning of their relationship, but he becomes hers at the last, the allusion to the blood with which the one witness to his death is 'covered from head to toe' (p. 149) a final reminder of the potent blend of desire, violence and narcissism which has marked all the interactions between them. As Lorna Sage says, 'Though Jewel is the rapist, he is also the sex-object and victim. . . . And although Marianne is the victim, she is also the puppet-master's successor'.[28]

When she arrives at the conclusion that 'perhaps chaos is even more boring than order' (p. 82), Marianne does not then retrace her steps back across the line which divides the two. Instead, she drags order – her own kind of order – into chaos, and thus transforms it from the inside. During her stay with the Barbarians she has encountered the shaman of the Barbarian tribe and former Professor, Donally, and from him learned the political potential of illusion. Donally maintains his power through the ritual manipulation of myth and symbol, and when he is banished and Jewel is dead, Marianne takes his place. Having so singularly failed to find the glamorous objective Other, Marianne instead transforms her own self into an icon of otherness – the 'tiger lady' who will rule the Barbarians 'with a rod of iron' (p. 150). This self-knowing production of the self takes the reader back to Carter's first novel and Honeybuzzard, her definitive dandy, compelled 'to face the task of producing himself'[29] in the knowledge that there is no 'essential' self to fall back on. But unlike Honeybuzzard, Marianne's purposes extend further than the self. She is, after all, the product of what virtually amounts to a police state, and quite deliberately mixes mythic spectacle with steely political purpose, intending to 'frighten them so much they'll do every single thing I say' (p. 150).

A number of reversals have therefore taken place by the end of this book. The dandy has been seen through, and his mystique has been appropriated and used against him. The countercultural impulse for which he stands has been incorporated back into the centre and thus deprived of its capacity to shock and disturb, for it is now in the process of being codified into a system which will be used to centralise power. In that sense, *Heroes and Villains* is expressive of the awareness that the symbols and techniques around which much of Carter's writing has up until now been based are perhaps, as the decade draws to a close, no longer suitable.

But there is another important consideration to take into account here; that the transformed dandy figure is now, impossibly, female. It is a moment which signifies a meaningful change in Carter's portrayal of the female subject, for it implies that Marianne has now broken free of the stereotyped roles – daughter, victim, wife and whore – in which she has been complicit from the text's beginning; something which none of

Carter's other female characters have hitherto achieved so definitively. Even Melanie, the character who, after Marianne, has gone furthest along the road to emancipation, freezes in the face of autonomy, uncertain, it seems, what do with her new-found freedom – if freedom it is.

The biblical allusions with which both characters are surrounded are extremely significant; not only do they go a long way toward offering an explanation as to how Marianne may be able to apparently complete the voyage towards autonomy and control when Melanie doesn't quite manage it, they also bring my argument full circle back to the discussion of fairytale with which this chapter began. It should be stressed, however, that what Carter is writing is not biblical allegory; rather, she is exploiting another literary allusion, this time to Milton's *Paradise Lost*, a text of which she was fond.[30] Her early fiction in particular shows a fascination with lapsarian themes, such as transgression, damnation and falling from grace.

In Melanie's case, the Edenic references begin from the moment she puts on her mother's wedding dress and, feeling 'like the last, the only woman' stranded at 'the edge of the world' (p. 17), goes out into the garden in the middle of the night. Her identification with the biblical figure of Eve is obvious. It is reinforced even more strongly upon her discovery that she has locked herself out of the house, and in fear of its 'sinister poison' (p. 20) fruit, has to climb an apple tree to get to her bedroom window. Her guilt at her theft and accidental destruction of the wedding dress causes her to subsequently come to feel that by some sympathetic magic her act of transgression has caused her parent's death, and thus her first expulsion from the house of the father. It is an episode which foreshadows the novel's ending, where Melanie (along with Finn) experiences her second expulsion from patriarchy, with, this time, no way to get back.

The lapsarian imagery in *Heroes and Villains* is, if possible, employed even more blatantly, represented most obviously in the magnificent tattoo adorning Jewel's back which depicts the scene of Adam's temptation, complete with the tree, the serpent and Eve. Eve's 'perfidious smile' (p. 85) links her to Marianne, and Jewel, indeed, encourages her to take on that role. Much nearer to the mark, however, Donally sees her as Lilith, Adam's first, disobedient, wife.

And herein lies the difference between Melanie and Marianne, for in *The Magic Toyshop* Carter can take the analogy with Eve only so far. Hélène Cixous and Catherine Clément observe of conventional fairytale that it is always driving towards becoming a different kind of story altogether, one which will remove the heroine from centre stage to the narrative margins, and I think it is an aspect of the form Carter knowingly confronts in this novel through her persistent stress on Miltonic themes. In this context, Eve is only a potent figure for as long as she represents the temptation to Fall. Once Adam has accepted the apple and the expulsion has taken place, 'what follows is sociocultural: he makes her lots of babies, she spends her youth in labor; from bed to bed, until the age at which the thing isn't "woman" for him anymore'.[31] There are hints in *The Magic Toyshop* that this could indeed be Melanie's future – at one point she has a 'prophetic vision' that

> [she and Finn] would get married one day and live together all their lives and there would always be pervasive squalor and dirt and mess and shabbiness, always, forever and forever. And babies crying and washing to be done and toast burning all the rest of her life. And never any glamour or romance or charm. Nothing fancy. Only mess and babies with red hair. (p. 177)

In freezing Melanie on the edge of an unimaginable future, the narrative evades its own, perhaps inevitable, resolution which will take it away from the realm of story and trap the female subject in an unpalatable reality.

Lilith, however, is a different matter. She is a figure who exists on the margins of biblical myth, and who has never been codified into the 'official' canon of stories which make up that system of belief. She is potentially, therefore, a more potent symbol of female transgression, as she has never reached the point at which her disruptive presence can be neutralised. Through her identification with such a figure, Marianne is empowered to stay within the realm of story, and rewrite it to suit her own purposes and desires.

However, I think there comes a point when one should question how much of what Marianne gains for herself is either meaningful or desirable. Wilfully enmeshing oneself in myth and allegory, even if it does constitute a transgression against the patriarchal order, isn't necessarily a tactic that ultimately achieves anything very much. In taking on the mask of the dandy, Marianne certainly saves herself, but at the cost of becoming something less, or more, than human – an icon, a theatrical figurehead, who is always, always, conscious of being watched.

Taken together, Melanie and Marianne represent two, and perhaps the only two, strategies open to women in a society which persists in categorising them according to mythologically inspired stereotypes. Like Melanie, the female subject can try to avoid the inevitable and thus find that she's run out of options, or, like Marianne, she can embrace such roles and try to subvert them from the inside, with the awareness that such a thing might not be possible, and that she might simply be running more quickly towards her inevitable fate.

Love (1971)

While *Heroes and Villains* thus acts as a clear indication of Carter's growing interest in the myths through which female identity, in partic-ular, is defined, she did not immediately explore further the implica-tions raised by this novel's conclusion. Instead, the male dandy is revis-ited for the last time in *Love*, a novel which rounds off many of the themes Carter was constantly reworking during her first decade as a writer – façades, entropy, class mobility and the flirting with disillusion and dissolution. Written in 1969, but not published until 1971, this novel chronologically straddles the division between decades. However, its constant referencing of the kind of sixties culture and attitudes Carter describes in 'Truly, It Felt Like Year One' makes it recognisably of that period. As Lorna Sage points out, *Love* brings her work full circle in its many similarities to her first novel:

> In a sense, it's a rewrite of *Shadow Dance*, with the shadows (images, unrealities) taking over yet again. Glamorous, sinister Honey-buzzard from her first book has been split into two, the 'Honey' reborn as beautiful Lee, the Buzzard as Buzz, his dark half-brother. The girl who is their go-between ends up as a blasphemous sacri-fice to fantasies of power in both books – though Ghislaine is murdered, and Annabel in *Love* kills herself, the difference is not so great as it sounds, since both girls die of delusion, overdosed on role-playing, and complicit in their own destruction.[32]

But if it is a rewrite, it is far from being a straightforward one. Here, the familiar themes are presented in stark relief, pared to the bone and utterly bereft of the enriching perspective of fantasy. What Carter essentially concentrates on in *Love* is the relationship between the dandy and his victim, a theme which certainly evokes echoes of *Shadow Dance*. However, the way in which she portrays it is quite different. In *Shadow Dance*, the mutual tragedy of Honeybuzzard and Ghislaine takes place on the sidelines of the text, and thus its horror is somewhat ameliorated. Honeybuzzard has scarred Ghislaine before the narrative opens, and all subsequent encounters between them are narrated after the event, sometimes by Honeybuzzard himself, but also by other characters. Even the final act of murder, although pregnant with half-evoked horror, is glimpsed, as it were, out of the corner of one eye. Effectively, it takes place off-stage, with the protagonists not being discovered by Morris and Emily until the murder has already occurred.

At certain points in the text, though, it is impossible to avoid the direct intrusion of the evidence of the destructive nature of the relationship between Ghislaine and Honey, as in the case of, for example, Ghislaine's ugly, festering facial scar. Here, however, the horror implicit in this image is at least partially diffused by being camped up outrageously. When Morris looks at Ghislaine and sees her as vampire-woman, Frankenstein's bride, the reference does not evoke the dark Gothic fantasies of the eighteenth-century, but their contemporary reworking through the horror film, where the blood may look real, but is actually Kensington gore. Although throughout their encounter the real horror of Ghislaine's situation keeps knocking on the door of Morris's imagination, demanding to be let in, that does not prevent the camp dramatic references allowing Ghislaine's mutilation to be seen as much a 'mockup', 'fake' or 'forgery' as the bar in which she and Morris meet.

Such illusions are comforting, even if you know they're not true, but they're denied the reader of *Love*, which does not bother to disguise, even for a moment, the fascination with necrophilia which lies at the heart of the camp aesthetic.[33] Even Carter's prose style is different here, acting as a microscope through which the tortuous geometrical intersections of the novel's characters can be magnified for closer viewing. Described by Marc O'Day as 'frighteningly pellucid',[34] and by Lorna Sage as 'a glowing patina of craft and indifference',[35] it has none of the rhetorical asides and self-conscious theatricality of her other novels. Instead, the tone is calm to the point of being clinical, with even punctuation kept to a minimum.

The novel's opening paragraph is a good example of the way in which the stark tone precipitates the reader, with stomach-wrenching abruptness, into a world rendered into nightmare by being filtered through the insane imagination:

One day, Annabel saw the sun and the moon in the sky at the same time. The sight filled her with a terror which entirely consumed

her and did not leave her until the night closed in catastrophe for
she had no instinct for self-preservation if she was confronted by
ambiguities. (p. 1)[36]

Although *Love* resembles *Several Perceptions* in its adoption of an obviously unbalanced narrative point of view, in the earlier novel we are still
encouraged to read Joseph's predicament, like Ghislaine's, in terms of
self-dramatisation. Even in the depths of depression, he's still self-
consciously playing a role, regarding himself as an 'ambiguous villain'
out of Jacobean drama, or '(in certain ferocious moods of self-disgust)
a big, fat, soft, stupid, paper Valentine heart squeezing out a soggy tear
at the sorrows of the world' (p. 5).

The beginning of *Love*, however, is remarkable for the way in which
it so obviously falls short of theatricality; the nouns which should evoke
drama – 'terror', 'catastrophe' and 'ambiguities' – jarring uncomfortably
with the flat, emotionless tone. The overall effect is totally disorientating,
leaving the reader with no clues as to what position to adopt with
regard to Annabel's perspective, because the confusion between the
authentic and the inauthentic, which in Carter's former novels is foregrounded through camp narrative play, is rendered invisible by being
completely ignored. In the words of Sue Roe, '*Love* presents the world
as Annabel sees it: a messy collage of the imaginary and the real'.[37]

Carter described what she saw as the differences between Joseph and
Annabel to Les Bedford in 1977, saying that, while Joseph 'is not
insane, he's neurotic, just a neurotic . . . Annabel in *Love* is mad. She's
not responding to an insane society, she's utterly isolated in psychosis'.
In this sense, the reader's dilemma as to how to go about the impossible
task of disentangling the subjective from the objective point of view in
this novel stems from the fact that Annabel, rather than defending
herself against reality, as Joseph does, has instead 'remodelled it entirely
to her own requirements'.[38] It is a dilemma also shared by all the characters who are close to Annabel, for she places an enormous demand
upon the people around her to perpetuate her psychotic charade.

Although *Love* evokes fantastic symbolism recognisable from Carter's
earlier novels, it remains flat, two-dimensional, and unable to assume
any authenticating power, either for reader or character. When Annabel
first moves into Lee's room, for example, it is painted pure white, but
she soon transforms it into an exotic wilderness of the imagination. She
first covers the wall with an elaborate drawing of a single tree, which
casts 'a poisoned shade' (p. 32) on the new lovers; after their marriage,

however, she paints the tree over in dark green, then creates a riotous 'forest of trees, flowers, birds and beasts' (p. 29). The single tree in particular evokes the biblical imagery of *The Magic Toyshop* and *Heroes and Villains*, where in both cases it becomes symbolic of an attempted escape from patriarchal structures. But it has no such positive connotations in this novel, where it represents nothing more than 'the dreary paraphernalia of romanticism' (p. 7).

Denied the transformative power of the fantastic, the female subject in this novel can only achieve transfiguration through self-immolation, as opposed to self-determination. Annabel is regularly beaten both by Lee and Buzz, and it is something she quite deliberately provokes, since she gets a warped masochistic pleasure from her own victimisation. At one point in the text, for example, she and Lee play chess. When he wins, she hits him:

> Though, he recalled, not sufficiently brutally to require that he tie her wrists together with his belt, force her to kneel and beat her until she toppled over sideways. She raised a strangely joyous face to him; the pallor of her skin and the almost miraculous lustre of her eyes startled and even awed him. He was breathless with weeping, a despicable object.
> 'That will teach you to take my queen,' she said smugly. (p. 40)

What in Marianne is dogged intractability becomes in Annabel the grateful passivity of the martyr. According to the warped logic by which she orders her life, the greater her pain, the greater her triumph, because her power to inflict suffering on others is filtered through her self. Her 'ultimate, shocking transformation' (p. 112) as a suicide therefore comes as no surprise; indeed, so inevitable is it that it is bereft even of the aura of tragedy, since it is essentially meaningless. Although Annabel sets out on this course in order to pay Lee back for his infidelity, at their last meeting she is 'hardly aware who he was' (p. 105). 'She did not spare a thought or waste any pity on the people who loved her for she had never regarded them as anything more than facets of the self she was now about to obliterate' (pp. 109–10). Theatricality again has failed, leaving only death, which as Carter says, is 'irreparable' (p. 112).

Even though the dandy figure, as Lorna Sage says, is doubled in this text, he too participates in its slow, aimless, haemorrhage of meaning. Again, unlike Kay Kyte, Finn and Jewel, all of whom represent *something*, even if it isn't always clear what that is, Lee and Buzz are closer to Honeybuzzard in that they stand for the sign which points to nothing beyond itself. But while Honeybuzzard embraces unmeaning so actively that it achieves a kind of significance all of its own, Lee and Buzz passively accept meaninglessness simply because they don't see the point of doing anything else. David Punter succinctly observes that the characters in *Love* 'do not struggle for self-realisation, or indeed for survival; they are much too far gone for that'.[39] In this sense, even more definitively than Honeybuzzard, Lee and Buzz stand for a crisis of indifference very much of the kind envisaged by Baudrillard, which both causes, and is caused by, the gradual grinding to a halt of the historical process. Indeed, his argument in *The Illusion of the End* is extraordinarily close to the situation Carter creates in *Love*: 'History comes to an end here, not for want of actors, nor for want of violence (there will always be more violence), nor for want of events . . . but by deceleration, indifference and stupefaction'.[40]

Carter relates the story of Buzz and Lee's childhood in detail in a manner which links it directly to the cultural upheavals of the sixties, but which also recasts that upheaval in something less than optimistic mode. Their mother goes mad when both boys are young, and Buzz and Lee are subsequently raised by a Trotskyist aunt amongst 'quiet terraces of artisan's dwellings' (p. 10) which are pulled down soon after the brothers move to London. Lee, the product of grammar school, goes to university, and Buzz, who has progressed no further than the secondary modern, follows him because, united in their common alienation, 'it never occurred to either they might live apart' (p. 13). Together, then, they move

> disinterestedly in the floating world centred loosely upon the art school, the university and the second-hand trade and made their impermanent homes in the sloping, terraced hillside where the Irish, the West Indians and the more adventurous of the students lived in old, decaying houses where rents were low. (p. 13)

But, this being the book it is, this isn't a story of working-class-boys-made-good, but of classlessness-as-displacement. Again, aimlessness is the dominant trope here, with the spectacular flight into unreason represented by the mother and the hard-headed political idealism of the aunt both rejected in favour of disinterest, uninvolvement, and a mechanical posturing which substitutes for any kind of commitment, be it to society, others or even self.

Beautiful Lee is so far along the path of artifice that he virtually comes out the other side, for his consciousness of his own beauty is so extreme that he gives 'the impression of perfect naturalness, utter spontaneity and entire warmth of heart' (p. 12). Yet this illusion of genuineness is constantly being undermined by his eyes, which are reddened and weeping due to a chronic infection. Thus, when he appears to be crying, he often is not, which renders his tears 'ambivalent' (p. 26).

Buzz is Lee's antithesis in that, while Lee constantly strives for at least an appearance of verisimilitude, Buzz, living 'at a constant pitch of melodrama' (p. 12) valorises artifice. While Lee is at least 'an honest orphan' (p. 11), Buzz is the product of a largely invented history, for he knows nothing of his father's real identity. Most significantly, while Lee's gaze is blurred by tears, Buzz's is disturbingly filtered through a camera lens, which he uses 'as if to see with, as if he could not trust his own eyes and had to check his vision by means of a third lens all the time so in the end he saw everything at second hand, without depths' (p. 25). As Marc O'Day observes, one of the novel's 'most heavily ironic moments' is when Annabel's middle-class parents 'admire him because of his camera',[41] mistaking him for 'a respectable Bohemian' (p. 37) in the David Bailey mould, since Buzz's photographic interests lie chiefly in the area of the pornographic. Not only does he give a collection of pornographic photographs to Annabel (who yearns for the anonymity of 'the photographic whore', p. 4), he also takes numerous pictures of Lee and Annabel in bed together, with which he then decorates his room.

Lee's tears and Buzz's camera in the end both add up to the same thing; the counterfeiting of emotion in a world in which all efforts at feeling and connection amount to no more than the 'indifferent arrangements of bizarre intersecting lines' (p. 4). In this context, the title of the novel is highly ironic, for 'love' is an emotion of which the main protagonists understand nothing. Lee wears his heart on the outside 'laid bare for all to see' (p. 70), tattooed on his flesh in red and green. But it is not the symbol of romance it seems, but a visible sign of his tie to Annabel, which is compounded not of love, but of mutual pain, manipulation and delusion.

Notes

1. Angela Carter, Introduction to *The Virago Book of Fairy Tales* (London: Virago Press, 1991), p. x.

2. ibid., p. xii.
3. Andrew Ross, *No Respect: Intellectuals and Popular Culture* (London: Routledge, 1989), p. 145.
4. Olga Kenyon, *The Writer's Imagination* (University of Bradford Print Unit, 1992), p. 26.
5. Marina Warner, *From the Beast to the Blonde: On Fairy Tales and Their Tellers* (London: Chatto & Windus, 1994), p. 25.
6. ibid., p. 24.
7. Elaine Jordan, 'The Dangers of Angela Carter', in Isobel Armstrong (ed.), *New Feminist Discourses: Critical Essays on Theories and Texts* (London: Routledge, 1992), pp. 119–32 (p. 120).
8. Kenyon, p. 27.
9. Angela Carter, *The Magic Toyshop* (London: Virago Press, 1981). All subsequent references in the text are from this edition.
10. Moira Paterson, 'Flights of Fancy in Balham', in *The Observer Magazine* (11 November 1986), pp. 42–5 (p. 45).
11. Lorna Sage, *Angela Carter* (Plymouth: Northcote House Publishers, 1994), p. 15.
12. John Haffenden, 'Magical Mannerist', *The Literary Review* (November 1984), pp. 34–8 (p. 35).
13. Mikhail Bakhtin, *Rabelais and His World*, trans. Hélène Iswolsky (Bloomington: Indiana University Press, 1984), p. 40.
14. Lorna Sage, *Women in the House of Fiction: Post-War Women Novelists* (London: Macmillan, 1992), p. 170.
15. Gina Wisker, 'Weaving Our Own Web: Demythologising/ Remythologising and Magic in the Work of Contemporary Women Writers', in Gina Wisker (ed.), *It's My Party: Reading Twentieth Century Women's Writing* (London: Pluto Press, 1994), pp. 104–28 (p. 111).
16. Sage, *Angela Carter*, p. 16.
17. Les Bedford, 'Angela Carter: An Interview' (Sheffield: Sheffield University Television, February 1977).
18. Lorna Sage, 'The Savage Sideshow', *New Review* 4/39–40 (July 1977), pp. 51–7 (p. 52).
19. Angela Carter, *Heroes and Villains* (Harmondsworth: Penguin, 1981). All subsequent references in the text are from this edition.
20. Sage, *Angela Carter*, p. 18.
21. Roz Kaveney, 'New New World Dreams', in Lorna Sage (ed.), *Flesh and the Mirror* (London: Virago Press, 1994), pp. 171–88 (p. 178).
22. Paulina Palmer, 'From "Coded Mannequin" to Bird Woman: Angela Carter's Magic Flight', in Sue Roe (ed.), *Women Reading Women's Writing* (Brighton: Harvester Press, 1987), pp. 179–205 (p. 188).
23. ibid.
24. ibid.
25. Dorothy Allison, 'Love Among the Ruins', *Village Voice Literary Supplement* 75 (June 1989), p. 15.

26. Elaine Jordan, 'The Dangerous Edge', in Sage (ed.), *Flesh and the Mirror*, pp. 189–215 (p. 198).
27. David Punter, *The Literature of Terror: A History of Gothic Fictions from 1765 to the Present Day* (London: Longman, 1980), p. 397.
28. Sage, *Angela Carter*, p. 19.
29. Michel Foucault, 'What is Enlightenment?', trans. Catherine Porter, in Paul Rabinow (ed.), *The Foucault Reader* (Harmondsworth: Penguin, 1984), pp. 32–50 (p. 42).
30. She said to Les Bedford, for example, that she 'was the only person in my year [at university] who actually read it all through, including the footnotes'.
31. Hélène Cixous and Catherine Clément, 'Sorties: Out and Out: Attacks/ Ways/Forays', in *The Newly Born Woman*, trans. Betsy Wing (Manchester: Manchester University Press, 1987), pp. 63–132 (p. 66).
32. Sage, *Angela Carter*, p. 20.
33. Andrew Ross comments that 'It is no surprise . . . to find that Sontag had been researching an essay on death and morbidity before she decided to write "Notes on Camp". The switch, in her mind from thinking about "mortuary sculpture, architecture, inscriptions and other such wistful lore" to the sociability of camp wit was perhaps triggered by a quite understandable flight from the realms of chilled seriousness to the warmer climate of theatrical humour and gaiety. But it is also symptomatic, I think, of the necrophiliac economy which underpins the camp sensibility'. *No Respect*, p. 152.
34. Marc O'Day, '"Mutability is Having a Field Day": the Sixties Aura of Angela Carter's Bristol Trilogy', in Sage (ed.), *Flesh and the Mirror*, pp. 24–58 (p. 51).
35. Sage, *Angela Carter*, p. 20.
36. Angela Carter, *Love* [1971] (London: Picador, 1988). All subsequent references in the text are from this edition.
37. Sue Roe, 'The Disorder of *Love*: Angela Carter's Surrealist Collage', in Sage (ed.), *Flesh and the Mirror*, pp. 60–97 (p. 64).
38. Les Bedford, 'Angela Carter: An Interview'.
39. Punter, *The Literature of Terror*, p. 399.
40. Jean Baudrillard, *The Illusion of the End*, trans. Chris Turner (Cambridge: Polity Press, 1994), p. 4.
41. O'Day, pp. 53–4.

III

Mad Scientists, Drag Queens and Fairy Godmothers

CHAPTER 4

For Angela Carter, says Lorna Sage, the sixties were not necessarily an era of liberation in the simplistic sense, but rather 'the period when the illusions broke, dissolved, came out in their true colours'.[1] If this is so, then although the sixties' insubstantial pageant had well and truly faded by the time the seventies dawned, the movement from optimism to disillusion is already registered in the books Carter published at the latter end of the decade, *Heroes and Villains* and *Love*. In their different ways, both signal her withdrawal from a narrative approach characterised by its conspicuous linking of fiction and its contemporary cultural milieu through references to fashion, settings and various aesthetic and behavioural cultural codes. *Heroes and Villains* places the countercultural, revisionist impulse in the dubious service of the self-created matriarch, and reduces the dandy to the status of grubby hippy drop-out. Although *Love* reworks the themes of her first novel, *Shadow Dance*, with more skill and far greater control, it crucially changes the mood of the setting, exchanging the former novel's dark and dangerous delight in its own subversiveness for an insidious *ennui* and a hideous resignation in the face of horror.

In the seventies, Carter's fiction turned away from the kind of playful, subversive representation of its contemporary culture which is so striking a characteristic of many of her novels written in the sixties. Instead, as *Love* intimates, one of the dominant tropes of Carter's seventies narratives is disillusion and alienation, especially as far as the fiction I intend to explore in this chapter is concerned: the novel *The Infernal Desire Machines of Doctor Hoffman* and Carter's first collection of short stories, *Fireworks*. In both books, disenchantment is not just a mood which permeates the text, but a dominant plot motif which frequently controls its action.

Whereas Carter's ex-centric[2] impulses had found an echo and, to a certain extent, a pattern, in the countercultural movements of the sixties, by the end of the decade the counterculture had been largely absorbed into the social mainstream, and its disruptive potential safely defused, leaving her, still resisting and critical, on the edge. I therefore don't think that it is any coincidence that the seventies was also the period in which Carter began to establish herself as a non-fiction as well as a fiction writer, creating in the process an authorial persona which publicly constructs her as a marginal subject on the personal, cultural and historical level.

The bulk of her journalism was produced during this decade, as well as her only book-length piece of cultural analysis, *The Sadeian Woman*, a controversial analysis of the pornography of the Marquis de Sade. It is an unconventional, deliberately inflammatory, and consistently iconoclastic work, which, viewed in the context of Carter's writing as a whole, is more than it appears. A provocative piece of polemic it might be, but it is also a summary of the issues and controversies that she was absorbed in throughout the decade, and which she explored in her fiction, as well as her non-fiction, and it is for this reason that I am choosing to introduce it into the debate early on in this chapter.

Carter's cultural detachment was physically reinforced by her migration from England in 1969 with the proceeds of the Somerset Maugham Award won for *Several Perceptions*. In her description of her travels, an essay entitled, with school-girl dutifulness, 'My Maugham Award', Carter produces a kaleidoscopic assemblage of colourful and chaotic impressions, which are not constrained by being fitted into some overall narrative intent. The 'somewhat disconnected paragraphs' of which the piece is composed constitutes, claims Carter, a faithful attempt to reproduce 'the enormous barrage of imagery to which I had been subjected'.[3] It is a true tall traveller's tale, filled with images which strain the credulity through their distance from the norms of English life, and are thus imbued with a fantastic surrealism. Carter obviously delights in the relating of such bizarre, unlikely incidents. For example: 'In a cafe in Arles, I saw a madman remove the battered top hat he wore on his head, take from this receptacle the raw chicken which it contained, and eat it' (p. 175). True or false? It really doesn't matter, for this is a celebration of the perspective of the foreigner which makes of the unknown a never-ending theatrical spectacle, a point of view Carter was to adopt to good effect in her subsequent writing.

However, she did not only regard the truly foreign country, Japan, with the eyes of the anthropologist or the travel writer; returning, Carter subjects her own country to the same kind of scrutiny. But there is a crucial difference, for, transferred to home, the point of view of the foreigner (who has, after all, chosen to take on the mantle of foreignness) becomes modulated into that of the alienated subject, who looks at the place she once belonged with the eyes of disenchantment. As she wryly comments on her return to London from Tokyo: 'The cure for homesickness is worse than the disease; all you have to do is to come back'.[4]

In his collection of essays on various aspects of French culture, *Mythologies*, Roland Barthes states that his intention is to deconstruct 'the "naturalness" with which newspapers, art and common sense constantly dress up a reality which, even though it is the one we live in, is undoubtedly determined by history'.[5] I think the fundamental difference between the sixties and the seventies as far as Carter is concerned can be built around that statement. She was an astute cultural observer from the beginning of her career – that was nothing new. However, when she commented on the sixties, she was regarding a society which celebrated its own tendency to artifice, and made of it, in itself, an art form. George Melly describes sixties 'pop' culture as 'an ambivalent thing, part tongue in cheek, part sincere, but never unconscious',[6] and it was this very self-consciousness which Carter both admired and adopted as her own. She regarded the seventies with a jaundiced eye, however, precisely because it seemed to her to have rediscovered the habit of 'universalisation', normalising cultural codes by encoding them as 'natural', and hence unchallengeable. Her role, as an onlooker both alien and alienated, was to defamiliarise that which has been constructed as familiar, thus inculcating an echo of her own detachment in the reader.

'Fin de Siecle' (1972)

Carter's adoption of a 'stranger's eye' with regard to her own culture is well illustrated by an article published in *New Society*, 'Fin de Siecle' [sic]. Only two years after it has begun ('It looks like the *fin* has come a little early to this *siècle*'), she does a thorough hatchet job on the new decade which she regards as having reneged on the optimism of the 'dear, dead days' of the sixties when, 'for a brief season, it seemed the old barriers of class and privilege were, if not actually down, at least crumbling'(p. 354).

Now, however, London is 'melting sweetly in her own decay', and violent graffiti has been scrawled over the hopeful, thoughtful slogans of the previous decade.

The controlling metaphor throughout this piece is fashion – even London itself is portrayed as an 'infinitely accommodating whore, painted thickly over the stratified residue of yesterday's cosmetics' (p. 354). Carter's persistent references to dress and make-up recall her 1967 article 'Notes for a Theory of Sixties Style' in which she echoes Elizabeth Wilson in her assumption that 'everywhere dress and adornment play symbolic, communicative and aesthetic roles'.[7] Although similar in orientation, however, 'Notes for a Theory of Sixties Style' and 'Fin de Siecle' are very different in mood. The former is frankly celebratory of the 'logic of whizzing entropy'[8] that is sixties style, eclectic, dandified and, as the essay's identical opening and closing sentences ('Velvet is back, skin anti-skin, mimic nakedness', p. 85) indicate, also sensual. In 'Fin de Siecle', however, 'whizzing entropy' has given way to 'a feverish, hysterical glamour' (p. 354). What Carter finds particularly disturbing is the way that seventies fashion is a 'parody of femininity', in which women 'are once again precariously elevated in a display of masochism' (p. 355). 'Certainly the girls who stump along in their enormous shoes, with their bellies thrust out and their eyes painted red so they look as if they have been weeping, have the iconography of sexual oppression scrawled all over them' (p. 355).

The adjective 'scrawled' directs the reader back to Carter's earlier comment on graffiti, making of the female body a canvas on which the dominant discourses of the period are inscribed, overwriting the sixties adherence to oppositional dress-codes. The notion that seventies style made of the fashion victim an image of female victimisation was reiterated by Carter in 1975 in an article entitled 'The Wound in the Face', when again she makes a crucial distinction between the self-knowing pastiche of the sixties and the seventies return to the habit of normalising the artificial. In this essay, she contrasts the extreme cosmetic fashion of the late sixties, in which women painted their *eyes* red, with the return of red lipstick in the seventies. While the former was 'cosmetics used as satire on cosmetics. . . . The best part of the joke was that the look itself was utterly monstrous',[9] red lipstick signals the return to that ubiquitous term 'glamour'. It makes of the mouth 'a bloody gash, a visible wound . . . [which] bleeds over everything', but because it carries with it such strong cultural connotations of sophisticated sexual seduction ('lipstick traces on a cigarette stub; the perfect imprint, like a half heart, of a scarlet lower lip on a drained Martini glass', p. 94), the red mouth becomes the essence of femininity, reinforcing rather than challenging the idea that girls dress up to get their men.

As always when looking at Carter's non-fiction, however, it would be a mistake to take her pronouncements purely at face value, for there is undoubtedly an element of disingenuousness at work here. Just as Carter uses the autobiographical mode as a way more of fictionalising her life than recording it, so she employs the tone and techniques of journalistic cultural analysis in such a way as to render her social situation as fantastic as her fiction. While these pieces should not, therefore, be naively approached as straightforward examples of social history, they can become a means by which the marked differences between Carter's fiction of the sixties and her fiction of the seventies can be aligned with the changing mood of the times. The real function of such essays as 'Fin de Siecle' and 'The Wound in the Face' is to redraw the demarcation lines between margin and centre, and reposition Carter's work relative to both.

Although Carter's exploitation of the fashion, settings, attitudes and politics of the counterculture was never straightforward, it did at least give her a discourse through which to articulate her differences with the mainstream. As she portrays it, however, this position is no longer satisfactory in the seventies. The political dissension of the counterculture has metamorphosed into an inarticulate hooliganism, and can thus no longer function as a valid vehicle for protest. Moreover, the fact that women are again making themselves into the mirror of male desire, through fashion codes taken to grotesque extremes, exposes as a failure the attempt to redefine gender roles through permissiveness.

The Sadeian Woman (1979)

This latter observation, however, pinpoints the changing orientation of Carter's fiction. Although no longer linked to the concept of the counterculture in the sixties sense of the word, it finds new expression of protest in the language of feminism. Carter herself said she moved towards a feminist position at some time in the late sixties, a process which her experiences in Japan only intensified. In 'Truly, It Felt Like Year One', Carter links her feminist conversion to the dying days of sixties optimism, when she found that sexual liberation did not necessarily equate with female liberation. In spite of the simplification of sexual relationships between the sexes, 'still and all there remained

something out of joint and it turned out that was it, rather an important thing, that all the time I thought things were going so well I was
in reality a second-class citizen'.[10] She echoes this in 'Notes From the
Front Line', in which she attributes 'my own questioning of the nature
of my reality as a woman' to 'that sense of heightened awareness of the
society around me in the summer of 1968'.[11] And in Japan, she says, she
'learnt what it is to be a woman and became radicalised'.[12] However, in
the context of the subsequent controversy concerning the feminist view
expressed in her fiction, exactly what kind of woman Carter learnt to
be in Japan is a matter for debate.

Carter consistently portrayed herself as 'a very old-fashioned kind of
feminist', concerned with 'abortion law, access to further education,
equal rights, the position of black women',[13] all of which sounds pretty
politically irreproachable. However, throughout her career, Carter was
consistently at odds with the feminist mainstream, to the extent that,
according to Paul Barker, when she was on a teaching stint at New York
State University in the 1980s, 'she wrote back to Lorna Sage that she
was being boycotted by the department of women's studies'.[14]

The fact was that Carter never felt herself obliged to toe any kind of
feminist party line, and the feminist ideology she espoused was defiantly idiosyncratic. Indeed, at various points in her writing she appears
to deliberately set out to be outrageous – in 'Notes From the Front
Line', for example, she caustically dismisses Marilyn French's *The
Women's Room* as an example of 'bourgeois fiction', whose aim is 'to
teach people how to behave in social circles to which they think they
might be able to aspire' (p. 76). But the most controversial aspect of
Carter's work as far as feminism is concerned undoubtedly centres on
the issue of sex, and it is here that the term 'pornography' rears its ugly
head.

To a certain extent, Carter's fascination with pornography can be
traced to her experiences in Japan, a country in which, as she portrayed
it, the sadomasochistic fetishisation of the female body is common-
place. Whereas on one level Carter certainly abhorred the exploitation
of women in Japanese society, on another she became fascinated with
the bizarre extremism of pornographic forms. It is a fascination which
permeates all the fiction she wrote during this period, and which
extends the interest in the dynamics of death and desire evident from
her earliest work. However, following such exquisitely discomforting
studies of Japanese sadomasochism as 'Once More into the Mangle' and
'People as Pictures', Carter's attention turned to the pornography of the

West, perhaps because, while it is easy to become seduced by the exoticism of a culture so far removed from one's own experience, to explore the pornographic output of one's own culture situates the debate much closer to home.

Her attitude towards the issue was staunchly matter-of-fact, and she consistently maintained that she certainly didn't see the need for all the fuss over pornography when there were so many more pressing social issues to worry about. As she pronounced in one interview, 'I don't think it's nearly as damaging as the effects of the capitalist system'.[15] She clearly became irritated, too, about what she saw as the double standards surrounding pornography. In a 1977 article entitled 'The Power of Porn', for example, she questions the criteria by which pornography is condemned. What is the use of taking exception to the way it 'degrades the image of women' whilst ignoring that most of the advertising industry routinely does the same thing? Instead, she suggests, censorship should be reserved for the Army, which is 'freely allowed to advertise killing as a fine career for a young man'. Furthermore, all kinds of false distinctions surround the classification of pornography as opposed to erotic art. If a book is 'both a dirty book and a work of literature', she argues, it is assumed that 'the art . . . [will] disinfect the filth'. Her conclusion is typically controversial: 'I'd say bad dirty books never did anyone any harm, except make their teeth rot or give them hairy palms. But *good* dirty books do the real damage'.[16]

Carter rounded off her literary output of the seventies with a defiant analysis of a collection of what are most definitely *bad* dirty books. *The Sadeian Woman* took her five years to write, and she found it extremely hard work: in 1977, for example, while in the midst of her research, she lamented that 'I must have done something awful in a previous life to have embarked on this impossible task. It's like emptying the sea with a cup with a hole in it'.[17] Hovering as it does between celebration and critique, the book is a showcase for the paradoxes of Carter's response to pornography. It has been too often misinterpreted as an unequivocal defence of de Sade – Andrea Dworkin, for example, condemns it as 'a pseudofeminist literary essay'[18] while Susanne Kappeler sees Carter as fatally 'misreading' de Sade, 'dazzled by the offer of equal opportunities'.[19]

Dworkin's and Kappeler's criticism, however, is neither wholly unfounded nor terribly surprising. Dworkin is particularly savage in her condemnation of Carter, arguing that *The Sadeian Woman*, in portraying de Sade as 'something unnaturally marvellous',[20] shows Carter's disregard for the actual degradation endured by the victims of his perversities.

While this isn't Carter's intent at all, it is obvious that the two analyses are fundamentally incompatible in their feminist orientation. For example, Dworkin picks out for particular condemnation Carter's retelling of a celebrated scandal involving de Sade's kidnapping and whipping of a woman, Rose Keller, who later escaped and reported him to the authorities. Eventually, she received a large sum of money out of court on condition she withdraw her charge against him. In Dworkin's version the woman is the helpless object of de Sade's lust, further victimised by subsequent critics' belittling of her ordeal in their attempts to vindicate him. In Carter's, however, Keller becomes the astute agent of her own revenge:

> Rose Keller, who expected, perhaps to have sex with the Marquis but for whom the whip came as a gratuitous, unexpected and unwelcome surprise, turns her hand to blackmail and who can blame her? An ironic triumph for the beggar woman; the victim turned victor. (p. 29)[21]

While Dworkin is passionate in her defence of the female victim of the sex crime, Carter steadfastly refuses to regard such women as victims at all; indeed, one of her primary purposes in the book is to urge women to repudiate the dubious status of passive, suffering martyr.

To read Dworkin's and Carter's retellings of the Rose Keller episode, therefore, is to read two completely different stories, which pit the perspective of the feminist sociologist against that of the feminist fabulator. While Dworkin treats her interpretation as *fact*, and upholds its claim to that status by juxtaposing it against the 'literary affectation'[22] of other de Sade critics, Carter *knows* she is telling tales. In Lorna Sage's description of *The Sadeian Woman*, one particularly apposite word keeps recurring; it is, she says, 'an ironic exploration of women's plight in a world authorized by patriarchy. . . . The strategy is to *follow through* the monster Marquis's plots in ironic paraphrase'.[23] It is irony, therefore, which is the dominant mode of expression in this text, although it is indeed a risky one to adopt, in the circumstances. As Dworkin's scathing critique shows, Carter's dry, mocking tone leaves her open to accusations of callousness and collusion by those, such as Dworkin and Kappeler, who either miss the irony, or see it as an inappropriate response to the subject matter.

But *The Sadeian Woman* is in fact less of an apologia than such critics make it appear. As Elaine Jordan says of Kappeler, 'she ignores Carter's final rubbishing of de Sade, once she's used his writing as a springboard for whatever she can get from it for women'.[24] And Carter has described her intentions in terms which are hardly a ringing endorsement for pornography: her purpose was, she said, 'to contrast what our culture does to women's views of themselves. . . . Pornography doesn't allow progress, it reflects static views of women'.[25]

Both Kappeler and Dworkin are therefore either taken in by, or else choose to ignore, the provocative aspect of Carter's rhetoric. Indeed, Carter herself slyly describes her debate at one point as an 'exercise of the lateral imagination' (p. 37), a phrase which can be read two ways at once. While on the one hand she is engaging in a genuinely subversive, sideways reading of her chosen material, she does not disassociate herself from the possibility of deliberately inflammatory exaggeration. While the book's first chapter, the mock-seriously entitled 'Polemical Preface', for example, is on one level a perfectly correct summary of Carter's analytical intentions, to a certain extent it also wilfully misrepresents the spirit in which such an analysis is being undertaken, veiling its seriousness in an elaborate display of its own contentiousness. Although Carter later engages in a more rigorously critical anatomisation of de Sade's intentions, here she makes sweeping generalisations in language calculated to shock and offend. De Sade appears here as some kind of profane early feminist, 'urg[ing] women to fuck as actively as they are able, so that powered by their enormous and hitherto untapped sexual energy they will then be able to fuck their way into history and, in so doing, change it' (p. 27).

It is also in the Polemical Preface that Carter creates the controversial description of a 'moral pornographer'. Such a figure, she argues,

> would be an artist who uses pornographic material as part of the acceptance of the logic of a world of absolute sexual licence for all the genders, and projects a model of the way such a world might work. A moral pornographer might use pornography as a critique of current relationships between the sexes. His [sic] business would be the total demystification of the flesh and the subsequent revelation, through the infinite modulations of the sexual act, of the real relations of man and his kind. (p. 19)

So the moral pornographer, in stripping the sexual act of romanticism, brings it into history by making his reader aware that any erotic encounter carries with it the baggage of socio-economic status. In

Carter's words, it is 'a direct confrontation of two beings whose actions in bed are wholly determined by their acts when they are out of it' (p. 9).

Such a claim would be problematic even were it not attached to the monstrous de Sade. But if one looks again at Carter's description of the moral pornographer quoted above, one should notice her use of the conditional, which is echoed in her provocative conclusion to the Polemical Preface: 'Sade remains a monstrous and daunting cultural edifice; yet I *would like to think* that he put pornography into the service of women, or, *perhaps*, allowed it to be invaded by women' (p. 37, my italics).

Indeed, de Sade's claim to the status of moral pornographer remains a matter of dispute throughout the text, and the apparent defence of him and his work with which the book opens is speedily abandoned in the rest of Carter's analysis, which steadily gains in critical intensity. It is in the final chapter of her study, however, that she fully confronts the nightmarish equation on which the whole of de Sade's vision is based: 'if flesh plus skin equals sensuality, then flesh minus skin equals meat'. Who is readied for the table, and who eats, therefore, is of crucial importance: 'My flesh encounters your taste for meat. So much the worse for me' (p. 138). Regarding the fictional careers of the sisters Justine (who suffers horribly) and Juliette (who causes horrible suffering) Carter concludes that in the Sadeian universe the only way in which women can avoid being regarded as no more than flesh – in both the sexual and the culinary meanings of the word – is to join the predators. But, she argues, this is no escape, merely a route to another kind of captivity:

> Justine is the thesis, Juliette the antithesis; both are without hope and neither pays any heed to a future in which might lie the possibility of a synthesis of their modes of being, neither submissive nor aggressive, capable of both thought and feeling. (p. 79)

The fact is that the purpose of *The Sadeian Woman* is not to defend de Sade so much as to fit his pornographic intent to Carter's own radical practice, a point which can be illustrated by quoting Carter's own description of the process which led to her 'radicalisation' in the late sixties. It was, she said,

> a moment when many of the things of which you have a theoretical knowledge actually apply to oneself. You could walk your calf past

the butcher's shop for days, but it's only when he sees the abattoir that he realises that there is a relation between himself and the butcher's shop – a relation which is mediated, shall we say, by the abattoir.[26]

Put side by side with the kind of language she uses in relation to her study of de Sade, the similarity in metaphorical terminology reveals that her valorisation of the monster is not all that it seems. Undoubtedly, *The Sadeian Woman* demonstrates Carter's fascination with the erotic extremism of de Sade's work. However, the quotation from Foucault with which the book opens is an open declaration of its ultimate intention to be a work of cultural evisceration which systematically strips Sadeian pornography of its superficial glamour in order to uncover and contest the issues of power and control which it disguises. In so doing, she reveals herself, rather than de Sade, as the real moral pornographer – in spite of the fact that throughout her argument she consistently envisages such a figure as male.

The dominant metaphors in Carter's writing of the sixties were all to do with surface, costume and sensuality, summed up in the recurring refrain in 'Notes for a Theory of Sixties Style': 'Velvet is back, skin anti-skin, mimic nakedness'. Velvet, in other words, becomes a second skin, a superannuated nakedness more sexually suggestive than the merely unclothed body could ever be, a fact which her Baudelarian dandies well know. *The Sadeian Woman*, however, is the final, most explicit, indication of the alteration in Carter's literary focus in her fiction of the seventies. Now, her perspective is focused below the surface, below skin itself, to find the meat beneath.

From de Sade's cannibalistic necrophiliacs, to the man-beasts which populate *The Bloody Chamber*, to the disintegrating, violent tyrant-states of *The Infernal Desire Machines of Doctor Hoffman* and *The Passion of New Eve*, therefore, Carter's main preoccupation in her writing throughout the seventies is with the alliance between the powerful and the powerless – how it is constructed, how maintained, by whom and to what ends. Taking on herself the controversial mantle of moral pornographer is one way in which such ideologies can be defamiliarised. Stripped of their veneer of 'naturalness', they can be exposed as the constructions they are, and thus capable of being dismantled and rebuilt in different forms. In the wake of their wreckage, Carter cultivates an extraordinary fluidity in which nothing is incontrovertible, nothing is set – the boundaries between story and history, male and female, logic and irrationality all dissolve into the surreal narrative anarchy which is the hallmark of Carter's fiction of this decade. Unlike de Sade, whose final failure of vision exposes him as 'a simple pornographer' (p. 132) all along, in spite of his spectacular perversity 'still in complicity with the authority which he hates' (p. 136), Carter is consistently audacious in her outrageous mingling of pornography and feminism in the interest of cultural critique.

Fireworks (1974)

Although *The Infernal Desire Machines of Doctor Hoffman* was the first book written and published by Carter in the seventies, it was followed by her first short-story collection, *Fireworks*, which is a suitable starting point for the investigation of her fiction of this period. With the exception of 'Flesh and the Mirror', this group of stories written while in Japan has received very little critical attention to date, yet it provides excellent introductory examples of the way in which Carter's narrative technique, never straightforward to begin with, became more intricately self-referential in terms of both form and content. In these short stories, she challenges her readers with portrayals of violence and desire which shock and disturb, and which intensify their effects by pushing against the boundaries of conventional narrative representation. The collection consists of first-person narratives set in Japan interspersed with surreal fantasies, in which Carter's response to the 'lyrically bizarre holocausts'[27] of Japanese pornography is dramatically displayed in evocative depictions of incest, sadism and sexual domination. Taken as a whole, this is an entire collection of traveller's tales, records of a journey not just into another culture, but also into the dark and dangerous landscape of taboo.

'The Loves of Lady Purple' is probably one of the darkest stories in the collection and, although it predates *The Sadeian Woman* by about five years, presents the same arguments in microcosm. Stripping the pornographic narrative of its superficial glamour in order to reveal its vicious underpinnings, this story is a perfect demonstration of the point Carter makes in *The Sadeian Woman* that a 'free woman in an unfree society will be a monster' (p. 27). It is the Gothic fable of a life-size marionette who under the 'godlike . . . manipulations' (p. 23)[28] of her puppet-master nightly re-enacts the monstrous career of Lady Purple, a courtesan who took to murdering her lovers before eventually becoming consumed by her own sexual voracity.

The reader of *The Sadeian Woman* will be reminded of Juliette, described by Carter as a woman who, having 'attained the lonely freedom of the libertine', is thus precipitated into 'a tautological condition that exists only for itself and is without any meaning in the general context of human life' (p. 99). In their endlessly self-perpetuating quest for new sexual atrocities to commit, Juliette and her partners in crime become no more than automata who 'define their own pleasure in mechanical terms, so much friction, so many concussions of the nerves' (p. 104). In 'The Loves of Lady Purple', Carter exploits the possibilities of fiction in order to render the same argument on a horribly literal level. In this context, the joyless mechanical contortions of the female libertine cause her to quite literally *become* a machine. Even when consumed by the diseases born of her own sexual voracity, outcast and alone, Lady Purple still robotically performs a ghastly imitation of the actions of desire, 'when, outrageous nymphomaniac, she practised extraordinary necrophilies on the bloated corpses the sea tossed contemptuously at her feet for her dry rapacity had become entirely mechanical' (pp. 32–3).

The Professor draws his audience on the basis of his claim that Lady Purple is eventually transformed into the very marionette who nightly re-enacts the story which is, in fact, her own. However, in a further horrific metamorphosis which transforms the relationship between puppet and puppet-master portrayed by Carter in previous books, she vampiristically feeds on his innocent desire for her in order to '[re]gain ... entry into the world by a mysterious loophole in its metaphysics' (p. 36). Her independence from the puppet-master achieved, she immediately takes herself off to the nearest brothel to repeat her career – and the events of the story itself – all over again.

The entire narrative, therefore, is founded on the ambiguity of whether 'the marionette [had] all the time parodied the living or was she, now living, to parody her own performance as a marionette?' (pp. 37–8). In the world of the story itself, to comment on such a paradox is essentially meaningless, for it really doesn't make any difference. Whether she begins or ends as a woman or as a puppet, Lady Purple's rapacious desires lock her into a savage cycle of endless replication and self-destruction which makes her the very epitome of the Sadeian subject, at least as much a prisoner of her own 'limitless presumption of appetite'[29] as her victims.

However, the issue of Lady Purple's in/authenticity does have a very real effect on an increasingly tautological text in which the dividing lines which separate the interlocking levels of narrative keep collapsing into one another. The story opens with Lady Purple as a marionette enacting a drama which purports to be both story and history at one and the same time: a paradox conveyed through the Professor's assertion that the marionette is the *real* Lady Purple. If he is telling the truth, then we are listening to history; if not, then pure fantasy. But if it *is* true, then we're still in the realm of fantasy, because such a claim – a woman has turned into a marionette – carries with it the implication of the transgression of the boundaries which divide the impossible from the possible, for in reality a woman *can't* turn into a marionette. Lady Purple's subsequent progression into the text's actuality does nothing to resolve this dilemma except throw it into a self-referential loop which cannot be untied. Making her way to the town's brothel 'like a homing pigeon, out of logical necessity' (p. 38), she becomes a disturbing symbol of the story that will not stay put, but will persist in trying to wander out of its category as fiction.

'The Loves of Lady Purple' is therefore a typical example of the way in which Carter can be seen to be moving towards a more overtly postmodernist form of fiction in the early seventies, creating narratives which play about with notions of meaning, truth and interpretation in such a way as to render them problematic in the extreme. However, the pieces in *Fireworks* which echo the non-fiction essays Carter was simultaneously writing for *New Society* – and which thus invite a more personal or autobiographical interpretation – are even more overt in their dismantling of such narrative certainties.

I have already discussed the problems encountered in attempting to read such pieces as straightforward autobiography. In the context of the development of Carter's fiction at this point in her career, however, such apparently autobiographical narratives demonstrate the growing self-consciousness of the authorial subject. Always narcissistically aware of its own effects, Carter's work now flowers into full-blown metafiction, which, in the words of Linda Hutcheon, 'is fiction about fiction – that is, fiction that includes within itself a commentary on its own narrative and/or linguistic identity'.[30] 'The Smile of Winter' is a typical example, reflecting even more overtly than 'The Loves of Lady Purple' on the compositional components out of which it is constituted.

Its setting is a fishing village on the coast of Japan, in all probability the place where Carter wrote *The Infernal Desire Machines of Doctor Hoffman*.[31] The central motif of this story is isolation. Separated from her environment by barriers of race and cultural expectation, the narrator watches the inhabitants of the village watching her, each divided from the other by ineradicable difference. So alien does the narrator's environment seem to her, that at one point she envisages it as an underwater world: 'when the women move among trays of fish I think they, too, are sea creatures, spiny, ocean-bottom-growing flora and if a tidal wave consumed the village ... there, under the surface, life would go on just as before'.

But isolation also breeds solipsism, for in this alien topography the only thing the narrator can presume to know is herself. In this sense, she carefully cultivates her emotions and her actions to make them imitations of the world around her 'to procure a moving image of poignant desolation' (p. 41):

> I collect driftwood and set it up among the pine trees in picturesque attitudes on the edge of the beach and then I strike a picturesque attitude myself beside them as I watch the constantly agitated waves, for here we all strike picturesque attitudes and that is why we are so beautiful. (p. 42)

In a narrative which depends on the juxtaposition of the solitary 'I' against the communal 'they', however, the introduction of the plural 'we' at this point in the text is somewhat startling. What it does, however, is foreground the extent of the narrator's role-playing, and thus cast doubts upon the reliability of her narrative voice. Although the story dwells persistently upon the sadness experienced by the narrator, the exact relationship between setting and emotion is difficult to disentangle. As the above quotation hints, her emotion may be no more than a way of integrating herself into her setting in a way which validates her position as outsider by encoding it in the overblown terms of romance. One of the repeated references in the text, for example, is of the narrator as Mariana in the moated grange, portrayed in such a way as to recall, not the character in *Measure for Measure*, but Tennyson's extravagantly love-lorn Victorian heroine.

The final twist is that the narrator reveals herself to have been all along perfectly aware of the paradoxes of her narrative position, suspended as it is between involvement and detachment. As she warns her readers:

> Do not think I do not realise what I am doing. I am making a composition using the following elements: the winter beach; the

winter moon; the ocean; the women; the pine trees; the riders; the
driftwood; the shells; the shapes of darkness and the shapes of
water; and the refuse. These are inimical to my loneliness because
of their indifference to it. Out of these pieces of inimical indifference, I intend to represent the desolate smile of winter which, as
you must have gathered, is the smile I wear. (p. 46)

The narrator is performing a complex and contradictory balancing trick
here. On the one hand, surrounded by the indifference of the alien
landscape, she is utterly alone. But on the other, her act of narrative
composition brings her into precarious harmony with her surroundings,
since she can arrange them to 'represent the desolate smile of winter'
which is also 'the smile I wear'. So she is at once part of the scene,
yet also outside it – simultaneously actor in and director of her own
personal melodrama in which her setting is meticulously arranged to
provide a fitting backdrop to her carefully cultivated solitary pose.

Moreover, the forceful way in which such paradox is foregrounded
signals the narrator's lack of interest in fulfilling the conventions of
fiction which demand the illusion of verisimilitude, since it reduces all
the poetic images within the narrative to no more than an assemblage
of two-dimensional cut-out devices out of which a story – any story –
can be assembled. In the final analysis, therefore, this is not so much
narrative as theatre (or perhaps a puppet show?), presented in such a
way as to constantly draw attention to its own artificiality.

Lady Purple's obsession with gaining a life independent of her
puppet-master is echoed in the almost neurotic self-awareness of the
narrative voice of 'The Smile of Winter', for both maintain their subjectivity, their essential sense of self, through nothing more than the
grim exercise of will. It is this mechanical act of self-creation which
is the hallmark of Carter's emblematic subject of the seventies. This
figure may posture like a dandy, and be similarly in love with artifice,
but he (it is still almost always 'he') does not share the dandy's easy,
though duplicitous, charm. Like de Sade himself, who in many ways
functions as the blueprint for this figure, he is sustained by an egocentricity which seeks to bend the entire world to the fulfilment of his
desire. Yet behind his single-minded self-centredness, exactly what that
'self' might be remains a matter for debate.

The Infernal Desire Machines of Doctor Hoffman (1972)

The most immediately obvious thing about *The Infernal Desire Machines of Doctor Hoffman* is how little it resembles the novels which came before it, thereby acting as a dramatic focus for Carter's changing response to her cultural setting. In her introduction added to 'Notes for a Theory of Sixties Style' on its republication in *Nothing Sacred* in 1982, Carter retrospectively describes the sixties as a period in which 'The pleasure principle met the reality principle like an irresistible force encountering an immovable object, and the reverberations of that collision are still echoing about us'.[32] *Hoffman* takes this idea and builds it into an elaborate and surreal fantasy which, while it echoes the disillusion voiced by Carter in such pieces as 'Fin de Siecle', also uses it as a starting point for radical deconstruction of the cultural status quo.

Like *Heroes and Villains*, *Hoffman* employs tropes drawn from science fiction, but, while Marianne's and Jewel's actions exist in (more or less) rational correspondence to their fictionally constructed world, *Hoffman* plays much more daring narrative games. The action is set in an anonymous South American country which comes under siege from the reality-modifying machines of Dr Hoffman. Under his direction, the country's capital is transformed into a place where the most hidden, most fantastic desires attain objective reality: as in 'The Loves of Lady Purple', story won't stay story but persists in trying to hijack fact. 'Hardly anything remained the same for more than one second and the city was no longer the conscious production of humanity; it had become the arbitrary realm of dream' (p. 33),[33] says the novel's narrator, Desiderio. The action of the novel follows Desiderio on the mission given to him by the Minister of Determination, Dr Hoffman's implacable foe, to find and destroy the unreality machines, and thus restore the country to its former rational state.

The novel's picaresque structure is an overt declaration of its liminal status. Carter described it as a 'dialectic between reason and passion, which it resolves in favour of reason',[34] but Desiderio's journey through the perpetually fluctuating landscape of Nebulous Time, however, allows the suspense between the two states to be maintained as long as possible before the inevitable denouement. As one review of the book points out, 'if the whole ends in a somewhat dying fall, this is only because the book's last page is prefigured and dictated by its first; of necessity, only the passage between chaos and order has flexibility, and hence, potential'.[35]

As another of the outsiders with which Carter's fiction has always been populated, however, Desiderio himself is an embodiment of the text's commitment to the avoidance of conclusion: in the words of Bakhtin, he is little more than 'a point moving in space'.[36] There is a difference here, however, which can be used to examine the exact nature of the change in Carter's fiction in the seventies. In many ways, Desiderio recalls male protagonists from her earlier novels, such as Morris in *Shadow Dance*, Joseph in *Several Perceptions*, and even Lee in *Love*, all of whom perceive of themselves as outsiders in a world both alien and alienating. But none of them possess Desiderio's acute self-awareness, an echo of his author's new commitment to theorising her narrative strategies. His narration, particularly in the book's opening chapter, is imbued with self-conscious irony, studied boredom and irritation with the irrational. On the occasion of 'Dr Hoffman's first disruptive coup' (p. 17), for example, Desiderio is watching a performance of *The Magic Flute* when the entire audience are turned into peacocks, He, however, is affected only by boredom, 'my first reaction to incipient delirium' (p. 16):

> I felt as though I was watching a film in which the Minister was the hero and the unseen Doctor certainly the villain; but it was an endless film and I found it boring for none of the characters engaged my sympathy, even if I admired them, and all the situations appeared the false engineering of an inefficient phantasist. (p. 25)

Which, in a sense, is exactly what they are. Desiderio comes very close here to recognising his role as narrative function, and allows Carter to briefly send up her own role as author in the process. Like the short stories in *Fireworks*, this is a narrative about narrative, locked into the kind of metafictional dialectic described by Patricia Waugh as 'the construction of a fictional illusion (as in traditional realism) and the laying bare of that illusion'.[37] Waugh's summary of the intentions of metafiction could function equally well as a description of Desiderio's role in the text, *in* the fictional illusion, but not *of* it, and thus, in the final analysis, committed to its deconstruction.

But it would be inaccurate to thus conclude that *Hoffman's* attention is focused totally inwards upon the issue of its own formation. On the contrary, it engages with the world of the 'real' more radically than any of Carter's novels have so far done. In this sense, it particularly corresponds to Linda Hutcheon's definition of historiographic metafiction which, she says,

> refutes the natural or common-sense methods of distinguishing between historical fact and fiction. It refuses the view that only history has a truth claim, both by questioning the ground of that claim in historiography and by asserting that both history and fiction are discourses, human constructs, signifying systems, and both derive their major claim to truth from that identity.[38]

Such master narratives as time, truth, identity and historical causation are systematically, deliberately, mangled in *Hoffman*, and although the ending apparently sees them restored, it is not to their former state. They may only have been dismantled once, but once is enough to see that they are not incontrovertible, but chosen. Again, it is Desiderio who functions as an excellent example of this intent, his claims to a rational, independent subjectivity growing increasingly desperate as the narrative proceeds. Although he begins the narrative as an exemplary example of the Baudelairean *flâneur*, in whom 'the joy of watching is triumphant',[39] by the end he is a shaken shadow of his former self, having been very nearly seduced into active participation within a world of seductive illusions and complex desires.

It is not accidental, as Lorna Sage also observes, that the setting of this novel is South America, which is 'very much the right setting for this vertiginous frontier-crossing – in literary terms, that is'.[40] This is the territory of magical realism, a form described by Mario Vargas Llosa as 'fantastic literature [which] . . . has its roots in objective reality and is a vehicle for exposing social and political evils'.[41] While it may be straining a point to place Carter, the white, Anglo-Saxon product of a white, Anglo-Saxon culture, alongside Latin American authors who write out of a history of political oppression and cultural domination, there is nevertheless a clear parallel. The label 'magical realist' was freely applied to Carter throughout her later career, and it was one she was happy to accept, citing Gabriel García Márquez and Alejo Carpentier, for example, as major influences on her own work.

What her adoption of the magical realist mode essentially offers Carter is a way of engaging with the world outside the text in a critical way – David Punter, for example, evocatively describes *The Infernal Desire Machines of Doctor Hoffman* as a 'metaphysicalisation of the political'.[42] For all its fantastic content, this novel is an extremely politicised analysis of power and colonisation. The major reason for Desiderio's disaffection, for example, is his racial background, for he bears the genetic stamp of his country's indigenous Indian population, an inheritance disowned and diluted by successive waves of colonisation from without. Throughout the book he can be seen both trying to belong and refusing to do so, a contradictory stance which is occasionally manifested in syntactic confusion: 'You could not', he says at one point,

> have said we were an undeveloped nation though, if we had not existed, Dr Hoffman could not have invented a better country in which to perform his experiments and, if he brought to his work the ambivalence of the expatriate, then were we not – except myself – almost all of us expatriates? (pp. 67–8)

The glaring contradiction between 'we' and 'me' here indicates a profound displacement of the subject, who has no home, and thus no history; consequently, what motivates the action of the novel is Desiderio's contradictory engagement with his desire to move from margins to the centre. In the realm of Nebulous Time, in which his desires gain an objective reality, each episode within the text offers him a different kind of belonging. When he joins the reclusive society of the river people, for example, he has the opportunity to marry into their extended family, feeling a racial solidarity with them which gives him 'the strongest sense of home-coming' (p. 76). The travelling fair offers him 'the unique allure of the norm' (p. 101), for compared to the freaks and misfits with which he is surrounded, race is a difference too trifling to worry about.

One of Desiderio's most significant encounters, however, is with a figure who echoes his position as outsider on the most grandiloquent and blasphemous of terms. The monstrous Count is the embodiment of the Sadeian sensibility which so fascinates Carter throughout her writing of this period: a master of polymorphous perversity, he is a self-styled 'connoisseur of catastrophe' (p. 122). His self-vaunting rhetoric is absurd in its elaborate extremism, yet his terrible solipsism – Desiderio describes him as 'the emperor of inverted megalomaniacs' (p. 123) – is also profanely glorious.

That the Count is the latest in Carter's procession of dandies is emphasised in Desiderio's first view of him, which recalls *Shadow Dance*'s final sight of Honeybuzzard in all the horror of his elemental self. Just as Honey appears as a living skeleton, his 'daytime flesh carved

off his bones' (*Shadow Dance*, p. 179), so the Count's 'diabolical ele-
gance could not have existed without his terrible emaciation; he wore
his dandyism in his very bones, as if it was a colour that had seeped out
of his essential bones' (p. 122). Yet perhaps it is not so much that the
dandy's role has changed here, as that he has been rendered down to his
essential elements, no more than 'a corpse animated only by a demonic
intellectual will' (p. 126). There is, indeed, something geometrical and
stark about the Count, which makes his enacting of his diabolic passions
no more than the programmed movements of an automaton and thus,
though horrible, also slightly ludicrous.

The threat offered by the Count is that those who come into his
orbit run the risk of being trampled beneath his 'self-regarding dia-
bolism which crushed and flattened the world as he passed through it'
(p. 168). Desiderio, however, escapes such a fate, for in this encounter,
as well as in every other he experiences in the realm of Nebulous Time,
his inability to surrender his ex-centric position proves to be his salvation
as well as his curse, showing that a place on the margin has its merits,
after all. He is not so enchanted by the river people as to switch off his
critical faculties entirely, and his anthropological knowledge helps him
to escape before they kill him in a bloodthirsty traditional marriage
ceremony. His life at the travelling fair comes to an abrupt and painful
conclusion when, in an unasked-for and somewhat extreme act of
solidarity, he is raped by all nine of the troupe known as the Acrobats
of Desire; but it is also this event which enables him to escape the
cataclysm which overwhelms the fairground and all the people in it.
The Count, meanwhile, ends up in a cannibal cooking-pot, and dies in
triumphant pain, victim of his own drive towards non-being; while,
ever the inveterate observer, Desiderio watches and narrates in horri-
fied fascination from the sidelines.

In seeking inclusion, therefore, Desiderio only experiences repeated
exclusions, and the ultimate object of his quest is no exception. His
allegiance to the Minister's absolutely rational vision has never been
entirely wholehearted, not least 'because I was aware of what would
have been my own position in that watertight schema' (p. 60). He thus
enters the domain of Dr Hoffman with the ultimate object of his
desire, Hoffman's daughter Albertina, covertly hoping to find 'a palace
dedicated only to wonder' (p. 209). Instead, he finds only 'the powerhouse
of the marvellous, where all its clanking, dull, stage machinery was
kept' (p. 201), and which he destroys more out of a fit of pique than
anything else. In doing so, he finally discovers a kind of identity –

however, he has to live for the rest of his life with the knowledge of the emptiness of the role he has chosen:

> In this city I have been, as you know, a hero. I became one of the founders of the new constitution – largely from the negative propulsion of my own inertia for, once I was placed and honoured on my plinth, I was not the man to climb down again, saying: 'But I am the wrong man!' for I felt that, if what I had done turned out for the common good, I might as well reap what benefits I could from it. The shrug is my gesture. The sneer is my expression. . . . I am the check, the impulse of restraint. (pp. 220–1)

In fact, what Desiderio has really gained by the end of the novel is not inclusion so much as a position which validates his role as sneering, passionless and detached malcontent. The price he has had to pay for it is the destruction of his female alter ego, Albertina, 'my Platonic other, my necessary extinction, my dream made flesh' (p. 215), whom he has pursued through all the worlds of Nebulous Time. The text's crowning irony is that it is Albertina all along who offers him that which he both fears and desires; the dangerously seductive possibility of the surrender of detachment. If it comes about, the consummation of their picaresque courtship will absorb Desiderio completely in the world of desire.

But Desiderio's murder of Albertina only confirms what his earlier experiences have already hinted at – that, while he may dream of inclusion, he does not actually want it. And certainly, on the terms offered by Albertina, inclusion is not an attractive prospect. Were Desiderio to accept her offer to be her partner in the mechanic generation of 'eroto-energy' (p. 214), he would exchange the dubious freedom of life on the margins for an even more dubious slavery to Dr Hoffman's scientific manipulation of the imperatives of passion.

Yet Desiderio's recounting of his murder of Albertina, even as it excludes him forever from inclusion, in itself signals a momentary loss of his habitual control over both himself and his narration. Striking out in a fit of blind panic and frustrated lust, love and hate intermingle in a savage outburst of eroticised violence which marks 'the grotesque dénouement of my great passion':

> She bit me and tore my clothes and I bit her and pummelled her with my fists. I pummelled her breasts until they were as blue as

her eyelids but she never let go and I savaged her throat with my teeth as if I were a tiger and she were the trophy I seized in the forests of the night. (p. 216)

The undercurrents of sadistic sexuality in this passage are disturbing, containing as they do an echo of the Count's own valorisation of the relationship between predator and prey, and in particular his proclamation that 'My crises render me utterly bestial and in that state I am infinitely superior to man, as the tiger, who preys on man if he has any sense, is superior' (p. 126). However, rather like the rape scene in *Heroes and Villains*, appearances are deceptive, for the roles of predator and prey are somewhat difficult to ascertain here. Her Daddy's girl through and through, Albertina's adventures with Desiderio have only been steps on the way towards the desire machine in her father's laboratory, and Desiderio, until this point, has been as much the hunted as the hunter.

The intermingling of the terminologies of death and desire in this passage forcefully signal the deeply equivocal nature of Desiderio's response to Albertina and all she represents: both a fate worse than death and the fulfilment of his most deeply held desires. No sooner has the murder been committed, though, than Desiderio rushes to reclaim the position of spectator, finding, as he says, the 'habit of sardonic contemplation . . . the hardest habit of all to break' (p. 201). With a detachment which is a distinctly disturbing contrast to his killing frenzy of a moment before, he regards his blood-stained knife with the assessing eye of an aloof commentator: 'It was a common kitchen knife, such as is used to chop meat fine enough for hamburger and so on' (p. 217).

But although Desiderio ends the novel having finally made the choice between order and chaos, he is haunted by 'the insatiable regret with which we acknowledge that the impossible is, *per se*, impossible' (p. 221). As Andrzej Gąsiorek says, Desiderio's pervasive sense of loss 'resists a dualistic conception of reality that can only pit philosophy and poetry against one another',[43] and shows that a choice between two extremes is always a hopeless one.

Notes

1. Lorna Sage, *Angela Carter* (Plymouth: Northcote House, 1994), p. 25.
2. I have drawn this term from Linda Hutcheon, *A Poetics of Postmodernism: History, Theory, Fiction* (London: Routledge, 1988).

3. Angela Carter, 'My Maugham Award', *Author* (Winter 1970), pp. 173–5 (p. 175).
4. Angela Carter, 'Fin de Siecle', *New Society* (17 August 1972), pp. 354–5 (p. 354).
5. Roland Barthes, *Mythologies*, trans. Annette Lavers (London: Vintage Books, 1993), p. 11.
6. George Melly, *Revolt Into Style: The Pop Arts in the 50s and 60s* (Oxford: Oxford University Press, 1989), p. 14.
7. Elizabeth Wilson, *Adorned in Dreams: Fashion and Modernity* (London: Virago Press, 1985), p. 3.
8. Angela Carter, 'Notes for a Theory of Sixties Style', in *Nothing Sacred: Selected Writings* (London: Virago Press, 1982), pp. 85–90 (p. 86).
9. Angela Carter, 'The Wound in the Face', in *Nothing Sacred*, pp. 90–5 (p. 93).
10. Angela Carter, 'Truly, It Felt Like Year One', in Sara Maitland (ed.), *Very Heaven: Looking Back at the 1960s* (London: Virago Press, 1988), pp. 209–16 (p. 215).
11. Angela Carter, 'Notes from the Front Line', in Michelene Wandor (ed.), *On Gender and Writing* (London: Pandora Press, 1983), pp. 69–77 (p. 70).
12. Angela Carter, introduction to her Japanese essays reprinted in *Nothing Sacred*, p. 28.
13. Mary Harron, '"I'm a Socialist, Damn It! How Can You Expect Me to be Interested in Fairies?"', *The Guardian* (25 September 1984), p. 10.
14. Paul Barker, 'The Return of the Magic Story-Teller', *The Independent on Sunday* (8 January 1995), pp. 14, 16 (p. 16).
15. Harron, p. 10.
16. Angela Carter, 'The Power of Porn', *The Observer* (10 April 1977), p. 9.
17. Les Bedford, 'Angela Carter: An Interview' (Sheffield: Sheffield University Press, February 1977).
18. Andrea Dworkin, *Pornography: Men Possessing Women* (London: The Women's Press, 1981), p. 84.
19. Susanne Kappeler, *The Pornography of Representation* (Cambridge: Polity Press, 1986), p. 135.
20. Dworkin, p. 88.
21. Angela Carter, *The Sadeian Woman: An Exercise in Cultural History* (London: Virago Press, 1979). All subsequent references in the text are from this edition.
22. Dworkin, p. 84.
23. Sage, *Angela Carter*, p. 38 (italics are Sage's).
24. Elaine Jordan, 'The Dangers of Angela Carter', in Isobel Armstrong (ed.), *New Feminist Discourses: Critical Essays on Theories and Texts* (London: Routledge, 1992), pp. 119–32 (p. 120).
25. Olga Kenyon, *The Writer's Imagination* (University of Bradford Print Unit, 1992), p. 29.

26. John Haffenden, 'Magical Mannerist', *The Literary Review* (November 1984), pp. 34–8 (p. 34).

27. Angela Carter, 'Once More into the Mangle', in *Nothing Sacred*, pp. 38–44 (p. 42).

28. Angela Carter, *Fireworks* (London: Virago Press, 1987) [rev. edn]. All subsequent references in the text are from this edition.

29. Michel Foucault, *Madness and Civilisation*, quoted in Angela Carter, *The Sadeian Woman*, p. 3.

30. Linda Hutcheon, *Narcissistic Narrative: The Metafictional Paradox* (London: Methuen, 1984), p. 1.

31. See Susan Rubin Suleiman, 'The Fate of the Surrealist Imagination in the Society of the Spectacle', in Lorna Sage (ed.), *Flesh and Mirror: Essays on the Art of Angela Carter*, pp. 98–116. Suleiman says Carter 'wrote the novel [*Hoffman*] in three months, in a Japanese village where she seems to have been the only European' (p. 100).

32. Angela Carter, *Nothing Sacred*, p. 84.

33. Angela Carter, *The Infernal Desire Machines of Doctor Hoffman* (Harmondsworth: Penguin, 1982). All subsequent references in the text are from this edition.

34. Quoted by Lorna Sage in *Angela Carter*, p. 34.

35. George Hay, 'Marionettes with Metaphysics', *Foundation: The Review of Science Fiction*, vol. 3 (1973), pp. 69–71 (p. 70).

36. Mikhail Bakhtin, 'The Bildungsroman and Its Significance in the History of Realism (Toward a Historical Typology of the Novel)', in *Speech Genres and Other Late Essays*, trans. Vern W. McGee (Austin: University of Texas Press, 1986), pp. 10–59 (p. 10).

37. Patricia Waugh, *Metafiction: The Theory and Practice of Self-Conscious Fiction* (London: Methuen, 1984), p. 6.

38. Hutcheon, *A Poetics of Postmodernism*, p. 93.

39. Walter Benjamin, *Charles Baudelaire: A Lyric Poet in the Era of High Capitalism*, trans. Harry Zohn (London: Verso, 1983), p. 69.

40. Sage, *Angela Carter*, p. 33.

41. Mario Vargas Llosa, 'Social Commitment and Latin American Writer', in Doris Meyer (ed.), *Lives on the Line: The Testimony of Contemporary Latin American Authors* (Berkeley: University of California Press, 1988), pp. 128–38 (p. 133).

42. David Punter, *The Hidden Script: Writing and the Unconscious* (London: Routledge, 1985), p. 29.

43. Andrzej Gąsiorek, *Post-War British Fiction: Realism and After* (London: Edward Arnold, 1995), p. 131.

CHAPTER 5

When asked by Olga Kenyon in 1992 whether she had a personal favourite amongst the novels she'd written, Angela Carter chose *The Infernal Desire Machines of Doctor Hoffman*. Elsewhere, however, she represented that piece of work as the one that very nearly scuppered her burgeoning novelistic career. The fact that it received a lukewarm critical reception obviously rankled with her – in interview with Susannah Clapp, for example, she satirically described it as 'the novel which marked the beginning of my obscurity. I went from being a very promising young writer to being completely ignored in two novels'.[1] The other of the 'two novels' to which she refers here was *Love*, and the analogy between them one she had made before, employing, moreover, very much the same half-humorous, half-resentful tone. Whilst *Love*, she said on that occasion, 'had been a small book, mildly commercially unviable, *Hoffman*, a big book, was magnificently commercially unviable'.[2]

Given her feelings, it is perhaps not surprising that Carter, formerly a prolific author who in the early years of her career wrote a novel a year or thereabouts, waited five years before publishing another. On her return to England from Japan in 1972, and now finally divorced from her first husband, Carter fell on difficult times. 'Times are hard & getting harder', she wrote in a private letter in 1974. 'I sit in the city of Bath & watch capitalism crumble; I regret my misspent youth. Is all'.[3] Not only did she discover that her writing did not make enough money to live on, she didn't have the security of a permanent publisher. Geographically speaking, she was equally displaced, for although she returned to the south-west of England in 1973 and bought a house in Bath, economic necessity forced her to travel in order to earn her keep. Amongst other forays abroad, she briefly returned to Japan in order to gather the material for some more *New Society* essays.

Eventually, however, Carter's search for new sources of income led to her appointment as Arts Council for Great Britain Fellow in Creative Writing at the University of Sheffield, a post she held from 1976–8. Although she had previously poured scorn on the notion of working in a university ('When I really want to humiliate myself, I apply for a job at a British University',[4] she wrote in 1974), this nevertheless marked a new chapter in her professional life, for her role as educator was to subsequently take her to other universities both at home and abroad, and also to gain her a steadily increasing academic audience.

The Passion of New Eve (1977)

This was the backdrop for the writing and publication of Carter's seventh novel, *The Passion of New Eve*, which proved that, in spite of her creative hiatus, the hope of gaining a wider audience hadn't caused her to compromise her art one iota. Taking Carter's constant fascination with the performative aspects of gender to surreal extremes, it is at least as difficult, bizarre and experimental as *Hoffman*. Its author later claimed it to have been 'intended as a piece of black comedy',[5] although the humour is often difficult to discern in the general bleakness of vision which pervades the text. Her final verdict on the book, however, was very different, for in an interview for the BBC filmed shortly before her death in 1992, Carter talked about *The Passion of New Eve* at length, describing it as 'my great bid for the European serious novel'.[6]

The author's own contradictory opinions concerning *New Eve* have their echo in its wider critical reception – for every person who admires it, one can find another who dismisses it as pretentious, incomprehensible, or just plain silly. Olga Kenyon summed it up when she said that, although she regards it as 'a really successful feminist novel', 'I can't make many of my friends or students admire it'.[7] Peter Ackroyd, reviewing *New Eve* in *The Spectator*, dismissed it as an unsuccessful attempt to resist the conventions of realism, resulting in an uneasy 'shuffling between pastiche and allegory'.[8] The overall effect, he sniffed, 'is of languorous but cheap sentiment that doesn't have the substance to match its style'.[9] Even Lorna Sage exhibits a certain reservation, describing *New Eve* as 'a raw and savage book' which showed Carter having 'sacrificed some of her habitual charm'.[10] Yet it does seem to be experiencing something of a renaissance of late, not only on the back of Carter's presently high level of academic popularity as a whole, but also because this text is particularly amenable to readings which utilise currently fashionable theories concerning the body, gender and technology.[11]

Carter claimed in 'Notes from the Front Line' that *The Passion of New Eve* was intended as an 'anti-mythic novel',[12] written with the intent to break down the processes by which 'the social fictions which regulate our lives'[13] are created. Although the text is saturated with references to religious mythology, from New Eve to Earth Mother, 'myth' in this context can be used to describe any stereotype accepted unquestioningly as 'real': although establishing where 'myth' ends and 'real life' begins is itself a matter for debate in this text. In this it echoes the Reality War waged in *Hoffman*; but where the earlier novel finally commits itself, however regretfully, to the real, *New Eve* raises questions concerning whether such a thing as the 'real' exists at all. Also like *Hoffman*, it rehearses issues to do with power and sexuality which Carter subsequently proceeded to air in a non-fictional form in *The Sadeian Woman*.

The novel opens with the male narrator Evelyn watching a film starring the object of his prepubescent fantasies, Tristessa de St Ange, a figure who has quite surpassed the limitations of realism: 'the dream itself made flesh although the flesh I knew her in was not flesh itself but only a moving picture of flesh, real but not substantial' (pp. 7–8).[14] Already the boundaries between 'dream' and 'flesh' are dissolving here, and in the course of the novel they will become almost completely indistinguishable. While Evelyn at this stage thinks he knows the difference between fantasy and reality – Tristessa the fantasy on the screen, himself firmly in the real world of the audience – his narration, imbued with the privileged perspective of hindsight, is already strongly signalling the breakdown of such an order:

> I thought I was bidding a last goodbye to the iconography of adolescence; tomorrow, I would fly to a new place, another country, and never imagined I might find her there, waiting for revivification, for the kiss of a lover who would rouse her from her perpetual reverie, she, fleshy synthesis of the dream, both dreamed and dreamer. I never imagined, never. (pp. 8–9)

In fact, at this moment in the text, the cinema screen functions as the point at which fantasy and reality intersect. It is, after all, the window into the quintessential 'dream factory' where, in a process analagous to Dr Hoffman's unreality machines, desires are synthesised and produced for mass consumption. Figuratively speaking, Evelyn is poised on the brink of that point of intersection, about to pass into and through the screen into a different realm altogether. In that sense, his subsequent journey is absolutely familiar to any reader of Carter's fiction, for it resembles Melanie's transferral from home to toyshop; Marianne's from the Professor's white tower to the filthy Barbarian encampment; Desiderio's from the beleaguered rationalism of the city to the endlessly fluctuating landscapes of Nebulous Time. Here, Evelyn's picaresque journeying takes him to the home of Hollywood, USA, where he becomes the hero of his own cinematic-style drama, for as Lucie Armitt has observed, there is more than a touch of the 'road-movie'[15] about *The Passion of New Eve*. In the process his journey will take him towards Tristessa – not the artfully presented symbol of 'romantic dissolution' (p. 7) preserved on scratched and faded film stock, but the 'real' thing – and also into the depths of his own disassembled and reassembled self. In neither case does he find what he expects.

We have not, however, seen quite such a dark and nihilistic landscape since the moral and emotional wastelands of Carter's earlier novels, *Shadow Dance* and *Several Perceptions*, where violence erupts in the midst of the most terrible indifference, and events form random heaps of disassociated experiences. In *The Passion of New Eve*, as Evelyn himself notes, 'I found, instead of hard edges and clean colours, a lurid Gothic darkness that closed over my head entirely and became my world' (p. 10). While the first chapter of the novel, set in an English cinema, has at least a superficial aura of realism, America is the place of fantasy and nightmare, where even the 'skies were of strange, bright, artificial colours' (p. 12). Society is in the process of fragmenting into its component parts – blacks against whites, women against men, muggers run amok.

At first, however, Evelyn retains the role of detached spectator, unable to believe that he is not still in a movie theatre: 'That the city had become nothing but a gigantic metaphor for death kept me, in my innocence, all agog in my ring-side seat. The movie ran towards its last reel. What excitement!' (p. 15). Baudrillard describes Evelyn's narrative trajectory precisely when he says that to understand the American city, 'you should not begin with the city and move inwards to the screen; you should begin with the screen and move outwards to the city'.[16] Evelyn 'knows' America through cinema; but what he has yet to grasp is that America *is* cinema. For both Carter and Baudrillard, America is characterised by a condition Baudrillard terms 'hyperreality', in which, roughly speaking, the 'real' is validated entirely through reference to fictions, copies and models:

> Today it is quotidian reality in its entirety – political, social, historical and economic – that now incorporates the simulatory dimension of hyperrealism. We live everywhere already in an 'esthetic' [sic] hallucination or reality. The old slogan 'truth is stranger than fiction,' that still corresponded to the surrealist phrase of this estheticization of life, is obsolete. There is no more fiction life could possibly confront – even victoriously – it is reality itself that disappears utterly in the game of reality.[17]

However, whether viewing the last convulsions of the American dream in person or through the television set, Evelyn is at this point unable to grasp that the laws which he believes still separate reality from illusion have ceased to operate. Perilously secure in this delusion, like Desiderio before him he self-consciously adopts the Baudelairean role of the modernist hero or *flâneur*, starkly outlined against the swirling mass of the city's population through his privileged difference and detachment. However, says Walter Benjamin, while 'In the *flâneur*, the joy of watching is triumphant. . . . it can stagnate in the gaper; then the *flâneur* has turned into a *badaud*'.[18] Benjamin goes on to quote Victor Fournel:

> [While the] simple *flâneur* is always in full possession of his individuality . . . the individuality of the *badaud* disappears. It is absorbed by the outside world . . . which intoxicates him to the point where he forgets himself. Under the influence of the spectacle which presents itself to him, the *badaud* becomes an impersonal creature; he is no longer a human being, he is part of the public, of the crowd.[19]

This is precisely what happens to Evelyn, for once he falls under the sexual spell of the black prostitute Leilah, he is drawn from his role as spectator into one of performer, from modernist *flâneur* to *badaud* – a crucial shift which, containing an implicit intimation of anonymity and loss of self, implicates him irretrievably in the postmodern topography of the text. Ensnared by Leilah's blatant seductions, Evelyn is led 'deep into the geometric labyrinth of the heart of the city' (p. 21), now nothing but a priapic manifestation of predatory male desire, 'All my existence . . . gone away into my tumescence; . . . nothing but cock' (p. 25). Not so much individuals as stereotypes of male and female, Evelyn's and Leilah's sexual interactions are presented with the stark exactitude of the pornographic text, which spurns the discreet veilings of romanticism.

Even here the dividing line between predator and prey, reality and its simulation, is being redrawn in ways which deprives Evelyn still further of identity and control. While he thinks of himself as 'a bird of prey' (p. 25), and of Leilah as 'a born victim' (p. 28) – a notion which neatly excuses his sadistic treatment of her – he is nevertheless forced to acknowledge that 'my prey, throughout the pursuit, had played the hunter' (p. 25). Tigerish Leilah, who reeks of musk and furs and who, though 'dressed meat', herself controls the process by which she is 'carnalised' (p. 31), resembles Albertina in *Hoffman* in that she is not all that she seems. Although Evelyn makes her pregnant, then abandons her after the abortion, thus seemingly sealing her status as victim, in retrospect it appears that it is actually Leilah who has controlled every step Evelyn makes towards the desert and the all-engulfing embrace of the Mother who will act as the agent for his metamorphosis. Indeed, much later in the text the now transformed Evelyn is belatedly inspired to wonder whether Leilah had not 'all the time been engaged on guerilla warfare for her mother' (p. 172), a conclusion which is supported by Leilah's own admission that her real purpose in the city was 'to lead the wary into temptation' (p. 174).

Although Evelyn subsequently attempts to regain his position of conceptual distance from the city through the tactic of distancing himself from it geographically, his attempt to flee into the desert now only takes him deeper into the very situation from which he is trying to escape. Rather like Alice, who finds everything reversed in a looking-glass world, all the time Evelyn thinks he's running away he is in fact only 'speeding towards the very enigma I had left behind – the dark room, the mirror, the woman' (p. 39). Carter, again, resembles Baudrillard in presenting the American desert as more symbolic condition than place, finding there 'an ecstatic critique of culture, an ecstatic form of disappearance'.[20]

Baudrillard's work, like Carter's, is constantly circling and returning to the desert, which he regards as the ultimate symbol of America, 'because you are delivered from all depth there – a brilliant, mobile, superficial neutrality, a challenge to meaning and profundity, a challenge to nature and culture, an outer hyperspace, with no origin, no reference points'.[21] In *The Passion of New Eve*, the desert is the place of death, transformation and of simulation taken to the ultimate degree, for it is here that, kidnapped by the militant women of the underground city of Beulah, Evelyn becomes Eve, 'the object of all the unfocused desires that had ever existed in my own head . . . my own masturbatory fantasy' (p. 75).

Beulah has been founded by Mother, whose ultimate aim is to restart the faltering course of history in the feminine mode, a project which involves not just social and political revolution, but also, through the utilisation of 'a complicated mix of mythology and technology' (p. 48), an extensive rewriting of the world's belief systems. She has already transformed herself through plastic surgery into 'an incarnated deity . . . she has undergone a painful metamorphosis of the entire body and become the abstraction of a natural principle' (p. 49), and has chosen Evelyn to take on the role of new Eve, intended to be fertilised with his own sperm to become the parent of a new Messiah, the institutor of a new world order in which women will no longer be 'the antithesis in the dialectic of creation' (p. 67).

Only the most uncritical of readers, however, could interpret such claims literally, for Carter's demythologising sentiments are blatantly manifested through satire, exaggeration and grotesque hyperbole.[22] Natalie M. Rosinsky's analysis of the text as a lampooning of feminist gynocentric essentialism is, I think, a point well taken.[23] The very corridors of Beulah are 'unnatural, slippery, ersatz, treacherous, false-looking' (pp. 55–6), but it is Mother who is the ultimate embodiment of its absurdity, huge, 'breasted like a sow' (p. 59), and 'bay[ing] like a bloodhound bitch in heat' (p. 64). Once the most detached of spectators, even Evelyn is almost 'crudely seduced . . . into a form of belief' (p. 57), but his description of Mother as both 'a piece of pure nature' and an 'artefact' who 'had reconstructed her flesh painfully, with knives and with needles' (p. 60) reveals the illogical nature of the Beulah belief system.

This slippage of the differentiation between what is natural and what is artefact echoes Evelyn's earlier inability to distinguish between life and cinema, and therefore implicates Beulah as only another manifestation of the hyperreal. Indeed, Mother's idea of teaching Eve the true nature of womanhood consists of enforced viewings of kitsch and sentimental Hollywood films. What this implies is that there is no authenticity to be found outside the culture of simulation, since the real can now only be guaranteed by references to the fake.

Although Eve escapes both Beulah and her fate as a virgin mother, she cannot undo what has been done to her and become Evelyn again.

And although the product of an absurd scenario, Eve herself plays a far from absurd role in the text. As a narrative device, she becomes the means by which Carter can interrogate the very categories of gender she transgresses. Returning to the desert, Eve falls into the hands of the misogynistic poet Zero, who rapes her, then adds her to his harem of wives. Under his savage rule, she is initiated into a womanly role which is the reversed mirror-image of what Beulah has attempted to teach her, since Zero believes women are to be degraded and reviled, deprived of language, dignity and autonomy. Married to him, Eve is condemned to sterility and slavery, rather than to the fertile future promised to her by Mother.

It is Zero, however, who finally brings Eve to Tristessa. He is obsessed with the insane belief that Tristessa has rendered him infertile, and that only 'her ravishment, then death, would restore the procreativity to his virility' (p. 98). Consequently, he does not rest until, in the heart of the desert, he finds her glass house surrounded by sculptures of tears. Her very name an evocation of 'whispered rumours of inexpressible sadness' (p. 122), Tristessa in life loses none of the doomed pathos of her screen persona, and regarding her, Eve feels a sense of kinship with another being 'without a history . . . mysteriously twinned by our synthetic life' (p. 125). At this stage in the narrative, this statement is more true than Eve herself knows, for under Zero's assault, Tristessa is subsequently revealed to be a man.

When Zero and his wives force Eve and Tristessa into an act of mutual rape following a mock marriage, however, the linguistic circumlocutions of Eve's narration reveal the potential challenge posed by these two equally improbable beings to the binary essentialism represented by both Zero and Mother. 'So he made us man and wife although it was a double wedding – both were the bride, both the groom in this ceremony' (p. 135). The union of the woman who was once a man and the man who has made himself into the perfect woman has profound implications, for in this action not only gendered language but gender itself has been cut adrift from the body, completely reducing sexual identity to a matter of performance. Although only Tristessa's adoption of femaleness is voluntary, and hence reversible, both she and Eve,[24] in the words of Judith Butler, represent the subversive potential of drag 'to the extent that it reflects on the imitative structure by which hegemonic gender is itself produced and disputes heterosexuality's claim on naturalness and originality'.[25]

However, as Butler also argues, drag is also

the site of a certain ambivalence, one which reflects the more general situation of being implicated in the very regimes of power by which one is constituted and, hence, of being implicated in the very regimes of power that one opposes.[26]

Although it is tempting to read Tristessa as an emancipatory figure in terms of the gender slippage she represents, the issue is not quite as straightforward as it initially appears if one studies the kind of woman she aspires to become. In all her great screen roles, the melancholic figure of Tristessa legitimises the spectacle of female suffering, creating a stereotype of masochistic femininity to which real women are educated to aspire and men to desire. The book's early chapters make clear, for example, that Evelyn's adoration of Tristessa has influenced his view of women in general. Now a woman herself, however, Eve reflects on Tristessa's romantic meanderings on the subject of femininity with a new cynicism: 'If a woman is indeed beautiful only in so far as she incarnates most completely the secret aspirations of man, no wonder Tristessa had been able to become the most beautiful woman in the world' (p. 129).

In fact, there is more than a hint of Sadeian solipsism about Tristessa. Like the Count in *Hoffman*, who 'had subjected his personality to a most rigorous discipline of stylization' to the extent that he 'had scarcely an element of realism and yet he was quite real' (*Hoffman*, p. 123), 'the thing that had chosen to call itself "Tristessa" . . . exist[s] only by means of massive effort of will and a huge suppression of fact' (p. 129). To this extent, the accusation Carter levels at de Sade, that he eliminates emancipatory possibilities for women even as he invokes them, can also be applied to Tristessa. (The link with de Sade, indeed, is emphasised by the fact that Tristessa de St Ange's namesake is the female libertine Madame de Saint-Ange, who appears in de Sade's *Philosophy in the Boudoir*.)[27]

While Tristessa's act of self-creation hints at a multiplicity of potential gender identities, the being she chooses to become is nevertheless created out of her own essentialist notions of 'woman'. As she tells Eve: 'I was seduced by the notion of a woman's being, which is negativity. Passivity, the absence of being' (p. 137). Related within the context of Eve's experience, this statement would be laughably simplistic were it not for the fact that the figure of Tristessa has reinforced its status as a universal condition of femininity which affects the lives of real women.

Tristessa would, one feels, agree with Warhol's description of the drag queen as 'living testimony to the way women used to want to be, and the way some people still want them to be, and the way some women still actually want to be';[28] a statement which is capable of being read as redolent with nostalgia for the masculine ideal of the properly 'feminine' woman. Carter described her as 'doomed' for precisely this reason. Because she is 'a male projection of femininity . . . her life is completely based on false premises. This character only had the notion of his idea of a woman before he set out to become one'.[29]

Transvestite, drag queen, and icon of cinematic sexuality, Tristessa is also, of course, irredeemably camp, although she herself completely lacks the sense of irony that would allow her to identify herself as such. In this respect, she functions as an example of what Sontag terms 'pure Camp', which, she argues, is 'always naive'.[30] The camp effect in this instance emerges at the moment when seriousness fails, where the camp subject 'proposes itself seriously, but cannot be taken altogether seriously because it is "too much"'.[31] Like her predecessor the Count, Tristessa is a figure both tragic and ridiculous in the theatrical extremities of her assumed persona. Realism, as far as she is concerned, is something that happens to other people, for she has based not only her career, but her very self, on a blatant refusal to acknowledge its constraints.

In spite of exhibiting this uniquely camp brand of heroism (or perhaps, more precisely, because of it) Tristessa remains a static, introverted figure, incapable of any real development, or of love for anything beyond her own idealised self-image. While Eve falls in love with Tristessa, portraying their brief and passionate sojourn in the desert as a romantic idyll during which she learns what it is like 'to be inside a woman's skin' (p. 149), Tristessa will not, or cannot, disentangle herself from her 'fictive autobiography' (p. 152) which renders all her experience into the stuff of tragic theatre. Even though bereft of costume and cosmetics, she manages to die in character, 'revert[ing] entirely to the sinuous principle of his notion of femininity' (p. 156). Although through Eve's eyes this episode takes on the aura of an elegiac idyll, she and Tristessa are only the latest in the series of would-be lovers which permeate Carter's fiction who, however earnestly they try, never quite succeed in establishing a mutually reciprocal romantic relationship.

While there is no doubt that Tristessa is a compelling addition to Carter's theatre of grotesques, in the end it has to be acknowledged that she, too, like the Hollywood star system which gives her fiction an illusion of life, exists only on the level of simulation. Precisely because her female persona is pure fiction, she appears more authentic than the real thing. But although she is the book's most striking example of gender configured as performance, she is not its only one. Both Zero's militant maleness and Mother's supra-femaleness are maintained just as stringently and consciously. Tristessa's extravagant paint and costume serve the same grotesquely exaggerated signifying function as Zero's obscenely priapic wooden leg and Mother's multiple breasts.

To a great extent, Eve – who is, after all, Tristessa's inverted mirror-image – also participates in this aspect of the text. For much of the narrative, she regards her new body as if it were a costume which disguises, rather than represents, the 'real' Eve/lyn within, and is constantly assessing the quality of her experiences as a woman. But her name, with its biblical echoes, hints at the possibility that she might – just might – stand for something else. The novel ends ambiguously with Eve, in an echo of her earlier entry into Beulah, making a second symbolic descent into the earth. By this time, Mother has been neutralised, transformed into nothing more than a mad, pitiable old woman. Eve, however, believing 'Mother could not abdicate from her mythology as easily as that' (p. 179) still fully expects her descent to reunite her with a universal maternal principle. But she is mistaken, for her journey through the cave is in fact a journey away from Mother and the consolations of mythology, for what she brings back into the world is the new knowledge that Mother is no more than 'a figure of speech' (p. 184):

> I emitted, at last, a single, frail, inconsolable cry like that of a new-born child. But there was no answering sound at all in that vast, sonorous place where I found myself but the resonance of the sea and small echo of my voice. I called for my mother but she did not answer me.
>
> 'Mama – mama – mama!'
>
> She never answered. (p. 186)

The hope that Carter is holding out at the end of *The Passion of New Eve* is, therefore, the hope of escape from the dream factory, in which performance is the condition for existence, and where 'male' and 'female' are not so much biological categories as roles people play. The continually recurring trope of dualism within this text, however, indicates its awareness that the notion of the performative subject itself conveys a dual, contradictory, significance. On the one hand, it can be seen as a liberatory concept, indicative of the multiple, malleable subject capable of an infinite degree of self-creation. On the other, though, the actual number and character of the roles accessible to the subject may well be limited by the ideological structure within which it finds itself placed. The ambiguous Tristessa, embodiment of an absolutely unambiguous socially conditioned femininity, is a figure whose very reason for existence is to act as a vehicle for this paradox.

I don't think the text ever escapes from such contradictions, or even that it wishes to. Indeed, the confusion surrounding its ending is an effective narrative underscoring of the thematic points Carter is trying to make within the narrative. During her time in the sea-cave, Eve gets the impression that time itself is running in reverse, so that the world into which she re-emerges is one free of myths, symbols and stereotypes. It is apt in the context of this generally film-conscious novel that this action is evocatively conveyed through the use of cinematic metaphor:

> Rivers neatly roll up on themselves like spools of film and turn in on their own sources. The final drops of the Mississippi, the Ohio, the Hudson, tremble on a blade of grass; the sun dries them up, the grass sinks back into the earth. (p. 185)

But this carries with it the inevitable question of whether this is a genuinely new start, or merely the beginning of the second showing. As the first sentence of the final chapter states, we 'start from our conclusions' (p. 191), but it remains debatable whether the direction of our trajectory is 'away from', or 'back to'. If it is the latter, we have become bound up ever more tightly in the 'entangled orders of simulation'.[32] If it is the former, the novel's lack of a definite conclusion indicates that it is unimaginable and unrepresentable.

To use another cinematic metaphor, the 'freeze-frame' effect with which *The Passion of New Eve* ends is reminiscent of Carter's earlier novel, *The Magic Toyshop*. In both cases, Carter either refuses or is unable to commit her narrative to a definitive resolution of the issues it so provocatively raises, leaving Eve and the text through which she both speaks and is spoken hesitating between the risk offered by the acquisition of new knowledge and the dubious security of obedience to the old.

The Bloody Chamber (1979)

Having thoroughly debunked myth in *The Passion of New Eve*, Carter's interests returned to a literary genre she had long been fascinated by, and whose subversive potential she had already explored in *The Magic Toyshop* – fairytale. Lest one might be mistaken in thinking that myth and fairytale are merely different sides of the same coin, Carter elaborated on the distinction she drew between mythology and folklore (which she uses here as a term synonymous with fairytale) in 'Notes from the Front Line'. The relationship between the radical writer and myth, she implies, has necessarily to be contentious because, as 'extraordinary lies designed to make people unfree', myths have to be argued with, dismantled through the act of writing. Folklore, however, is an ideal tool for an author 'in the demythologising business', because it is 'a much more straightforward set of devices for making real life more exciting and is much easier to infiltrate with other kinds of consciousness'.[33]

Precisely why fairytale is so suitable for this task is, as I have already observed, something that Carter began to engage with in her fiction as early on as *The Magic Toyshop*, and she outlined her views in a more theoretical form in the introduction to the first collection of fairytales she edited for Virago Press in 1990. Here she argued that, while the novel is always tied to the figure of the author, whose name legitimises its status as a unique, original work of art, fairytale is a more democratic art form. Originally transmitted orally, it was passed from teller to teller, all of whom freely modified it to suit the specific requirements of their audience. For Carter, this willingness to accommodate is what makes the fairytale indispensable for, as Marina Warner similarly argues, the form's innate flexibility thus allows it to

illuminate experiences embedded in social and material conditions ... [and] reveal ... how human behaviour is embedded in material circumstances, in the laws of dowry, land tenure, feudal obedience, domestic hierarchies and marital dispositions, and that when these pass and change, behaviour may change with them.[34]

In a modern period where 'the mythologies of advanced industrialized countries'[35] are disseminated through a global media, fairytale's willingness to adapt to suit the specific circumstance has never been more valuable.

For both Carter and Warner, another important attribute of the fairytale is that, precisely because it is regarded as a domestic and personal narrative form, 'a medium for gossip, anecdote, rumour',[36] it has always been identified with women, who have played a large part in its development both as tellers and as writers. In rewriting such traditional tales as 'Bluebeard', 'Beauty and the Beast' and 'Puss-in-Boots', Carter was not only exploiting the potential inherent in fairytale for demonstrating how experiences are 'embedded in material and social conditions', but also doing so through a specifically feminist sensibility which consciously recovered a female tradition of storytelling obscured by the popularity of such male adapters as Charles Perrault, the Brothers Grimm and Hans Christian Andersen. The fact that Carter had herself published a translation of Perrault's collection in 1977 adds another pleasing twist to this scenario, so that *The Bloody Chamber* can be regarded as a gleeful, subversive, commentary on her own earlier work.

The steady growth of Carter's popularity throughout the 1980s can to a large extent be traced back to the publication of this collection of stories, most particularly because they provided her with material that could be transposed into other media, thus bringing her name to the attention of people who might not necessarily read her books. She adapted 'Puss-in-Boots' and 'The Lady of the House of Love' (re-entitled *Vampirella*) for radio,[37] while the 'The Company of Wolves' was not only made into a radio play, but also into a film.[38] Shortly before her death, Carter edited two collections of fairytales for Virago (the latter, *The Second Virago Book of Fairy Tales*, was published posthumously with an introduction by Marina Warner).[39]

Merja Makinen has argued that the public perception of Carter as a writer owed a great deal to the success of *The Bloody Chamber* and its adaptations, and backs up the point with references to Carter's obituaries, many of which characterised her as a 'Fairy Godmother' (Margaret Atwood), 'friendly witch' (J. G. Ballard), 'very good wizard' (Salman Rushdie).[40] Makinen, however, is suspicious of 'this concurrence of white witch/fairy godmother mythologizing'[41] for, however sincerely meant, it smacks of the very process of false universalisation that Carter spent most of her career protesting against and thus runs the risk of fatally misrepresenting her work. As Makinen says, 'the books are not by some benign magician. The strengths and the dangers of her texts lie in a much more aggressive subversiveness and a much more active eroticism than perhaps the decorum around death can allow'.[42]

The idea of Angela Carter as Mother Goose also misrepresents *The Bloody Chamber* itself, for it's not nearly as straightforward a rewriting of the traditional fairytale collection as such an image might suggest. Firstly, as recent critics have begun to realise, all the stories are interconnected. Rather than being a series of segregated little narratives, therefore, each tale 'bleeds' into the other to form an intricately interlinked whole. Makinen, for example, observes that 'each tale takes up the theme of the earlier one and comments on a different aspect of it';[43] while Lucie Armitt argues that the collection 'functions less as a collection of individual short stories and more as a single narrative which uses the short story medium to work and rework compulsive repetitions'.[44] Armitt, indeed, speculates that this refusal to remain enclosed within the parameters of the short-story form is encoded in the book's title, observing that the 'bloody chamber' of the title need not necessarily be read as 'room' but as 'vase or vessel'. 'In this case the blood is the liquid with which the vessel is filled. . . . The associated excesses are those of overspill, not those which threaten containment'.[45]

Exactly what Carter is so compulsively circling and reworking within the blurred boundaries of these stories constitutes another departure from the traditional image of the fairytale narrative, for these are no children's bedtime stories or cosy fireside flights into fabulation. On the contrary, they are fierce, dark, erotic, gothic and, as the title itself suggests, frequently dripping with gore. Margaret Atwood argues, I think very perceptively, that *The Bloody Chamber* is best understood as a kind of fictionalised companion volume to *The Sadeian Woman*, for it constitutes an exploration of the same predator/prey equation that preoccupies the de Sade study. In a description that could equally as well be applied to the latter text, Atwood reads *The Bloody Chamber* as 'a "writing against" de Sade, a talking-back to him',[46] and sees this as informing the organising principle underlying the book as a whole:

> *The Bloody Chamber* is arranged according to categories of meateater; three cat family stories at the beginning, followed by 'Puss-in-Boots' as a kind of comic coda; three wolf family stories at the end; and three ambiguous supernatural creatures – erl-king, snow-child, female vampire – in the middle.[47]

Such parallels aren't that surprising when one considers that Carter was working on *The Sadeian Woman* at the same time as writing the stories that make up *The Bloody Chamber*. Indeed, in her interview with Les Bedford it is obvious that she considered the writing of the latter light relief from the monumental task of sorting out her thoughts on de

Sade. His influence is particularly apparent in the collection's title story 'The Bloody Chamber', of which Carter said with evident satisfaction that it 'did manage to get in most of de Sade, which pleased me'.[48]

However, while all these stories share a Sadeian interest in predation, which is why they're populated with carnivores, they also convey Carter's concern with renegotiating the relationship between predator and prey, which is why metamorphosis is such a prevalent theme within the collection as a whole. A good example of how Carter utilises these elements within a fairytale setting is provided by her two Beauty and the Beast stories, 'The Courtship of Mr Lyon' and 'The Tiger's Bride'. The first contains most of the elements of the familiar tale, although brought up-to-date – the Beast is a country squire, while Beauty is a modish, cigarette-smoking, debutante. In fact, in many ways this is a relatively tame rewrite. Beauty is another of Carter's daddy's girls, who 'would have gone to the ends of the earth for her father, whom she loved dearly' (p. 58);[49] and the story ends, as all good traditional fairy-tales should, in marriage and the promise of future domesticity: 'Mr and Mrs Lyon walk in the garden; the old spaniel drowses on the grass, in a drift of fallen petals' (p. 66).

Ellen Cronan Rose's observation that this story shows Beauty 'simply chang[ing] masters – from a beastly father to a fatherly beast'[50] has a certain validity in this context, but I think there's more to the issue here than she allows. In the context of Carter's fiction as a whole, Beauty and the Beast's mutual avowal of love is a remarkable achievement, for it is the very first time a couple have succeeded in meeting on terms which are founded on genuine affection on both sides. It is an encounter which changes both of them, for it is not only the Beast, as he always traditionally does in this story, who gains humanity thorough the love of another; Beauty, too, is saved from a not-quite-human fate. The spoiled, petulant daughter of an indulgent father before she takes the step of commitment to the Beast, she hovers on the verge of becoming a kind of automaton born of the stasis of privilege, 'acquiring, instead of beauty, a lacquer of the invincible prettiness that characterizes certain pampered, exquisite expensive cats' (p. 63).

The motif of metamorphosis, therefore, works both ways, for these are not just stories where the once so submissive, so passive, fairytale heroine gets her own back. On the contrary, by giving as good as she gets, the heroine works towards a utopian space where both male and female benefit from the transformation of the old power relations. This is shown even more clearly in Carter's second reworking of 'Beauty and the Beast', where the same themes are explored on a far more explicitly radical level. The Beauty of 'The Tiger's Bride' has a negligent father who loses her to the Beast in a game of cards, while the Beast himself is a grotesque enigma awkwardly disguised as a man, 'a carnival figure made of papier mâché and fake hair' (p. 70). Beauty herself is a spiky, astute character who looks at the world with the eyes of a shrewd accountant. Having decided that the withdrawal of her father's support leaves her only 'my skin . . . [as] my sole capital in the world' (p. 74), she is determined to get as much out of the deal as she possibly can when the Beast tells her the price of her freedom is to allow him to see her naked. Beauty's mercenary ethics are severely shaken, however, when she sees the Beast in the magnificence of his true feline form. Realising that 'the tiger will never lie down with the lamb; he acknowledges no pact that is not reciprocal' (p. 84), Beauty gives herself freely to the Beast, 'white, shaking, raw, approaching him as if offering, in myself, the key to a peaceable kingdom in which his appetite need not be my extinction' (p. 88). And it isn't, for instead of devouring Beauty the tiger licks her into her proper shape, which is the mirror of his: 'each stroke of his tongue ripped off skin after successive skin, all the skins of a life in the world, and left behind a nascent patina of shining hairs' (p. 89). Both Beauty and Beast in this story thus shrug off the disguises that society forces them to assume, and in this way the predator/prey dichotomy is shattered with the establishment of a harmonic and mutually beneficial relationship between man and woman.

However, Carter's exploration of this relationship between the carnivore and his victim is carried to its most disturbing, and potentially problematic, extreme in 'The Company of Wolves'. Here, the beast takes the form of a wolf, and his metaphorical function within the text is barely disguised. As a lycanthrope, he represents the threatened destruction of the means by which human society differentiates itself from nature; in particular, as the story clearly conveys, its own animal nature. Through his metamorphosis into wolf and back again, he escapes the social regulations by which human society is structured, with the concomitant threat that he might bring the law of the (primitive) forest back into the (civilised) village upon his return. And according to the prim and censorial voice which dominates the first part of the narrative, the law of the forest is not only predatory – 'if you stray from the path for one instant, the wolves will eat you' (p. 149) – but also specifically sexual: 'Before he can become a wolf, the lycanthrope strips stark naked. If you spy a naked man among the pines, you must run as if the Devil were after you' (p. 152). In this context, therefore, the wolf's hunger for flesh has an acknowledged double meaning.

This Red Riding Hood, however, is more than a match for the wolf when she meets him, and little resembles the shrinking violet of Perrault's version of the tale. For a start, she's not a small girl, but an adolescent who has just reached sexual maturity: 'Her breasts have just begun to swell . . . her cheeks are an emblematic scarlet and white and she has just started her woman's bleeding' (p. 152). In other words, the girl is in herself a variation on the 'bloody chamber' trope, with all the connotations of the risk of overspill already discussed by Armitt. But although the heroine's menstrual blood is already flowing, she is still a virgin, 'inside her a magic space the entrance to which is shut tight with a plug of membrane' (p. 153); and this is what constitutes both her particular vulnerablity and her peculiar defence. It is what marks her out as the lycanthrope's prey, for the shedding of her hymeneal blood is what he specifically desires. However, Carter's description of the heroine as 'a closed system' (p. 153) is reminiscent of the Sadeian subject's willed invulnerability; like them, 'she does not know how to shiver' (p. 153).

This heroine, therefore, is trapped in a double bind, precariously secure in the closed circle of her virginal state, but unable to progress without becoming prey. Unlike the Count and Tristessa, however, whose intense preoccupation with self she to a great extent shares, the girl finds her way out of this conundrum by running towards, rather than away from, the sexual threat of the lycanthrope. In her assertion that she is 'nobody's meat' (p. 158), she refuses to confirm his own perceptions of her as his natural victim, and thus ends the story sleeping 'sweet and sound . . . in granny's bed, between the paws of the tender wolf' (p. 159). In opening out the closed circle of her self (represented here by the spilling of her blood beyond her body's boundaries), and by giving it 'freely' (p. 158), the implication is that she and the wolf enter into a relationship of complete equality. As Atwood says:

> [This may be a] consolatory nonsense perhaps – don't try this technique on a street mugger – but at least [it is] a different kind of consolatory nonsense, one that tries for the kind of synthesis Carter suggested in *The Sadeian Woman*: 'neither submissive nor aggressive'.[51]

Yet this story is more explicit than most in the disturbing echoes it arouses, and it is therefore not surprising, perhaps, that it has become a focus for those critics who regard this collection as less liberatory than it obviously purports to be, for how much choice, in actuality, does the poor child have? Patricia Duncker, for example, says the ending of 'The Company of Wolves' shows Red Riding Hood realising 'that rape is inevitable . . . and decides to strip off, lie back and enjoy it. They want it really. They all do'.[52] Her views are closely echoed by Robert Clark who argues that although the story finally 'represents the woman enjoying her own sexuality and using this as a power which tenderizes the wolf', such

> positive aspects are achieved at the cost of accepting patriarchal limits to women's power. . . . the implication may be that the girl has her own sexual power, but this meaning lies perilously close to the idea that all women want it really and only need forcing to overcome their scruples.[53]

The opinions of Duncker and Clark are distinctly reminiscent of the concerns voiced by critics of *The Sadeian Woman*, in that none of them see Carter as able to transcend the limitations of her chosen medium. In spite of Carter's best efforts to radicalise such forms, they argue, pornography and fairytale are literary modes whose conventions will always lean towards the status quo: compare, for example, Patricia Duncker's argument that 'the infernal trap inherent in the fairy tale, which fits the form to its purpose, to be the carrier of ideology, proves too complex and pervasive to avoid',[54] with Susanne Kappeler's view of *The Sadeian Woman*:

> Sade is more subtle than Carter gives him credit for. He does not rattle her chains in order for her to escape them, and she should suspect his 'liberating spirit' bred from hatred. . . . While his options are strictly binary – to suffer or to cause suffering, to belong to one half of 'mankind' or the other – these are not for her to choose from: they are gender specific.[55]

It is interesting in this context to note that Carter changed the ending of 'The Company of Wolves' slightly but significantly on each of its subsequent rewrites. In the radio play, the heroine's increased assertiveness robs the ending of much of the hidden connotations of rape that Duncker and Clark read into the original version. Whereas there the lycanthrope loses none of his threatening connotations, and it is entirely up to the girl to rise to the challenge he represents, here the predator is left thoroughly nonplussed by the heroine's unexpected enthusiasm for her defloration:

> RED RIDING HOOD. I do believe, since you got here before me, that you owe me a kiss.
> What big teeth you have!
> WEREWOLF. (*Choking – grabbing at straws.*) All the better . . . to eat you with.
> RED RIDING HOOD. Oh, I say!
> *She goes into peals of laughter.*
> Well, each to his meat but I am meat for no man! Now I shall burn your clothes, just like I burned my own . . .
> WEREWOLF. Not that!
> RED RIDING HOOD. Why, anybody would think you were scared of being a good wolf all the time . . .[56]

Carter's destabilising of the power relationship between girl and werewolf in the heroine's favour is taken still further, although I would argue with less success, in her screenplay for the film of 'The Company of Wolves'. The heroine (here named Rosaleen) burns the lycanthrope's discarded clothing in the fire along with her own, thus trapping him in his wolfish form; an aspect of the narrative which is entirely absent in the original story, although, as the above quotation demonstrates, it is hinted at in the radio play. Completely outmanoeuvred in this version, the lycanthrope grovels and howls, his head in Rosaleen's lap, who addresses him as if he were a pet: 'Come on, old fellow, old dog. Good boy, good . . .'.[57] Although the notion of an equal relationship between the two is belatedly (re)established with Rosaleen's final implied metamorphosis into wolf, as Maggie Anwell says, this does nothing to reinstate the overtly expressed sexuality of the original story. Instead of the disruptive, implicitly taboo, image of the girl asleep in the arms of the wolf, we are left with two wolves running off into the forest together; a manifestation of the film's 'coy reluctance . . . to allow an image of successful sexual initiation'.[58]

Carter would have it that one of the things that so attracted her to fairytale was the anonymity of the teller, who acts only as a vehicle for the transmission of stories that both pre- and post-date her literary intervention. It is distinctly ironic, therefore, that the publication of *The Bloody Chamber* contributed to the formation of a popular identity which brought her, if not exactly into the mainstream of British fiction writing – she still remained rather too contentious for that – at least an established and distinctive literary voice. Indeed, what fairytale did was to offer Carter a way to be *more herself*, which is, perhaps, why she always claimed to have 'relaxed' into it.[59] As a rather kitsch fantastic form with, nevertheless, a subversive past, it provided her with a model that corresponded exactly to what she was already doing in novels such as *The Infernal Desire Machines of Doctor Hoffman* and *The Passion of New Eve* – the interrogation of master narratives and, particularly, of the divergence between the roles male and female are permitted to play within them. Such a demythologising impulse is doubly shocking when applied to cherished traditional fairy stories, yet Carter would argue that it is only bringing them back in line with their original function. As she said to Helen Cagney Watts, 'The tales in my volume *The Bloody Chamber* are part of the oral history of Europe, but what has happened is that these stories have gone into the bourgeois nursery and therefore lost their origins'.[60] While there was a side of the oral fairytale tradition that Perrault considered unsuitable for bourgeois consumption, Carter's aim is to reintroduce her readers to such discomforting aspects – with a vengeance.

Notes

1. Quoted in Susannah Clapp, 'On Madness, Men and Fairy-Tales', *The Independent on Sunday* (9 June 1991), pp. 26–7 (p. 26).
2. Quoted in Alex Hamilton, 'Sade and Prejudice', *The Guardian* (30 March 1979), p. 15.
3. Letter from Angela Carter to Neil Forsyth, 26 August 1974, *The European English Messenger* V/1 (Spring 1996), pp. 11–13 (p. 11).
4. Letter from Angela Carter to Neil Forsyth, p. 12.
5. John Haffenden, 'Magical Mannerist', *The Literary Review* (November 1984), pp. 34–8 (p. 36).
6. *Omnibus: Angela Carter's Curious Room* (produced by Kim Evans), BBC1, 15 September 1992.
7. Olga Kenyon, *The Writer's Imagination* (University of Bradford Print Unit, 1992), pp. 23–33 (p. 31).
8. Peter Ackroyd, 'Passion Fruit', *The Spectator* (26 March 1977), pp. 23–4 (p. 23).
9. ibid., p. 24.
10. Lorna Sage, *Angela Carter*, (Plymouth: Northcote House, 1994), p. 36.
11. At a conference I recently attended on contemporary fiction, *The Passion of New Eve* was without doubt the text most frequently referred to.

Given that the subject of the conference was twentieth-century fiction as a whole, the amount of attention paid to Angela Carter was startling.

12. Angela Carter, 'Notes from the Front Line', in Michelene Wandor (ed.), *On Gender and Writing* (London: Pandora Press, 1983), pp. 69–77 (p. 71).

13. ibid., p. 70.

14. Angela Carter, *The Passion of New Eve* (London: Virago Press, 1977). All subsequent references in the text are from this edition.

15. Lucie Armitt, *Theorising the Fantastic* (London: Arnold, 1996), p. 172.

16. Jean Baudrillard, trans. Chris Turner, *America* (London: Verso, 1988), p. 56.

17. Jean Baudrillard, trans. Paul Foss, Paul Patton and Philip Beitchman, *Simulations* (New York: Semiotext(e), 1983), pp. 147–8.

18. Walter Benjamin, *Charles Baudelaire: A Lyric Poet in the Era of High Capitalism*, trans. Harry Zohn (London: Verso, 1983), p. 69.

19. Victor Fournel, *Ce qu'on voit dans les rues de Paris*, quoted in Benjamin, *Charles Baudelaire*, p. 69.

20. Baudrillard, *America*, p. 5.

21. ibid., p. 124.

22. It has been done: see, for example Robert Clark's essay, 'Angela Carter's Desire Machine', *Women's Studies* 14 (1987), pp. 147–61, which is extremely critical of the novel for its portrayal of 'negative and reductive' (p. 157) feminist alternatives. His reading, however, is based entirely on the assumption that Carter is absolutely serious in her portrayal of Beulah as a valid feminist society.

23. Natalie M. Rosinsky, *Feminist Futures: Contemporary Women's Speculative Fiction* (Ann Arbor: UMI Research Press, 1984).

24. Discussion of Eve/lyn and Tristessa, one a man who becomes a woman, the other a woman who is revealed to be a man, contains the potential to degenerate into a confusion of pronouns. Although by no means consistent on the matter, Carter tended to refer to Tristessa as 'she', and I have chosen to follow her example.

25. Judith Butler, *Bodies That Matter: On the Discursive Limits of "Sex"* (London: Routledge, 1993), p. 125.

26. ibid.

27. Carter discusses the book, and Madame de Saint-Ange's role in it, in Chapter 4 of *The Sadeian Woman*.

28. Andy Warhol, quoted in Andrew Ross, *No Respect: Intellectuals and Popular Culture* (London: Routledge, 1989), p. 165.

29. Helen Cagney Watts, 'Angela Carter: An Interview', *Bête Noir*, 8 (1985), pp. 161–76 (p. 165).

30. Susan Sontag, 'Notes on "Camp"', in *Against Interpretation* (New York: Dell Publishing, 1966), pp. 275–92 (p. 282).

31. ibid., p. 284.

32. Baudrillard, *Simulations*, p. 23.

33. Angela Carter, 'Notes from the Front Line', p. 71.

34. Marina Warner, *From the Beast to the Blonde: On Fairytales and Their Tellers* (London: Chatto & Windus, 1994), pp. xviii–xix.
35. Angela Carter, Introduction to *The Virago Book of Fairy Tales* (London: Virago Press, 1991), p. xxi.
36. ibid.
37. The radio plays are collected in *Come Unto These Yellow Sands: Four Radio Plays by Angela Carter* (Newcastle upon Tyne: Bloodaxe Books, 1985), and also in *The Curious Room: Collected Dramatic Works* (London: Chatto & Windus, 1996).
38. *The Company of Wolves*, directed by Neil Jordan (ITC Entertainment/ Palace Production, 1984). Carter's screenplay is collected in *The Curious Room*.
39. Angela Carter (ed.), *The Second Virago Book of Fairy Tales* (London: Virago, 1992).
40. Merja Makinen, 'Angela Carter's *The Bloody Chamber* and the Decolonization of Feminine Sexuality', *Feminist Review* 42 (Autumn 1992), pp. 2–15 (p. 2).
41. ibid.
42. ibid., p. 3.
43. ibid., p. 10.
44. Lucie Armitt, 'The Fragile Frames of *The Bloody Chamber*', unpublished manuscript, forthcoming in Treva Broughton and Joe Bristow (eds), *The Infernal Desires of Angela Carter* (London: Longman, 1997).
45. ibid.
46. Margaret Atwood, 'Running with the Tigers', in Lorna Sage (ed.), *Flesh and the Mirror: Essays on the Art of Angela Carter* (London: Virago Press, 1994), pp. 117–35 (p. 120).
47. ibid., p. 122.
48. Les Bedford, 'Angela Carter: An Interview' (Sheffield University Television, February 1977).
49. Angela Carter, *The Bloody Chamber* (Harmondsworth: Penguin Books, 1981). All subsequent references in the text are from this edition.
50. Ellen Cronan Rose, 'Through the Looking Glass: When Women Tell Fairy Tales', in Elizabeth Abel, Marianne Hirsch and Elizabeth Langland (eds), *The Voyage In: Fictions of Female Development* (University Press of New England, 1983), pp. 209–27 (p. 223).
51. Atwood, 'Running with the Tigers', p. 130.
52. Patricia Duncker, 'Re-Imagining the Fairy Tales: Angela Carter's Bloody Chambers', *Literature and History* X:I (Spring 1984), pp. 3–14 (p. 7).
53. Robert Clark, 'Angela Carter's Desire Machine', *Women's Studies* 14 (1987), pp. 147–61 (p. 149).
54. Duncker, 'Re-Imagining the Fairy Tales', p. 6.
55. Susanne Kappeler, *The Pornography of Representation* (Cambridge: Polity Press, 1986), p. 135.

56. Angela Carter, *The Company of Wolves*, in *Come Unto These Yellow Sands*, p. 80.

57. Angela Carter, screenplay for *The Company of Wolves*, in *The Curious Room: Collected Dramatic Works*, p. 241.

58. Maggie Anwell, 'Lolita Meets the Werewolf: *The Company of Wolves*', in Lorraine Gamman and Margaret Marshment (eds), *The Female Gaze: Women as Viewers of Popular Culture* (London: The Women's Press, 1988), pp. 76–85 (p. 81).

59. Angela Carter, 'Notes from the Front Line', p. 71. It was a phrase she reiterated in interview with Olga Kenyon, in *The Writer's Imagination* (University of Bradford Print Unit, 1992), p. 29.

60. Cagney Watts, 'Angela Carter: An Interview', p. 170.

IV

Flying the
Patriarchal Coop

CHAPTER 6

If Angela Carter began the 1970s regarding her culture from a perspective of disenchanted alienation, by the 1980s she had found her
niche in both personal and professional terms. She had grown up in
London, which made her settling in Clapham in the late seventies a
kind of homecoming. It is a move which is echoed in Carter's later
fiction, for her use of the urban landscape in her final novels *Nights at
the Circus* and *Wise Children* is in some ways reminiscent of her use of
Bristol as the setting for her early work. Although *Nights at the Circus*
is primarily structured around the picaresque form, and so moves constantly from place to place, the strident Cockney voice of the heroine
nevertheless ties it irrevocably to London. The action of Carter's final
novel, *Wise Children*, is based more firmly in defiantly unfashionable,
slightly down-at-heel Brixton. But for neither the author nor her books
did this settling-down preclude the occasional excursion off into the
exotic elsewhere. Just as Carter now spent much of her time travelling,
both in Britain and abroad, so the characters in her novels journey to
America, Russia or Siberia. Unlike the rootless wanderings of so many
of her earlier picaresque characters, however, these travel secure in the
knowledge that they always have a home to come back to. The dominant voice in Carter's fiction changed too, becoming more gossipy,
colloquial and stridently female.

If Carter had 'come home' geographically speaking, she had also
found a place for herself professionally. Her reputation by now established, she was an exceedingly busy person. She continued to write
short stories, essays, radio plays and screenplays (as well as the 1984 film
The Company of Wolves, she also adapted *The Magic Toyshop* for Granada
Television in 1987). She still contributed to *New Society* (although less
often now that she didn't need the money), edited a collection of short
stories for Virago in 1986, *Wayward Girls and Wicked Women*, and was

a popular book reviewer. She was also in demand as a teacher of creative writing, working at universities in both the USA (1980–1) and Australia (1984), as well as the University of East Anglia (1984–7). In addition, Carter gave birth to a son in 1983. The role of mother was one she clearly relished, and journalists and academics who came to her house to interview her did so in the presence of the baby and among domestic clutter.

Given all this, it is not surprising that Carter's output of fiction slowed down quite dramatically. While she wrote five novels in the sixties (an impressive figure, considering she didn't even begin publishing her work until 1966) and only two in the seventies, *Nights at the Circus* was her sole extended piece of fiction of the 1980s. Critics and readers alike, however, considered it worth the wait; published in 1984, it became without doubt the most acclaimed of her novels. Many critics expressed surprise that it was not shortlisted for that year's Booker Prize, although it did win the James Tait Black Memorial Prize. A year later, she published her third volume of short stories, *Black Venus*.

'Masochism for the Masses' (1983)

This not to say, however, that Carter retreated into domestic cosiness and professional success, and thus ceased to be a questioning and critical cultural observer. Although her pieces for *New Society* and similar publications were rarer now, they were no less articulate and strident in their social critique. Indeed, in the Britain of the 1980s as Carter portrays it, strident resistance against 'the system' is of the utmost importance. While she might have criticised the seventies for its reactionary return to the status quo, creating fictions and mistaking them for reality, Carter regarded the eighties as continuing this tendency to naturalise artifice. But while it is one thing to be mistaken, it is quite another to deliberately capitalise on that mistake. In essays such as 'Masochism for the Masses', written in an election year, Carter draws a bitterly satirical picture of a political system which knowingly influences the voting population through the cynical manipulation of image.

In this piece, Margaret Thatcher is portrayed as nothing *but* image, a purely 'symbolic entity'[1] created for the sole purpose of the acquisition of political power. One of Carter's particular concerns in this essay is analysing how such a 'complex of signs'[2] is put together, and her concentration on Thatcher's personal appearance recalls her earlier pieces on fashion and cosmetics: 'That face of Thatcher is more stylised than even her voice, and nothing about it is comic, especially its striking Aryan quality. The blonde, immaculate hair; the steel blue eyes glittering like bayonets'.[3] For Carter, fashion has always been an index of social attitudes, but now the stakes are higher than they've ever been before. With her 'voice as artificial . . . as that of a duchess in a farce or a pantomime dame', and 'her lady magistrate's two-piece costumes and her lady doctor's "sensible" shoes',[4] Thatcher becomes a symbol of fiction run out of control and of government through the exercise of pure simulation, in which 'the image is more important by far than the meaning behind it'.[5] Indeed, there's something about this piece that invites comparison with such obsessive figures as Lady Purple or Tristessa (because isn't there more than a hint of the male impersonator about this portrayal?), who is self-created by pure effort of will and the burning desire to escape from the realm of story.

Carter particularly stresses the inherent ridiculousness possessed by such a figure through ironic reference to the Thatcher voice: 'a voice with connotations so richly comic it's a wonder her perorations aren't drowned by peals of mirth each time she opens her mouth, and unpleasantly significant that they are not'.[6] The ludicrous nature of such a blatant 'construct'[7] should, therefore, positively invite laughter – the kind of laughter that punctures pretensions and brings everything down-to-earth again. The fact that it doesn't allows the fantasy to proceed unchecked without any need to acquiesce to the pressures of reality.

'Masochism for the Masses', therefore, is an indicator of the kind of concerns that motivated the writing of Carter's fiction throughout the 1980s, in which she demonstrates a growing need to re-establish the relationship between fantasy and fact, in order to prevent precisely the problem that she has the Thatcher phenomenon represent in this essay – that of the runaway sign which has ceased to stand *for* something, and attempts to gain significance in its own right. This doesn't mean that her chosen mode of writing becomes any more mimetic, but that it is increasingly overt in the way in which it draws attention to the limitations of the fantastic form. Carter's fictions have always had a tendency to run themselves up against a conceptual brick wall – *The Magic Toyshop* and *The Passion of New Eve* are both proof of that – but her later novels are more considered, more deliberate, in the way they point to the moment when fantasy fails. History, both personal and social, becomes an increasing thematic preoccupation in her texts, fore-grounding her efforts to find a new synthesis between the practice of fabulation and the world of actual, lived, experience.

In a somewhat paradoxical manner, this becomes particularly apparent through Carter's increased use of broad humour in her fiction, which is expressed primarily, in the novels at least, through the distinctively raucous voices of over-blown, gin-swigging Cockney heroines such as Fevvers and the Chance sisters. I have already argued that Carter's writing of the sixties, in particular, participates in what Bakhtin terms the 'Romantic grotesque', and for Bakhtin, one of the primary differences between the Romantic and medieval grotesque is the tone of laughter they employ. In Romantic grotesque, he claims, 'laughter was cut down to cold humor, irony, sarcasm. It ceased to be a joyful and triumphant hilarity. Its positive regenerating power was reduced to a minimum'.[8] In contrast, one of the most defining characteristics of the medieval grotesque is the way in which laughter is at once both 'degrading and regenerating';[9] a 'festive folk laughter [which] presents an element of victory not only over supernatural awe, over the sacred, over death; it also means the defeat of power, of earthly kings, of the earthly upper classes, or all that oppresses and restricts'.[10]

Carter's later work is clearly motivated by the attempt to re-educate her readers in the subversive potential of carnivalesque laughter, and to thus erode the seriousness which enables the palpably ridiculous to be rendered unremarkable and hence acceptable. However, Marina Warner, in her essay 'Angela Carter: Bottle Blonde, Double Drag', makes the interesting point that Carter's use of humour in her later writing is primarily defensive

> because she saw, with her sharp-eyed mordancy, that in her struggle for change she was losing ground – that through Thatcher's eight-ies and in the world they were creating, all too many were able to resist – by turning a deaf ear to 'the truth of laughter' and much besides.[11]

Although I think it would be incorrect to see this aspect of Carter's work in wholly defeatist terms, laughter, as Warner's argument indicates, is a double-edged concept which conveys a defiant fatalism along with utopian hope for change and renewal. Apart from *Several Perceptions*, where it sits somewhat at odds with the dark tone of the rest of the book, Carter's fiction up to this point is not particularly strong on utopian endings, and it wasn't a habit that an increased accent on the humorous was necessarily going to change. While novels such as *Nights at the Circus* and *Wise Children* deliberately cultivate utopian expectations, it is in a manner which provocatively holds them perpetually just out of reach, which means they're therefore never allowed to become unequivocally certain. While Carter hung onto her sense of humour and her hope for change against all the odds, by this time she had been introduced to Bakhtin's work, and thus was also well aware that the reversals initiated by carnival are temporary. As Warner says, 'She knew that humour was a last-ditch stratagem, even an admission of defeat: this is the nub of the irony. She understood the limits of merrymaking, burlesque and masquerade'.[12] They are limits Carter began to explore in the stories published in *Black Venus*.

Black Venus (1985)

The stories collected in *Black Venus* had all been published separately elsewhere between 1977 and 1982, and thus do not function in the same interlocking manner as the narratives in *The Bloody Chamber*. Nor do they wholly share the bawdy humour of the later novels (although 'Overture and Incidental Music for *A Midsummer Night's Dream*', which cuts Shakespeare's pastoral fantasies down to size, is a glorious exception). Nevertheless, these narratives demonstrate that the demythologising project which had preoccupied Carter throughout the 1970s had not come to an end; indeed, with its very obvious preoccupation with history, this collection shows the beginning of a new compromise being negotiated between 'fact' and 'fiction' in Carter's work, whereby the exercise of her extravagant imagination returns us increasingly definitively to the realm of the real, although, crucially, with our belief in accepted versions of the 'truth' somewhat shaken.

It also demonstrates how Carter's expression of her feminism grew increasingly overt as her career progressed. Several of the stories in the collection are concerned with familiar, almost iconic, figures in Western literary and popular culture – Baudelaire, Edgar Allan Poe, Shakespeare and Lizzie Borden – and even those that aren't are still concerned with establishing origins in such a way as to interrogate received historical assumptions and recuperate women's place within them.

Probably the best example of this is the story which opens the collection, 'Black Venus'. It is the story of Jeanne Duval, the mistress of Baudelaire and the figure around which he based his 'Black Venus' cycle of poems. Muses, traditionally, don't have a voice, but are the silent focus of the (male) artist's adulation and inspiration. While the narrative does not flatter itself that it can retrieve the 'real' Jeanne Duval from the little that is actually known about her, it does give her a fictional space from which she can resist the process of mythification that will be her fate; something of which she does have some intimation:

> Therefore, you could say, not so much that Jeanne did not understand the lapidary, troubled serenity of her lover's poetry but, that it was a perpetual affront to her. He recited it to her by the hour and she ached, raged and chafed under it because his eloquence denied her language. It made her dumb. (p. 18)[13]

As Carter, interviewed on the publication of *Black Venus*, says of this story, 'I just can't imagine anything more awful than being Baudelaire's mistress – the *symbolism* put on one's frail shoulders!'[14]

The story, however, takes on an antiphonal quality as the voices of Baudelaire and Jeanne mingle and clash, foundering on the rock of Baudelaire's refusal to allow Jeanne anything other than the mystical role of feminine Other: 'He thinks she is a vase of darkness; if he tips her up, black light will spill out. She is not Eve but, herself, the forbidden fruit, and he has eaten her!' (p. 15). She, meanwhile, understands him only all too well – '"Sucker!" she said, almost tenderly' (p. 12) – although she is also unable to fully utilise that understanding because, the inheritor of an entire racial history of exclusion and dispossession, she has 'only the haziest notion of her own use value' (p. 13). But Carter gives Jeanne the last laugh, rewriting her story so as to allow her to extract a final, though silent, revenge on the world. Before Baudelaire dies, the ravages of syphilis have caused him to become 'so far estranged from himself that . . . when he was shown his reflection in a mirror, he bowed politely, as to a stranger' (p. 22). Jeanne, however, reduces the fruits of his artistic labour to hard cash and returns to her native island of Martinique, where 'she will continue to dispense, to the most privileged of the colonial administration, at a not excessive price, the veritable, the authentic, the true Baudelarian syphilis' (p. 23).

This technique of breaking apart received histories specifically in order to find the female experience which has been exiled to the subtext or the margins of the accepted narrative is one which Carter employs time and time again in *Black Venus*. In 'The Cabinet of Edgar Allan Poe', she imaginatively recreates Poe's childhood in order to find the spectre of the mother hidden there; denied, yet persistently returning through nightmares, phobias and, of course, Poe's art. In 'Peter and the Wolf', Carter rewrites not only the folk-tale made familiar by Prokofiev, but also psychoanalytic accounts of the procedure by which the subject is both formed and socialised. A baby is taken away by the wolves, but when she is reunited with her human family, the wolves come to reclaim her. It is not soon enough, though, to prevent her profoundly shaking her boy-cousin's faith in the order of things through the display of her absolute otherness, an experience which he encodes primarily in terms of gender difference:

> Peter's heart gave a hop, a skip, so that he had a sensation of falling; he was not conscious of his own fear because he could not take his eyes off the sight of the crevice of her girl-child's sex, that was perfectly visible to him as she sat there square on the base of her spine. . . . It exercised an absolute fascination upon him. (p. 83)

However, as a later scene in the story makes clear, it is not just gender which is at issue here, but the challenge the wolf-girl poses to the entire human order in the completeness with which she has passed out of it, possessor of 'a different kind of consciousness than ours is' (p. 86). Whereas theorists like Lacan and Freud would have it that the subject does not acquire an identity or a place in language until it is able to differentiate itself from others, here it is the supposedly socialised observer who is threatened, feeling himself to be exiled from this female being's 'marvellous and private grace' (p. 86).

The story which stands out in the collection, however, is Carter's reconsideration of the story of the American axe-murderess, Lizzie Borden. Borden was to become a figure which fascinated Carter, for not only did she write a second short story about her, published in 1991,[15] but was also planning a full-length novel on the Borden murders before she died. 'The Fall River Axe Murders' is a subtle, skilfully constructed narrative, which focuses on the morning before Lizzie murders her parents. The actual murder is not described, for that is the bit of the story everybody knows – instead, Carter is again concerned with revealing what the commonly accepted version of history keeps hidden.

Carter prefaces the narrative with the familiar nursery rhyme in which Lizzie gives her father 'forty whacks', thus drawing attention to

Borden's quasi-folkloric status. What she proceeds to construct, however, is not a nursery story, but rather a study in repression related under
the shadow of the inevitable foreknowledge both reader and author
share, which attempts to restore historical specificity to the familiar
narrative. In this way, she removes Lizzie's act from the realm of the
salaciously horrific and recasts it, more sympathetically, as the release of
a repression too great to be contained. The dominant trope within the
narrative is that of enclosure; a preoccupation which extends to the
text's own formation, for it is generated from within the very narrow
space which divides the drawing back of the hammer on top of a clock
from its striking the alarm which will set the tragedy in motion.
'Bridget's clock leaps and shudders on its chair, about to sound its own
alarm. Their day, the Borden's fateful day, trembles on the brink of
beginning' (p. 121).

The narrative voice itself, however, remains resolutely modern and
detached, its awareness of the events to come placing it beyond the
narrow temporal space within which the action of the text is itself
confined. Instead, it wanders freely between past, present and future in
order to build up a picture, almost unbearable in its nightmarish intensity, of confinement and repression. Under its knowing eye, the Borden
house itself takes on the surreal quality and distorted perspective of
an Escher engraving, 'full of locked doors that open only into other
rooms with other locked doors, for upstairs and downstairs, all the
rooms lead in and out of one another like a maze in a bad dream' (p. 107).
The sleepers enmeshed in this humid, fetid domestic space offer an
appearance of peacefulness which is patently no more than an illusion;
but the signs of impending catastrophe can be read most clearly in the
body of the woman who is to be its perpetrator:

> The hem of the nightdress is rucked up above her knees because
> she is a restless sleeper. Her light, dry, reddish hair, crackling with
> static, slipping loose from the night-time plait, crisps and stutters
> over the square pillow which she clutches as she sprawls on her
> stomach. (p. 113)

Glimpsed in the abandonment of sleep, Lizzie is temporarily released
from the constraints of middle-class spinsterhood which constrict her
waking hours, but as the static which 'crackles', 'crisps' and 'stutters' her
hair indicates, she is dry tinder on the verge of becoming a conflagration
born of anger and frustration.

Carter traces the origins of this frustration back to both its local and general sources. The Borden household itself is presented as a peculiar one. It is dominated by the figure of Lizzie's father – a diluted embodiment of the joylessly self-sufficient Sadeian spirit – whose iron-willed repression extends to himself as well as to others, and to every area of his domestic and professional life: 'At night, to save the kerosene, he sits in lampless dark. He waters the pear trees with his urine; waste not, want not. . . . He mourns the loss of the good organic waste that flushes down the WC' (p. 111).

But Old Borden himself is not the whole story, for behind him lies a whole culture which condemns Lizzie, as a middle-class New England spinster at the end of the nineteenth century, to a pitifully circumscribed form of existence. Her never-varying day begins with the donning of her viciously tight 'whalebone corset that took her viscera in a stern hand and squeezed them very tightly' (p. 103), and proceeds to a tedious round of genteel domestic tasks and charity work undertaken with the sole intention of filling in time ('What would the daughters of the rich do with themselves if the poor ceased to exist?', p. 117). In this context, her murder of her father and stepmother is no act of meaningless insanity, but a striking out at a system which cancels out her own will and desires and forces them to conform to the pattern of another's.

As well as continuing *Black Venus*'s general interest in reuniting history with popular myth, this story provides an interesting contrast with those collected in *The Bloody Chamber*. Denied the risky opportunity of progression represented in those tales by the figure of the wolf, the female subject can herself become a monster; a glassy-eyed automaton with an axe. Interestingly, though, it is the very first story in *The Bloody Chamber* which itself postulates a different possibility for the female subject which takes her in a different direction from that indicated either by Lizzie Borden or Red Riding Hood, and which adds an intriguing twist to Carter's perennial fascination with blurring the boundaries of gender difference. In 'The Bloody Chamber', the Sadeian subject is subjugated to the power of the matriarch, thus clearing the way for a new conception of woman in Carter's fiction – one with wings.

'The Bloody Chamber' (1979)

'The Bloody Chamber' is a rewrite of Carter's perennially revisited fairytale, 'Bluebeard', with, as she herself acknowledged, a good dash of de Sade thrown in. It opens with a young girl, full of romantic

expectations, being borne away by train 'from the white, enclosed qui-
etude of my mother's apartment, into the unguessable country of marriage'.[16] But the narrator's assumption that it is marriage which offers
the key to freedom from the claustrophobic enclosure of the maternal
space is, however, quite wrong, for her husband is the last of Carter's
Sadeian monsters. Her precarious safety lies in her innocence, but once
she loses it – as, confronted with her new husband's pornographic
desires, she is intended to – she is doomed to internment in the bloody
chamber which represents the deepest, darkest realm of the Sadeian
erotic fantasy: 'a room designed for desecration and some dark night of
unimaginable lovers whose embraces were annihilation' (p. 35).

However, the ending of the story is a calculated surprise. While the
girl kneels at the feet of her executioner husband expecting nothing but
death, her mother comes galloping into the narrative, freeing her
daughter and rewriting the Sadeian script with one well-aimed bullet
through the monster's head. This story, I would argue, is thus a bench-
mark in Carter's fiction in delivering the *coup de grace* to the Sadeian
subject. With his removal the rigid dichotomy of his eroticised power-
games is shattered, and the space he once occupied is recovered and
reconfigured; although within this particular short story, such a project
of recuperation remains implied rather than actual. In spite of the fact
that the stories that follow within the collection as a whole begin to
deconstruct the predator/prey conundrum in utopian terms, it is not
until her writing of the 1980s that Carter really begins to speculate in
detail on what might lie outside the Sadeian torture chamber, in which
one either wears the executioner's hood or the bloody stigmata of the
victim.

It is the redemptive role it allocates to the mother, however, that
makes 'The Bloody Chamber' unique, not only in terms of the collection itself, but within Carter's fiction as a whole. The other stories in
The Bloody Chamber follow the pattern of Carter's previous work in that
the mother is either lost, absent, or simply just not mentioned; registered, in other words, through vacancy (or in the case of Mother in *The
Passion of New Eve*, of course, monstrosity). Instead, it is the father who
tends to be inevitably present, either as an object of his daughter's
preadolescent attachment (think of Marianne or Albertina), or as the
oppressive patriarchal figure to be resisted (Uncle Philip or Dr
Hoffman, for example). Because of this tendency, and in spite of their
cultivation of fluidity, flexibility and metamorphosis in other areas,
Carter's novels have hitherto done little to deconstruct the fixed oppo-

sition of what Hélène Cixous and Catherine Clément call 'a binary system, related to "the" couple, man/woman'.[17] Even the transvestism of the later novels, *The Infernal Desire Machines of Doctor Hoffman* and *The Passion of New Eve*, doesn't pose as much of a challenge to the fixed boundaries of gender as may at first appear. Indeed, it is not until the stories in *The Bloody Chamber* that Carter, if not deconstructing 'the' couple as such, certainly begins to renegotiate the terms on which they meet through her speculation that a sincere exchange of affection between the sexes is possible.

The introduction of the mother, however, changes everything, for, just as in the story her intervention quite literally breaks up the victor/victim tableau in Bluebeard's castle courtyard, it introduces a wild-card third element into the fixed dualism of the couple. It is as if the greater consequences of the destruction of the Sadeian order, based as it is upon a remorseless dialectic of opposition, is the removal of an entire pattern of binary thought, thus opening out the possibility of a conceptual space in which one need not always be 'either/or', but can instead move between the poles of opposing signifiers in order to form a creative, consistently mobile, synthesis between them.

If read alongside Teresa de Lauretis's 1987 essay 'The Technology of Gender', this alteration of perspective in Carter's fiction, which she developed more fully in the work she published in the eighties, may be read as echoing a shift in feminist thought which was taking place at about the same time. De Lauretis suggests that feminist theory of the 1960s and 1970s was closely bound up in the notion of 'gender as sexual difference', which keeps feminist thought 'contained within the frame of a conceptual opposition that is "always already" inscribed in what Fredric Jameson would call the "political unconscious" of dominant cultural discourses and their underlying "master narratives"'.[18] However, she proceeds to argue for

> the possibility, already emergent in feminist writings of the 1980s, to conceive of the social subject and of the relations of subjectivity to sociality in another way: a subject constituted in gender, to be sure, though not by sexual difference alone, but rather across languages and cultural representations; a subject en-gendered in the experiencing of race and class, as well as sexual relations; a subject, therefore, not unified but rather multiple, and not so much divided as contradicted.[19]

The destruction of the single, unified subject, therefore, leaves room for many possibilities, and according to de Lauretis, one of the consequences of a shift away from such a fixed oppositional notion of gender is that it would, in particular, allow for a new conception of the female subject. Freed from her static role as man's unchanging Other, 'Woman' becomes 'women', in all their infinite, often contradictory, variety, because it thus becomes possible to articulate 'the differences among women or, perhaps more exactly, the differences *within women*'.[20] The consequences of such an apparently slight semantic alteration are therefore far-reaching, moving the female subject out of the realm of the ahistoric and apolitical into the world of social actuality.

But however desirable this emergent subjectivity might be, de Lauretis acknowledges the difficulties involved both in its discernment and encoding, for it both is and is not contained by the boundaries of discourse. To site it in 'some mythic distant past or some utopian future history' is incorrect, for that would involve rendering the concept unrepresentable. Instead, the perspective from which this new kind of subjectivity can be glimpsed is from within

> the elsewhere of discourse here and now, the blind spots, or the space-off, of its representations. I think of it as spaces in the margins of hegemonic discourses, social spaces carved in the interstices of institutions and in the chinks and cracks of the power-knowledge apparati.[21]

Although the radically different heroine of Carter's next novel, *Nights at the Circus*, possesses her utopian aspect, she also embodies all the problems of living and lurking in the gaps between categories, and thus is a potent symbol of both the drawbacks and possibilities of living on the margins.

Nights at the Circus (1984)

De Lauretis does not go on to explicitly argue for the value of female community, but in the context of a discussion of Carter's work it is evident that an acknowledgement of the differences between women also makes the forging of alliances between them a possibility. Although they do not by any means form an homogenous, individually indistinguishable group, Carter's female characters have always tended to exist in opposition to the male, whether that relationship be marked by open antagonism, covert suspicion or baffled good intentions. Consequently, her texts have not tended to include a consideration of the possibility of women managing to build up relationships between themselves, and what alliances do exist are fragile and temporary.

In *The Magic Toyshop*, for example, Melanie and Aunt Margaret are both subject to Uncle Philip's tyranny, but Aunt Margaret's dumbness precludes a close relationship developing between the two women, and they both take separate flights away from patriarchal confinement at the end of the novel. When Marianne joins the Barbarian encampment in *Heroes and Villains* she finds a motherly presence in Jewel's foster-mother Mrs Green, but she does nothing to help when Jewel's brothers threaten Marianne with rape. And although Leilah/Lilith helps the new Eve with rough, though impersonal, kindness, she is left behind when Eve sails off alone into an unimaginable future beyond the ending of the text.

Although the possibility of effective solidarity between women is not one which Carter addresses in either *The Bloody Chamber* or the *Black Venus* stories, it takes on a new, central importance in *Nights at the Circus*, where her heroine, the improbably winged Cockney trapeze artiste, Fevvers, is aided and abetted throughout by her irascible foster-mother Lizzy. Over and around the main storyline, as well, the novel features a varied and interesting female supporting cast. As well as benefiting from the fellowship of women, Fevvers also gets her man; in this case, the American journalist Jack Walser, who follows her into the wilds of Siberia via the topsy-turvy world of the circus.

In interviews, Carter stressed the amount of work that had gone into the novel, telling Ian McEwan, for example, that it had taken ten years to write because 'I had to wait until I was big enough, strong enough, to write about a winged woman'.[22] From the first, therefore, Carter identified *Nights at the Circus* as a work born out of confidence; and it shows. (Indeed, 'confidence', and all its possible meanings, is a dominant byword in the text.) In terms of length, it is the longest novel she wrote, but its sense of expansiveness doesn't have so much to do with the number of pages as with the sense of space, for the narrative itself mimics Fevvers's leisurely pace through the air, 'potter[ing] along the invisible gangway between her trapezes' (p. 17).[23] That is not to say that it isn't a novel packed with incident and adventure, but it certainly lacks the lurking sense of claustrophobia that was a characteristic of Carter's fiction from the beginning.

Novels such as *Shadow Dance*, *Several Perceptions*, *The Magic Toyshop* and *Love* are set predominantly in confined domestic spaces – bed-sits, houses, toyshops, night-clubs and pubs. When the characters do get outside, they go no further than parks or rural preserves which are themselves encroached upon by urban development. Even in those works of fiction within which the picaresque is an integral element, such as *Heroes and Villains*, *The Infernal Desire Machines of Doctor Hoffman* and *The Passion of New Eve*, the same intimation of enclosure exists, for the most important journey undertaken by the narrators is the one that takes them into the interior of their own minds. However fantastic the landscapes through which they pass may be, therefore, they are in fact dreamscapes which map the territory of the unconscious. In this text, Carter's own acute self-consciousness is passed on to the characters, so that, given the space to do so, they have the ability to reflect and philosophise on the nature of fiction, time and history on their travels with, and without, the circus. *Nights at the Circus*, therefore, is an example of Carter venturing into a more expansive, humorous and romantic form of fiction.

In an interview with Helen Cagney Watts, Carter was very specific about Fevvers's origins, claiming that she had been born out of the writing of *The Sadeian Woman*, in which she includes a quotation from Apollinaire:

> It was no accident that the Marquis de Sade chose heroines and not heroes. Justine is woman as she has been until now, enslaved, miserable and less than human; her opposite, Juliette, represents the woman whose advent he anticipated, a figure of whom minds have as yet no conception, who is rising out of mankind, who will have wings and who will renew the world.[24]

Fevvers is the literal embodiment of Apollinaire's fanciful winged woman, created not because Carter took his pronouncement at face value, but as another manifestation of her desire to debunk male pretensions:

> It just seemed to me that people, especially male intellectuals, say this sort of thing, and think how wonderful they are in making this sort of gesture, but I can't help feeling that they're not going to like it when it happens: that they are going to be immensely pissed off when it happens.[25]

True to her origins, therefore, Fevvers is a wonderful amalgam of the transcendent and the earthy. While on stage she appears as a 'fabulous bird woman' who appears 'twice as large as life' (p. 15), off it she is a big-boned, vulgar Cockney girl, her wings confined within

> a grubby dressing gown, horribly caked with greasepaint round the neck . . . under the splitting, rancid silk . . . her conspicuous deformity, the twin hills of the growth she had put away for those hours she must spend in daylight or lamplight, out of the spotlight. (p. 19)

No angel, Fevvers, and no fool either. Instead, like the prostitutes in the London brothel in which she is brought up, she finds her body is her most profitable investment, dreaming at night 'of bank accounts . . . to her, the music of the spheres was the jingling of cash registers' (p. 12).

Yet as Marina Warner argues in *Monuments and Maidens*, such down-to-earth individuality is more usually the province of the male, not the female, form, which 'tends to be perceived as generic and universal, with symbolic overtones'.[26] And the unique peculiarities of Fevvers's wings make her more vulnerable than most women to being considered purely in terms of 'form'. Throughout the book, they become the focus for male speculation, and thus function as a way in which the impulse to inscribe transcendental meanings upon the surface of the female body can be satirised. Most of the men with whom Fevvers come into contact echo Apollinaire's hyperbolic response to the notion of a winged woman. She serves her 'apprenticeship in *being looked at*' as a child in Ma Nelson's brothel, where, 'nought but the painted, guilded *sign* of love' (p. 23, Carter's italics), she impersonates Cupid for the benefit of the clients. When she gets older, she exchanges Cupid's bow for a sword and the role of Winged Victory, although this is less of a success, for as Fevvers herself comments, tongue firmly in cheek, 'it may be that a *large woman* with a *sword* is not the best advertisement for a brothel' (p. 38, Carter's italics). Yet her sword as well as her wings become her means of protection from those whose desire to mythify her have more threatening consequences, such as the Rosicrucisan pervert Mr Rosencreutz, who buys her out of the freakish brothel of Madame Schreck. Regarding Fevvers as a kind of all-purpose symbolic repository – 'Queen of ambiguities, goddess of in-between states, being on the borderline of species, manifestation of Arioriph, Venus, Achamatoth, Sophia' (p. 81) – he attempts to ritually sacrifice her, a fate she only escapes by the narrowest of margins.

As Carter was surely well aware, feminist critics have also been tempted to buy into the utopian myth of the winged woman – witness, for example, Cixous's statement in 'The Laugh of the Medusa':

> Flying is a woman's gesture – flying in language and making it fly. We have all learned the art of flying and its numerous techniques; for centuries we've been able to possess anything only by flying; we've lived in flight, stealing away, finding, when desired, narrow passageways, hidden crossovers. It's no accident that *voler* has a double meaning, that it plays on each of them and thus throws off the agents of sense. It's no accident: women take after birds and robbers just as robbers take after women and birds. They . . . fly the coop, take pleasure in jumbling the order of space, in disorienting it, in changing around the furniture, dislocating things and values, breaking them all up, emptying structures, and turning propriety upside down.[27]

Another instance of false mythification? Perhaps. After all, there's no reason why women should be immune to the seductive simplification such a process affords. But on the other hand, I would nevertheless maintain that Cixous's argument has very pertinent things to offer the reader of *Nights at the Circus*. In particular, her concept of a female refuge to be found in 'hidden crossovers' recalls de Lauretis's statement that a new perception of the female subject can be found in the interstices and 'blind spots' of discourse. In this context, Fevvers's need to maintain her aura of ambiguity is essential, because if the illusion fails,

> She would no longer be an extraordinary woman, no more the Greatest *Arialiste* in the world but – a freak. Marvellous, indeed, but a marvellous monster, an exemplary being denied the human privilege of flesh and blood, always the object of the observer, never the subject of sympathy, an alien creature forever estranged. (p. 161)

Her own history has provided Fevvers with abundant examples of the way in which the freakish are made the recipients of the 'normal' world's fears and perversions, from the tragic inhabitants of Madame Schreck's brothel to the acts in Colonel Kearney's circus. So although she may superficially appear to – and to some extent, does – embody the utopian aspects of flying, she also represents the same double meaning that Cixous points to in the word; 'flight' as in the sense of retreat or evasion. As Mary Russo observes in her analysis of the novel, the awkward amalgam that is Fevvers 'starts and stops in the intervals between points, hovering on the brink of possibility, instead of going forward'.[28] This is best represented by Fevvers's trapeze act in which, working on the maxim that it is better to hide in plain sight, she blatantly displays the freakish excesses of her body, all tits, wings and the tantalising illusion of nakedness. And although the most striking thing about her technique is the way in which she dawdles in the air, keeping to a 'modest chug at twenty-five m.p.h.' (p. 159), she never quite strains the credulity of her audience beyond what it will bear. In this way, however, she succeeds magnificently in preserving herself as a singularity whose whole existence depends on the maintenance of paradox, 'an object of the most dubious kind of reality to her beholders . . . who looks like a hallucination but is not' (p. 290).

In fact, the book's first section is largely constructed for the purpose of not only creating a tension between what Fevvers appears to be and what she actually is, but also of throwing the whole question, once posed, into confusion. Walser, at this point the sceptical journalist bent on proving Fevvers a fake, interviews her in her dressing room after a performance, his cynical observations interwoven with her relation of her increasingly fantastic life story. He is initially bent on quarrying verifiable facts – names, dates, events – out of the rich expansiveness of Fevvers's autobiographical narrative, although his efforts remain largely ineffectual. Indeed, his impulse towards scepticism becomes increasingly defensive as, confused by an increasing discrepancy between subjective and objective time caused by Big Ben's apparent tendency to keep striking twelve o'clock, and erotically discomposed by Fevvers's earthy physicality, Walser finds his detached journalistic point of view increasingly threatened, and himself confronted with the question 'Shall I believe in it? Shall I pretend to believe in it?' (p. 28).

As the above quotation, in which he considers the possibility of belief before the *pretence* of belief, perhaps indicates, the erosion of Walser's objectivity has actually begun before the interview takes place. He has already viewed Fevvers's performance, and although he begins with the assumption that her wings cannot possibly be real, the clumsiness of her stage act, the way in which it 'point[s] up the element of the meretricious spectacle' (p. 14), leads him to consider the question of whether it may not in fact be a kind of sophisticated double bluff, and that 'in order to earn a living, might not a genuine bird-woman –

in the implausible event that such a thing existed – have to pretend she was an artificial one?' (p. 17). The conundrum Fevvers is made through Walser's eyes to represent – of whether she is 'fact' or 'fiction' – is incapable of resolution if one can't distinguish between fact and fiction in the first place.

Fevvers, therefore, like the laughter with which she heralds the coming of the new century, is inherently contradictory. As I have already argued, she can readily be made to stand for utopian concepts, for in both her possession of wings and her profession as *arieliste*, she rearranges space to fit a world in which gravity is no longer a problem. By directing the gaze of her audience upwards to the air above their heads, she challenges their perceptions of where it is possible, or permissible, for a woman to go. Russo, for example, remarks that in many ways Fevvers's act induces 'a temporary reversal so that the male viewer appears childlike or at least diminished'.[29]

Indeed, Fevvers is often tempted to cast herself in a utopian role as the harbinger of the New Woman of the twentieth century, making ringing declarations that 'once the old world has turned on its axle so that the new dawn can dawn, then, ah, then! all the women will have wings, the same as I' (p. 285). But the slightly overdone rhetoric of this statement should act as a clue that perhaps such avowals should not be taken at face value. Indeed, at this point Fevvers is almost immediately deflated by the indefatigable Lizzie: 'It's going to be more complicated than that. . . . You improve your analysis, girl, and *then* we'll discuss it' (p. 286). Lizzie's common-sense philosophy has little truck with pie-in-the-sky utopian concepts for, she maintains, 'We live, always, in the here and now, the present. To pin your hopes upon the future is to consign those hopes to a hypothesis, which is to say, a nothingness. Here and now is what we must contend with' (p. 239).

In other words, a better future can only be brought about through the hard work of the present, and even then it cannot be guaranteed. Although several critics have read *Nights at the Circus* as exuberantly utopian – Andrzej Gąsiorek, for example, describes it as a novel which 'rewrites history as utopia, envisaging the closing of the last century as the opening of a brave new feminist world'[30] – I'm not convinced that such an interpretation is really capable of being sustained, given that whatever moments of utopia this text achieves are precarious and speculative at best. This is best demonstrated in one of the novel's sub-plots which not only shows Carter considering the value of female solidarity, but also acts as her final word on her on-going reconsideration of the relationship between predator and prey.

The Princess is a circus performer who can make tigers dance to her tune, although it is hard to maintain any illusion of harmony between human and animal for long in view of the ever-present gun on top of her piano. In fact, what she shares with her tigers is not so much fellowship as a strained suspension of hostilities. However, the Princess finds an unlikely companion and lover in the figure of the childlike innocent Mignon, whose singing adds a new dimension to the act in the tiger cage. Although the captive tigers are lost following the sabotage of the circus train in Siberia, the Princess and Mignon find refuge in an incongruously remote conservatory of music, where their music enchants the wild tigers 'who had never known either confinement or coercion; they had not come to the Princess for taming'. The beauty of the scene in which the house is 'roofed with tigers. Authentic, fearfully symmetric tigers burning as brightly as those who had been lost' (p. 249) conjures up the seductive notion that this signals the final cancelling out of the doctrine of predation. But the astute Fevvers realises that this event does not signify resolution so much as a different kind of danger:

> I thought to myself: when these tigers get up on their hind legs, they will make up their own dances – they wouldn't be content with the one she'd teach them. And the girls will have to invent new, unprecedented tunes for them to dance to. There will be an altogether new kind of music to which they will dance of their own free will. (p. 250)

However, the biggest challenge to the text's surface optimism is posed by the cruel and destructive humour of the circus clowns, representatives of performance taken to the ultimate degree. Their leader, the nihilistic philosopher Buffo, is yet another inheritor of the Sadeian philosophy of self-creation. As he says to Walser, now ex-journalist and apprentice clown, 'It is given to few to shape themselves, as I have done'. Yet Buffo's curse is to also understand that the freedom of self-creation has its limits, for 'what am I without my Buffo's face? Why, nobody at all. Take away my make-up and underneath is merely not-Buffo. An absence. A vacancy' (p. 122). While Buffo goes spectacularly mad in the circus ring, thus creating the greatest tragi-comic performance of his life, the other clowns dance themselves out of existence in the

Siberian wastes in the process of their lugubrious performance of the Clown's Funeral, at the heart of which lies 'the whirling apart of everything, the end of love, the end of hope' (p. 243). They become their true selves: that is, nothing.

As far as Fevvers is concerned, the clowns are her dark mirror-image, for there is always the risk that she may share their complete submersion in performance. Take away *her* make-up, after all, and what is left? This is what she has to contend with when stranded in Siberia after the sabotage of the circus train. Injured, lost and frightened, she momentarily appears on the verge of fading away altogether, 'as if', observes Lizzie, 'it was nothing but the discipline of the audience that kept you in trim' (p. 280). In order to avoid this fate, which is a very real one for her, she must renegotiate her position on the boundaries of possibility, a process in which her relationship with Walser plays a crucial role.

Jack Walser, like the majority of Carter's heroes, is given a particularly hard time in this novel. Fair-haired and square-jawed, he initially appears ideal hero material, a 'man of action' who 'subjected his life to a series of cataclysmic shocks because he loved to hear his bones rattle. That was how he knew he was alive' (p. 10). His aura of casual macho bravura is quickly punctured, however, for like Desiderio and Evelyn before him, he is subjected to a steady, calculated, separation from the privileged perspective of masculinity. He is a journalist who surveys the world from a position of 'habitual disengagement' (p. 10), and his determination to write 'a series of inside stories' (p. 90) of the circus – which he believes is motivated by his determination to unravel the paradox of Fevvers – signals that he has already begun the process that will remove him from his carefully cultivated role as detached spectator. And when an injury to his arm causes him to lose the ability to write, the boundaries between reality and make-believe begin to merge, drawing him into an ever deeper submersion within the text. 'Therefore, for the moment, his disguise disguises – nothing. He is no longer a journalist masquerading as a clown; willy-nilly, force of circumstance has turned him into a *real* clown' (p. 145). However, he reaches the lowest point of his narrative progression following the blowing-up of the circus train in Siberia, when a blow to the head renders him a complete blank, the 'empty centre of an empty landscape' (p. 236).

Deprived of memory, and thus of history, Walser is initiated into the mysteries of shamanism by an isolated tribe who adopt him as their own. Nevertheless, in spite of the fact that, like the community of clowns of which he was briefly a part, he has been shaken all to pieces, he is privileged to begin a slow process of self-reconstruction, although he never returns to that complete state of detachment he enjoyed before. What preserves him from regressing completely back to his old self, however, is not the memory of his picaresque adventures so much as his new willingness to love, and thus surrender detachment in favour of emotional involvement.

Although Fevvers is never catapulted into quite the same intense cataclysm of self-exploration to which Walser is subjected, in her own way she also has a journey to make, and towards the same end – the acceptance of love. Throughout her life, relationships between the sexes have been a matter of cold-blooded negotiation, entered into for what one can get out of it, and in that sense they therefore become merely another performance, reinforcing, rather than challenging, the para-doxical mystique which is Fevvers's best disguise. True love, however, carries with it the danger of being cut down to size, naturalised. When informed somewhat ironically by Lizzie that 'True lovers' reunions always end in marriage' (p. 280), Fevvers rejects the whole idea, identi-fying it as posing only another threat of dissolution: 'the essence of myself may not be given or taken, or what would be left of me?' (p. 281).

This fear teeters on the verge of coming true on her reunion with Walser. He is still completely subsumed in the mindset of the tribe, in which 'there existed no difference between fact and fiction; instead a sort of magic realism' (p. 260), and from the depths of his unknowing is thus able to accept her at absolute face value. However, the lack of his former scepticism initially horrifies Fevvers, who feels 'the hairs on her nape rise when she saw that he was looking at her as if, horror of horrors, she was perfectly natural' (p. 289). She is thus thrown into 'the worst crisis of her life: "Am I fact? Or am I fiction? Am I what I know I am? Or what he thinks I am?"' (p. 290). This moment of what Barthes might term an 'amorous catastrophe'[31] is only resolved when Fevvers obeys Lizzie's urgent instruction to 'Show 'em your feathers, quick!' Given an audience again, Fevvers blooms anew on seeing 'the eyes that told her who she was'.

But that is not, however, the ending of the story, which concludes with Walser and Fevvers meeting, like the fairytale protagonists of *The Bloody Chamber*, on equal and romantic terms at the very moment when the new century begins. For the new Walser, the observation that Fevvers indeed does not possess a navel, and thus is absolutely authentic, no longer matters, for he now accepts her entirely as she is. Recipro-cally, Fevvers has learnt that it is possible for her to be accepted as a woman, wings and all, without becoming either the embodiment of an abstract idea or a freak, although for both parties it also means accepting 'the meaning of fear as it defines itself in its most violent form, that is, fear of the death of the beloved, of the loss of the beloved, of the loss of love' (pp. 292–3). Practised dissimulator that she was, I think Carter momentarily drops her habitual mask of irony here, and is being absolutely serious in maintaining the desirability, as well as the perils, of romantic love.

Nights at the Circus, therefore, is a fantasy which ends up by negotiating its way out of fantasy. There comes a point, it implies, when the performance has to end, and the notion of being nothing more than the sum of your performance, a view by which Carter's fiction was once seduced, is now regarded as a threat. There is real experience, authentic emotion, to be had in the world outside the circus, and the novel concludes having firmly staked its claim there. Of course, Carter still manages to have it both ways: Fevvers remains a fabulous creature who still has a few tricks up her sleeve, as her final triumphant assertion to Walter, 'Gawd, I fooled you!' demonstrates. The novel ends on the 'spiralling tornado' (p. 295) of her laughter, which seeks to counteract the nihilistic, bitter humour of the clowns. It is Bakhtinian laughter, as well as the laughter of Cixous's subversive Medusa, whose role is 'to blow up the law, to break up the "truth"'.[32] But whether this signals anything more than a private happy ending for two individuals is left up to the reader to surmise.

Notes

1. Angela Carter, 'Masochism for the Masses', *New Statesman* (3 June 1983), pp. 8–10 (p. 10).
2. ibid., p. 8.
3. ibid., p. 9.
4. ibid., p. 8.
5. ibid., p. 9.
6. ibid., p. 8.
7. ibid.
8. Mikhail Bakhtin, *Rabelais and His World*, trans. Hélène Iswolsky (Bloomington: Indiana University Press, 1984), p. 38.
9. ibid., p. 79.
10. ibid., p. 92.
11. Marina Warner, 'Angela Carter: Bottle Blonde, Double Drag', in Lorna Sage (ed.), *Flesh and the Mirror: Essays on the Art of Angela Carter* (London: Virago Press, 1994), pp. 243–56 (p. 253).

12. ibid., pp. 253–4.
13. Angela Carter, *Black Venus* (London: Chatto & Windus, 1985). All further references are from this edition.
14. Anne Smith, 'Myths and the Erotic', *Women's Review*, 1 (November 1985), pp. 28–9 (p. 28).
15. It is included in Carter's final collection of short stories, *American Ghosts and Old World Wonders.*
16. Angela Carter, *The Bloody Chamber* (Harmondsworth: Penguin, 1981), p. 7.
17. Hélène Cixous and Catherine Clément, 'Sorties: Out and Out: Attacks/Ways/Forays', in *The Newly Born Woman*, trans. Betsy Wing (Manchester: Manchester University Press, 1987), pp. 63–132 (p. 64).
18. Teresa de Lauretis, 'The Technology of Gender', in *Technologies of Gender: Essays on Theory, Film and Fiction* (London: Macmillan, 1989), pp. 1–30 (p. 1).
19. ibid., p. 2.
20. ibid., p. 2 (De Lauretis's italics).
21. ibid., p. 25.
22. Ian McEwan, 'Sweet Smell of Excess', *The Sunday Times Magazine* (9 September 1984), pp. 430–4 (p. 44).
23. Angela Carter, *Nights at the Circus* (London: Vintage, 1984). All further references in the text are from this edition.
24. Helen Cagney Watts, 'Angela Carter: An Interview', *Bête Noir* 8 (August 1985), pp. 161–76 (p. 169).
25. ibid.
26. Marina Warner, *Monuments and Maidens: The Allegory of the Female Form* [1985] (London: Vintage, 1996), p. 12.
27. Hélène Cixous, 'The Laugh of the Medusa', trans. Keith and Paula Cohen, *Signs* 1 (Summer 1976), pp. 875–93 (p. 887).
28. Mary Russo, *The Female Grotesque: Risk, Excess and Modernity* (London: Routledge, 1994), p. 164.
29. ibid., p. 171.
30. Andrzej Gąsiorek, *Post-War British Fiction: Realism and After* (London: Edward Arnold 1995), p. 126. To give Gąsiorek his due, however, he does go on to say that 'Carter sets clear boundaries to the liberatory possibilities her texts release' (p. 134).
31. Roland Barthes, *A Lover's Discourse: Fragments*, trans. Richard Howard (Harmondsworth: Penguin Books, 1990), p. 48. Barthes defines the 'amorous catastrophe' as 'an extreme situation, "a situation experienced by the subject as irremediably bound to destroy him"', which seems a fair summary of Fevvers's experience.
32. Cixous, 'The Laugh of the Medusa', p. 888.

CHAPTER 7

Nights at the Circus demonstrates many of the contradictions operating within Angela Carter's later work, for while it acts as a superb demonstration of her continuing preference for the kind of narrative games and implausible fictions that characterise postmodernism, Carter also made claims for it as a character-led novel in the nineteenth-century mode. The paradox implicit in such an assertion is condensed within Fevvers's final 'Gawd, I fooled you!', a statement which is intended to reveal that the nature of Fevvers's con trick is nothing to do with her wings, which by this time have been shown to incontrovertibly exist, but everything to do with her much-vaunted virginity. In the end, it seems, her aura of knowing sexuality is as real as her feathers. However, it is still inescapably the case that Fevvers's wings gaining an objective reality within the world of the text does not make them any more plausible, for they cannot help but continue to point towards its status as a fictional construction.

There is thus a clear contradiction involved in attaching conventions associated with the nineteenth-century novel's presentation of character to a text which nevertheless continues Carter's postmodernist tendency to undermine any efforts to uphold the very 'consistency and continuity of the subject'[1] upon which such a concept depends. The kind of confusion this can engender is demonstrated in Carter's interview with John Haffenden soon after *Nights at the Circus* was published, during which she said that, quite apart from the way it acts to round off the plot, Fevvers's final triumphal assertion is 'actually a statement about the nature of fiction, about the nature of her narrative'. But when Haffenden attempted to draw from this remark the conclusion that *Nights at the Circus* therefore ends with 'a kind of gesture towards postmodernism', Carter retorted:

[E]nding on that line doesn't make you realise the fictionality of what has gone before, it makes you start inventing other fictions, things that might have happened – as though the people were really real, with real lives. Things might have happened to them other than the things I have said have happened to them. So that really is an illusion. . . . it is inviting the reader to take one further step into the fictionality of the narrative, instead of coming out of it and looking at it as though it were an artefact. So that's not postmodernist at all, I suppose: it's the single most nineteenth-century gesture in the novel.[2]

But surely, this is what Fevvers's final 'I fooled you!' is really all about, in that it is also the author's own celebration at having pulled off the meta-fictional equivalent of an aerial double-somersault. Although ostensibly directed at Walser, its implicit object of address is the novel's reader, who is thus faced with a particularly ingenious dilemma. On the one hand, they are being implicitly ridiculed for having taken Fevvers's story at face value, and not having noticed a significant omission that must have occurred in the narrative somewhere along the line. But on the other, to begin constructing alternative histories for the characters, as Carter herself points out in the interview quoted above, is to fall victim to the illusion that they are objectively real, and thus allow the fiction to overstep its boundaries.

Wise Children (1991)

Carter's final novel, *Wise Children* reiterates the invitation extended by *Nights at the Circus* to enter into the world of the narrative and accept the characters as real people with lives beyond the confines of the text. Indeed, while she was writing it Carter told one interviewer that it was part of an on-going experiment with 'nineteenth-century characterisation and narrative'.[3] However, while it does not dwell on implausibility quite so blatantly as its predecessor, *Wise Children* nevertheless persistently undermines its own claims to realism.

The presentation of this novel as a family saga in the best tradition of soap opera implies the insufficiency of the narrative to contain everything that happens to these characters. Like soap opera, in many ways it does not so much operate within the finite restrictions of 'beginning, middle and end', as consist of 'an indefinitely expandable middle'.[4] Such an illusion is ostensibly reinforced by the way in which

Carter structures the novel as a first-person autobiographical narrative. Its narrator is the ebullient Dora Chance, one half of a pair of identical twins who have made a living as music hall hoofers in the dying days of vaudeville entertainment. Her autobiography encompasses not only personal reminiscences but her entire family history which, given that she and her sister Nora are the illegitimate byblows of 'the imperial Hazard dynasty that bestrode the British theatre like a colossus for a century and a half' (p. 10),[5] is a significant one indeed.

Dora's gossipy, colloquial voice evokes memories of the autobiographical segments of Fevvers's narrative, in that both are endowed with a vibrant materiality through their energetic and distinctive speech patterns.[6] However, I have already argued that in Carter's hands, the concept of autobiography does not preclude equivocation, evasion or even downright mendacity in the interests of a good story, and it is a habit she has fictional alter egos such as Fevvers and Dora send up particularly outrageously. As Kate Webb has observed, Dora's status as autobiographer does not withstand much close examination, for:

> At the beginning of the book, Dora tells us that she is writing her autobiography on a word-processor on the morning of her seventy-fifth birthday, but the vernacular force of her speech is so great that later she magically appears to transcend the written word, becoming, instead, the old bird who's collared you at the local boozer.[7]

But although I agree with Webb's general point, I would challenge her on specifics; in particular, her assumption that we're ever meant to assume that we are reading the final, word-processed version of Dora's story, which the 'vernacular force of her speech' then 'magically appears to transcend'. In fact, Dora is quite explicit that she is only 'in the course of assembling notes towards my own autobiography' (p. 11, my italics). This is an early warning that her narration is probably not wholly reliable, for this is a draft which has yet to achieve the authenticity which will be implicit in the finished product. But I'm not sure that even notes come into what we read, for from the beginning of the story the reader is positioned as the audience of a verbal reminiscence:

> But, as to the question of origins and past history, let me plunge deep into the archaeology of my desk, casting aside the photo of Ruby Keeler ('To Nora and Dora, four fabulous feet, from your Ruby').

Here it is. A fraying envelope stuffed with antique picture postcards. We've put together quite a collection over the years. (pp. 11–12)

By the end of the novel, however, the venue for the meeting between reader and narrator has changed, having moved out of the cluttered confines of 49 Bard Road, Brixton, and down to the local pub: 'Well, you might have known what you were about to let yourself in for when you let Dora Chance . . . reeking with liquor, accost you in the Coach and Horses and let her tell you a tale' (p. 227). It's a slight move, but a significant one, away from the photographs, newscuttings and letters which are meant to act as material evidence for Dora's story, and into a setting which recasts her as the drunken teller of what is, in all probability, a tall tale.

A performer to the last, Dora never loses her consciousness of an audience. Indeed, one of the idiolectal markers of her discourse is the way in which she persistently addresses the reader in conversationally familiar terms. 'I told you, Brixton used to be everso convenient for public transport' (p. 82). 'There we are, see? On the front page of the *New York Post*, in our best suits – Schiparelli, I kid you not' (p. 112). Increasingly, however, Dora also uses her awareness of the reader's interpellating presence to draw attention to the way in which she is structuring her story. This tendency is apparent from the beginning of the narrative, for while it opens on the morning of the twins' seventy-fifth birthday, it is not long before Dora interrupts the action with her reminiscences, which then proceed to take up most of the length of the book:

Freeze-frame.
    Let us pause awhile in the unfolding story of Tristram and Tiffany so that I can fill you in on the background. High time! you must be saying. (p. 11)

As the story proceeds, however, these narrative pauses and redirections begin to multiply to the extent that it appears to be beginning to evade Dora's control, as she struggles to place events in their proper order, or even merely to recall them accurately. All of this is inscribed within her narrative, with the result that the reader is drawn not only to contemplate the means by which the text is being formulated, but also, crucially, to doubt the entire process. For example:

These days, half a century and more later, I might think I did not
live but dreamed that night, if it wasn't for the photos, see? This is
one of Bottom, being hugged by –

There I go again! Can't keep a story going in a straight line, can
I? Drunk in charge of a narrative. (p. 158)

Such a blatant working out of the structure of the novel in plain sight
of the reader is distinctly reminiscent of Tristram Shandy's appeal to his
audience to 'bear with me, – and let me go on, and tell my story in my
own way'.[8] In writing this novel, Carter must surely have had Laurence
Sterne in mind, for more than any of her other novels, *Wise Children*
shares what Linda Hutcheon calls *Tristram Shandy*'s 'dual interest in
the storytelling as well as the story told'.[9]

Ultimately, Dora's refusal to efface herself as narrator of her own
story can be seen as analogous to Fevvers's final narrative sleight-of-
hand, in that it renders the text more 'real' and more 'fictional' at one
and the same time. The very vitality invested in Dora's distinctive voice
imbues her with character, and her direct appeals to the reader draws
you into the world on the page to the extent that you, too, virtually
become part of its *dramatis personae*. But what she's telling you is that
she's unreliable, and not to be trusted – 'I've got a tale and a half to
tell, all right!' (p. 227). And in the process, of course, you should be
reminded that in the final analysis she is only a narrative device herself.

This slippery equivocation concerning reality and illusion, whereby
the nature of the illusion is simultaneously both celebrated and known,
extends beyond the formal arrangement of the text to become one of
the novel's main themes. It achieves this most obviously through its
persistent theatrical references, for both branches of Nora's and Dora's
family tree are in showbusiness, although on opposite sides of the tracks.
While the 'Lucky Chances' are song-and-dance girls who perform
mainly on the music-hall stage, they are the illegitimate products of a
dynasty of renowned Shakespearean actors. Seasoned hoofers that they
are, the Chance twins know how to carry off a performance: but they
also never fall for their own illusions. This is shown to wonderful effect
in Dora's description of dressing up for their distinguished father's
hundredth birthday party, in which they laboriously superimpose 'the
faces we always used to have on to the faces we have now':

Foundation. Dark in the hollows of the cheeks and at the temples,
blended into a lighter tone everywhere else. Rouge, except they
call it 'blusher', nowadays. Two kinds of blusher, one to highlight

the Hazard bones, another to give us rosy cheeks. Nora likes to put the faintest dab on the end of her nose, why I can't fathom, old habits die hard. Three kinds of eyeshadow – dark blue, light blue blended together on the eyelids with the little finger, then a frosting overall of silver. Then we put on our two coats of mascara. Today, for lipstick, Rubies in the Snow by Revlon. (p. 192)

In many ways, this passage quite consciously harks back to the long list of other characters in Carter's fiction who are obsessed with their own self-fashioning, such as Honeybuzzard, Kay Kyte, Lee, the Count and in particular, of course, Tristessa. In fact, Carter appears to deliberately evoke the spectre of Tristessa in a remark passed by Nora while survey-ing her freshly painted reflection: 'It's every woman's tragedy . . . that after a certain age, she looks like a female impersonator'. But whereas Tristessa's fantastic transformation is achieved through the rigorous exercise of a will which simply cannot accept that she is anything other than the being she desires to be, the Chance sisters know they exercise a much more mundane magic.

It's the inclusion of detail here that gives the game away, because all the references to brand names, colours and methods of application in the above passage demonstrate the sisters' awareness that their new faces are illusions created by nothing more extraordinary than over half-a-century's experience in theatrical make-up techniques. And they are also aware, as Tristessa and her ilk can never be, of their own innate ridiculousness. Having duly tarted themselves up, when Nora and Dora enter the party they are abruptly confronted with their own full-length reflections, which reveal to them 'two funny old girls, paint an inch thick, clothes sixty years too young, stars on their stockings and little wee skirts skimming their buttocks. Parodies' (p. 197). For an uncomfortable instant, the Chance sisters merely appear pathetically risible – but only for an instant. It is Nora who salvages the situation, demonstrating the Chance saving talent for not taking oneself too seriously:

'Oooer, Dor', she said. 'We've gone and overdone it.'
    We couldn't help it, we had to laugh at the spectacle we'd made of ourselves and, fortified by sisterly affection, strutted our stuff boldly into the ballroom. (p. 198)

In this context the Chances' ever-ready laughter is analogous to Fevvers's hilarity which closes *Nights at the Circus*, for in both cases it performs a destabilising function, puncturing pomposity and overturning propriety.

It is this kind of mocking humour, capable of being directed against the self as well as others, that makes *Wise Children* Carter's last, most celebratory, expression of her belief that 'the margin is more important than the page'.[10] From the beginning the novel foregrounds polarity, presenting the reader with a series of hierarchical oppositions which, while they clearly establish the boundaries of legitimacy, firmly position both narrator and reader outside them: 'My name is Dora Chance. Welcome to the wrong side of the tracks' (p. 1).

Hélène Cixous and Catherine Clément, among others, have argued that, while the margins are a place of repression and exclusion, they also extend the benefit of 'mobility'.[11] To a certain extent, this novel supports this point of view, but with certain qualifications. Although the margins may be a place where you can make your own rules, it's also where you learn the facts of life early. A large proportion of the Chance girls' clear-sightedness is due to the fact that they have never been under any delusions concerning their own status in the world. Never officially recognised by their father, they are brought up in shabby SW2 by an adoptive but much-loved grandmother, and quickly realise that their love of song and dance will only ever be of any use if it can be used to generate hard cash. Already 'hardened old troupers' (p. 77) by the age of fifteen, they also know that their market value as individuals is far outweighed by their attraction as a matching set: 'On our own, you wouldn't look at us twice. But put us together . . .' (p. 77).

Such exact imitation of the other which is also the self (which although natural in its origins, is also intensified through the use of artifice) aligns the twins with the 'image of the uncanny, grotesque body as doubled, monstrous'.[12] Just as it is Fevvers's physical excessiveness which makes her 'a figure of ultimate spectacularity',[13] so the twins' specular appeal is based on bodily superabundance, for they are more than one, yet not quite two. But while Fevvers fears that she will forever be trapped as the object of the spectacle, Nora and Dora deliberately court the gaze of others. In making a livelihood out of their freakish duality, they happily flaunt themselves both on and off stage.

In this sense, they exemplify Mary Ann Doane's notion of masquerade, through which she attempts to enable a theory of female spectatorship:

> The masquerade, in flaunting femininity, holds it at a distance. Womanliness is a mask which can be worn or removed. The masquerade's resistance to patriarchal positioning would therefore lie in its denial of the production of femininity as closeness, as

presence-to-itself, as, precisely, imagistic. . . . Masquerade . . .
involves a realignment of femininity, the recovery, or more accurately, simulation, of the missing gap or distance. To masquerade
is to manufacture a lack in the form of a certain distance between
oneself and one's image.[14]

The Lucky Chances, however, are more lucky than most, for while
Doane describes the masquerader as 'us[ing] her own body as a disguise',[15] Nora and Dora find their masquerading options doubled, for
they can also use each other's. They will happily swap identities or even
play at being both twins in order to cover up the other's absence. The
eagerness with which they make full use of the freedom their identical
appearance affords them foregrounds the way in which that which
makes them the object of the spectacle is also the very thing that
enables them to evade it.

The comparison with Doane can only be taken so far, however.
Doane herself acknowledged that the concept of masquerade carries
with it significant problems, not least that the theories from which it
is drawn do not make a distinction between 'femininity' and an autonomous female subjectivity. Instead, as a 'reaction-formation against
the illicit assumption of masculinity',[16] it is presented as a pathological
condition in which the female subject masquerades femininity in order
to cover up the fact that entry into language and the social order can only
be achieved through the assumption of a *masculine* subject position. In
other words, no such thing as an 'authentic' female identity exists,
because it is not capable of being encoded within a system in which, in
psychoanalytical terms, the phallus is the guarantee of meaning. In a
reworking of her earlier argument, Doane admits that her attempt to
'tear the concept of masquerade out of its conventional context'[17] and
to invest it with some notion of female empowerment – in this case
the hijacking of the specular gaze – does not completely succeed in
eradicating its original role as an indicator of female *dis*empowerment.

Although eventually proved wrong, this is the fear with which
Fevvers has to contend; the fear that she may amount to no more than
the image reflected back to her through the gaze of others. However,
the strident self-assurance implicit in Dora's narration is probably the
best indicator that this is not applicable to the Chance sisters. For a
start, the masks of femininity they assume are so bizarre that they
cannot possibly qualify as disguises. In accordance with the twins'
tendency to 'debate invisibility hotly' (p. 199), they flaunt rather than

conceal their eccentricity and their difference. But Nora's and Dora's recognition of illusion also makes it clear that the masks they elaborately construct are only façades which bear no relation to their interior sense of self.

Furthermore, in spite of the way they exploit their physical inter-changeability, the twins actually possess a strong sense of individual identity. In this case at least, to be identical does not necessarily mean to be the same. As Dora says, 'identical we may be, but symmetrical – never' (p. 5). Behind their play of sameness, Nora and Dora actually maintain a list of distinguishing characteristics which define them as individuals, and which people in the know can also use to differentiate between them. The moment of reconciliation with their father at the end of the book, for example, is marked by his realisation that they habitually use different perfumes: 'Now, my darlings, you must refresh my memory ... which of you is it who uses Shalimar and which Mitsouko?' (p. 200).

It has to be said, however, that much of this breezy self-confidence is gained through age and experience, rather than innate. At the age of seventy-five, the twins can assume masks of femininity so over-the-top that they almost appear to be concealing masculine, not feminine, iden-tities (which, given masquerade's original connotation as *disguising* the assumption of a masculine subject-position, is decidedly ironic). When they are younger and more impressionable, however, Nora and Dora hanker after belonging to the system which so persistently excludes them; a system which for them is not only represented by the legitimate theatre, but also acts as an embodiment of the elusive paternal figure.

On the day of the twins' thirteenth birthday, for example, a particu-larly poignant confrontation occurs between the legitimate and the unacknowledged, when Nora and Dora stand outside the theatre in Brighton where Melchior is starring in *Macbeth*. 'And here he was, treading the boards like billy-oh, in Shakespeare, and weren't we fresh from singing in the streets? We never felt quite so illegitimate in all our lives as we did that day we were thirteen' (p. 69). In this sense, their subsequent careers spring from a desire to win their father's attention and approval, although they also recognise the impossibility of ever stepping over the line which divides mere song-and-dance girls from authentic thespians.

What subsequently happens in this novel, however, is that this initially insurmountable line begins to dismantle itself. The book's clear-cut opening, in which Dora neatly draws a line between '*rive gauche, rive droite* ... the North and South divide' (p. 1) is deceptive, for these boundaries are quickly proved to be a good deal more blurred than they at first appear. On one level, *Wise Children* is Carter's homage to a playwright whose work she greatly admired, and in this context, the novel's title – an inversion of a line from *The Merchant of Venice*, 'It is a wise father that knows his own child' – is indicative of Carter's strategy in the text as a whole, which hinges on reversal and subversion, as opposed to outright rejection. As she said soon after the publication of *Wise Children*, 'It must be obvious that I *really like* Shakespeare'.[18] But this book does not seek to valorise him; on the contrary, it seeks to reclaim him for popular culture, and put him back on the side of the 'folk' where Carter believed he belongs. As she remarked, for example, to Lorna Sage:

> The extraordinary thing about English literature is that actually our greatest writer is the intellectual equivalent of bubble-gum, but can make twelve-year-old girls cry, can foment revolutions in Africa, can be translated into Japanese and leave not a dry eye in the house.[19]

As if to prove this point, the text of *Wise Children* itself is intricately woven out of Shakespearean quotations and plot allusions. Carter claimed to have attempted, in fact, to include references to every play in the Shakespearean canon, although after the book's publication she acknowledged that she hadn't quite managed it.[20]

However affectionate Carter's portrayal of the plays themselves might be, therefore, she nevertheless takes fervent issue with the notion that Shakespeare functions as some kind of guarantor of excellence. The rise of the house of Hazard coincides with the glory days of British imperialism, in which Shakespeare became the determinator of cultural superiority. According to Terence Hawkes, the second half of the nineteenth century in particular was a period in which Shakespeare became 'a kingpin in ... [the] project of welding native cultures abroad and local cultures at home into a single coherent imperial identity',[21] and in *Wise Children*, this imperialist missionary zeal is represented by the Chance twins' paternal grandparents, Ranulph and Estella Hazard, who end up touring the globe on a mission to take the civilising word of Shakespeare 'to the ends of the Empire' (p. 17). Although said Empire is fading into twilight by the time Nora and Dora come along, Shakespeare as 'an instrument of cultural meaning'[22] nevertheless remains the symbol of the legitimate English theatre, and the standard by which an aesthetic of cultural value is determined.

As the twentieth century gets underway, however, so the primacy of the theatre is steadily challenged, and the cultural divide that separates Melchior in *Macbeth* from the end-of-pier entertainment outside becomes increasingly negligible. While at the age of thirteen the twins are barely respectable enough to enter his dressing-room, by the age of eighteen, they're on the same West End stage as their father, and the implied intellectual gravitas of *Macbeth* has been replaced by a riotous musical revue on a Shakespearean theme suggestively entitled *What? You Will?*. It is the harbinger of a process by which Shakespeare, once comfortably enshrined in English theatrical tradition, will be put through the wringer by the new ascendant media of film and television in a thoroughly disrespectful fashion. In an episode which forms the comic centrepiece of the book, *A Midsummer Night's Dream* is made into a truly awful 1930s Hollywood spectacular (script by Peregrine Hazard, 'with additional dialogue by William Shakespeare', p. 108).[23] And by the 1980s the Hazard family are parodying their own theatrical reputation in margarine advertisements: 'To butter or not to butter . . .' (p. 38).

What Carter is charting here is the process by which objects of cultural value lose their ability to participate within a dominant aesthetic. In this way, theatrical institutions, once enshrined in high culture, become appropriable by contemporary, popular cultural forms. And this, of course, eventually brings us back to camp, Carter's dominant preoccupation in her early work. As Andrew Ross explains:

> The camp effect . . . is created not simply by a change in the mode of cultural production, but rather . . . when a much earlier mode of production, which has lost its power to dominate cultural meanings, becomes available, in the present, for redefinition according to contemporary codes of taste.[24]

It is this process which ensures that, by time of the Chance sisters' old age, the film of *A Midsummer Night's Dream* (starring Melchior as Oberon and featuring Nora and Dora as Peasblossom and Mustardseed), which was such a flop when it was made, is seen to be experiencing a modern resurgence. Itself now an anachronistic artefact in the television age, it has graduated to showings in art cinemas and is studied by students on film courses. Shakespeare, then, enjoys a renaissance, but it is a *camp* renaissance, which involves a deliberately parodic reassertion of his old cultural position. Although originally a perfectly sincere attempt on Melchior's part to bring the civilising benefits of Shakespeare to Hollywood, it only gains fame when hindsight endows it with the 'failed seriousness'[25] which defines the camp sensibility.

Throughout this novel, therefore, the line between the illegitimate and the legitimate is presented as an extremely fine one, repeatedly crossed and recrossed to create an exuberant and eclectic mixture of forms and references. Kate Webb, for example, describes it as a narrative which

> is itself patterned with intersecting tracks and grooves that are made by her characters 'crossing, crisscrossing' the globe; by the zigzagging lines of familial and artistic descent that reach across and into their lives; and by the writing itself, which passes through – often parodying – many genres and styles.[26]

Such a description foregrounds how the novel's narrative movement itself mimics the conceptual movement of camp, in that it does not travel in a straight line. Instead, just as camp 'involves a rediscovery of history's waste. . . . liberating the objects and discourses of the past from disdain and neglect',[27] Dora's story is persistently returning, circling, reappropriating and reconfiguring its subject matter. In this way, the novel participates in the very process of campification it is describing, grounded on the assertion that no boundaries, and certainly not those which govern hierarchies of taste, stay intact for long.

Illegitimacy, therefore, becomes a state which exists only in the eye of the beholder, underlined here by the fact that family relationships are constantly being defined and realigned. In fact, the entire Hazard family is founded on illegitimacy, for hardly any, or perhaps even none, of its children are the offspring of their supposed father, which makes any discussion of their family tree complicated in the extreme. Melchior and his twin Peregrine are not Ranulph's sons, nor is Melchior the biological father of certainly one, and possibly neither, of the two sets of twins that bear his name. In fact, they are the offspring of Peregrine, who also acts as the putative father of Melchior's actual children, Nora and Dora, thus confusing the issue still further. Moreover, the generations, rather than proceeding in a decorously straight chronological line, keep on getting tangled up, something which is reinforced by the Hazard men's tendency to marry their stage-daughters. Both Ranulph and Melchior, playing Lear, subsequently marry their Cordelias, an action which also neatly conveys a strong implication of incest. This may be literally justified in the case of Melchior's assumed son Tristram, who has a long-standing relationship with his much older half-sister Saskia. (If she is his half-sister, that is, for every family relationship is conditional in this book.) Incest is also implicit in Peregrine's sexual association with at least one of his brother's wives, and also, though belatedly revealed, with his own niece Dora.

While, as Peregrine says, paraphrasing Shakespeare, 'It's a wise child that knows its own father. . . . But wiser yet the father who knows his own child' (p. 73), it is therefore virtually impossible to exercise such wisdom in the midst of such a tangle of relationships as that presented by the Hazard family. But although paternity is permanently under dispute in this novel, one thing appears to remain certain: while '"Father" is a hypothesis . . . "mother" is a fact' (p. 223). It is Dora who says this, but her belief in the validity of maternal origins is about to be somewhat shaken. Although the twins have been raised on the romantic tale of their mother's seduction by Melchior and her subsequent death in childbirth, it is Peregrine who puts the thought in Nora's head that perhaps Grandma Chance had made up that story all along, and that Nora and Dora might be the products of her own 'last fling' (p. 223).

By this point in the text this is not, however, the revelation it might have been. At their age, the Chance girls know that 'that nothing is a matter of life and death except life and death' (p. 215). To put it another way, you make the most of what you've got while you've got it, and you don't question where it came from. Their down-to-earth, eccentric Grandma, so reminiscent of Carter's description of her own maternal grandmother, is all the mother they ever needed, and the matter of their possible biological relationship is irrelevant.

Indeed, the whole concept of 'family' is de-naturalised in the course of this text, no longer an automatic given, but something constructed out of affection and a sense of responsibility towards others. While in Carter's earlier novels in particular, the domestic space is configured as cluttered, claustrophobic and conflictual, *Wise Children*'s notion of family as artefact helps to get around that. It's the difference between being stuck within the same four walls with people with whom you have nothing in common except heredity, and choosing the people you want to live with of your own free will. While, under the rule of the patriarch, the supposedly legitimate Hazard family is riven with jealousy and Oedipal tension, Nora and Dora exemplify the matriarchal generosity of spirit which makes the 'found' family thrive. Not only do they take in their father's divorced first wife after Grandma's death, but also, at the very end of the book, they adopt their (possibly) half-brother's abandoned twin babies.

As they eventually come to realise, having spent their lives longing for a real father, the patriarch is extraneous to this family unit. When they are accepted at long last by a father whose new generosity of spirit owes more to senility than any true remorse, in their maturity they finally concede that he is actually no more a reality to them than their supposed mother was:

> D'you know, I sometimes wonder if we haven't been making him up all along.... If he isn't just a collection of our hopes and dreams and wishful thinking in the afternoons. Something to set our lives by, like the old clock in the hall, which is real enough, in itself, but which we've got to wind up to make it go. (p. 230)

However, although I agree with Lorna Sage that this is Carter's final, boldest, deconstruction of the patriarch,[28] it doesn't have the effect of rendering either mother or father unnecessary – although it does make them work harder for the *right* to play that role. On the contrary, it is the companionship of others that insulates the individual against inevitable tragedy. Although Dora's narrative ends having pledged its firm allegiance to 'the world of comedy' (p. 227), the fact that such an avowal has to be made at all alerts the reader to the alternative course it might have taken. After all, as Dora observes, glibly negating yet another comforting boundary-line, comedy is only 'tragedy that happens to *other* people' (p. 213). While the Chance girls end the novel looking forward to 'at least another twenty years' (p. 230) of life, playing, now, Grandma's role, death is only postponed, not negated. Kate Webb points out that death is a particularly 'strong presence in this book – not just the end of empire or the death of the patriarch, which Dora is happy to let go, but a sense of the presence of death in the midst of life'. And as she says, all deaths are 'untimely'.[29]

Dora, with seventy-five action-packed years behind her, knows her limitations. Her final, triumphant achievement in the novel is not the assumption of grandmotherhood (it is really Nora who has always yearned for babies), but her final, riotous fuck with Peregrine. It is an event which consciously breaks a number of taboos – against old people doing it, against uncles doing it with nieces, against doing it in your father's bedroom in the middle of a family party – but its greatest value is as an assertion of Dora's continuing commitment to life, and to happy endings. Although, from the perspective of the people in the room below, there is a moment when it seems possible they might 'fuck the house down' (p. 220), Dora knows that that really is, regretfully, impossible, for 'The carnival's got to stop, some time' (p. 222).

As critics such as Marina Warner, Lorna Sage and Kate Webb have noted, *Wise Children*, for all its ever-present humour, is imbued with a fatalistic defiance, its characters persisting in laughing in the very face of adversity. Carter aligns herself definitively with Bakhtin here, in portraying carnival very specifically as arising from repressive conditions, and as only ever constituting a temporary escape from them. Underneath the bawdy burlesque lies an awareness that nothing ever remains the same for long, and that it is not only culture that is subject to the entropic pull towards decline. Nora and Dora may have gained the wisdom of age, but they care very much indeed about getting old. In a text which specialises in dismantling boundaries, the line that divides the past from the present is very firmly established as one that cannot be crossed, except in reminiscence. This is movingly emphasised at the moment when the old twins confront their younger selves precariously preserved on celluloid:

> It took me donkey's till I saw the point but saw the point I did, eventually, though not until the other day, when we were watching *The Dream* again in Notting Hill that time, couple of batty old tarts with their eyes glued on their own ghosts. Then I understood the thing I'd never grasped back in those days, when I was young, before I lived in history. When I was young, I'd wanted to be ephemeral, I'd wanted the moment, to live in just the glorious moment, the rush of blood, the applause. Pluck the day. Eat the peach. Tomorrow never comes. But, oh yes, tomorrow does come all right, and when it comes it lasts a bloody long time, I can tell you. (p. 125)

But considering that this is a book preoccupied with asserting the inevitability of endings, it is strangely reluctant to commit to one itself. Dora nominally postulates the family party as the proper moment for the book to conclude, for during it everything has been resolved. The twins have finally been 'allowed to join in, legit. at last' (p. 226), but already Dora is beginning to pull away from finality:

[T]he barren heath was bloomed, the fire that was almost out sprung back to life and Nora a mother at last at seventy-five years old and all laughter, forgiveness, generosity, reconciliation.

Yes.

Hard to swallow, huh? (p. 227)

So at the very moment when Dora contemplates her narrative's happy resolution – a resolution particularly appropriate for comedy, her chosen genre – she also acknowledges the insufficiency of this event to act in any such a capacity. Life isn't like that, not just because happiness is ephemeral, but also because she and her story have already moved past that moment of conclusion, which is nothing but a narrative convention anyway. No ending is ever quite final because there is always the morning after the night before, even if it is a bit of an anti-climax.

In true metafictional fashion, therefore, Dora offers her reader a choice. If you want a happy ending, she says, you can 'choose to stop the story there, at such a pause, and refuse to take it any further' (p. 227). The novel itself, however, carries on for another few pages, which tantalise the reader with the dangling threads of new stories. The sisters plan their future as the rather incongruous mothers for a new generation of Hazard twins, while Peregrine and Tristram are on the point of going to South America to track down the infants' absent parents (if they find, them, of course, it will be a Hazard family first).

What *Wise Children* ultimately asserts, therefore, is not only the inevitability of death, but also the power of stories to generate themselves; and the latter, to a certain extent at least, acts as a counter to the former. One of the primary functions, if not *the* primary function, of family in this novel is to act, not only as the origin of story, but also as the vehicle through which it is perpetuated. And because it is part of the nature of story to always overrun its narrative boundaries, the perpetuity of the family structure is also ensured, a notion which implies a kind of immortality, however tenuous. Nora and Dora will inevitably bite the dust, sooner or later, but there will still be stories to tell of the Hazards and the Chances. As the renegade spirit of Grandma Chance conveys (itself a tantalising indication that, perhaps, even death does not quite remove one from the family circle), 'Memory Lane is a dead end' (p. 190), running counter to both life and fiction's tendency to keep on going in spite of everything.

Structured as it is around reminiscence, the concept of hindsight (which allows to you to look back to the past, reassess it from a new perspective, make it into the stuff of stories, but never to change it) is an extremely important element in *Wise Children*. Carter's audience, too, inevitably bring their own kind of hindsight to this book, which now cannot help but be read in the light of the knowledge that Carter died of cancer eight months after its publication. It is thus extremely tempting to regard it not just as Dora's fictional autobiography, but also, to a certain extent, as Carter's own. In this context, it could be interpreted as recording the author's own confrontation with mortality, putting up two defiant fingers at death and using her imagination to create the indecorous old age she would have loved to have had, but now would never know.

Certainly, there are elements in this novel which are distinctly reminiscent of Carter's autobiographical narratives. Grandma Chance, defiantly eccentric and fiercely loyal to her foundling children, possesses the kind of 'architectonic personality' Carter attributes to her own Gran in 'The Mother Lode', and the novel's general setting recreates Carter's own South London origins. An interview by Susannah Clapp is particularly intriguing in providing parallels between Carter's own life and the background of her last novel:

> The London of *Wise Children* is also the pre-war city . . . enjoyed by her [Carter's] mother. As a cashier in Selfridge's in the Twenties, she eyed with some envy the Dolly Sisters, the Hungarian mistresses of Gordon Selfridge, who spent lavishly in the store, and who appear on the cover of *Wise Children* with sequins like windmill sails on their heads and breasts, and ostrich feather skirts. In re-creating the past lives of the city, the novel also invents a happier life for the author's Aunt Kit, who, having failed her exams, was expected by her parents to 'go on the Halls', but was instead pushed by a prim headmistress into a life as a clerkess.[30]

Such references to Carter's own family history demonstrates in a very tangible way the novel's assertion that family is the origin of stories, and that both family and stories go on independently of any one individual. It also reiterates the ending of *Nights at the Circus*, in that it enunciates belief in a world beyond the text; indeed, in a world from which the text itself springs, in which human companionship, affection and love, are both possible and important. But what it does not indicate is that *Wise Children* was intended as any kind of personal *memento mori* – in fact, Carter's illness had not been diagnosed when she began it. That this novel is peculiarly susceptible to such a reading, therefore, is a suitable irony for a writer who habitually used invention to conceal, rather than reveal, the authorial self.

American Ghosts and Old World Wonders (1993)

Carter's last work, a collection of short stories written in the years leading up to her death in 1992, was published posthumously. Taken together, these narratives reprise many themes to be found in Carter's longer fiction, but are all imbued with the kind of down-to-earth perspective which is such an important element in *Wise Children*. Like Carter's last novel, these narratives are linked together by the double-edged tactic they all adopt in relation to illusion, simultaneously expressing delight in its creation but recognising that it is no more, in actuality, than a clever con trick.

One particularly good example of how this works is a story entitled 'The Merchant of Shadows', which is told from the point of view of a film student doing postgraduate research in America. His subject is the work of a 1930s Hollywood director named Heinrich Mannheim, and although Mannheim himself is dead, the narrator is delighted to receive an invitation to interview his widow in order to gather material for his thesis. Living in 'an austere cube of pure glass' (p. 71)[31] beside the ocean, this woman is, however, as the narrator anxiously reminds us, 'far, far more than a Hollywood widow; she was the Star of Stars, no less, the greatest of them all . . . dubbed by *Time* magazine the 'Spirit of the Cinema' (p. 69). In fact, Mannheim is famous more because he was married to her than for any of his independent achievements as a director.

To any habitual reader of Carter's fiction, this is all bound to be strangely familiar, evoking an extraordinarily close parallel with her greatest *femme fatale*, Tristessa de St Ange from *The Passion of New Eve*. The similarity is no coincidence either, as it turns out, for like Tristessa, this 'Spirit of the Cinema' is also no more than a masquerade. The elaborate artifice of the film star – 'that . . . one hundred per cent Max Factor look' (p. 76), as the narrator drolly observes – conceals, naturally, none other than Mannheim himself, while the Spirit's gruff companion who looks 'like a superannuated lumberjack' (p. 75) in her jeans and boots is actually his actress wife.

The narrator, too, is a familiar aspect of Carter's fictional topography. From the moment he introduces himself as 'a student of Light and

Illusion' (p. 66), he is exposed as the latest in a line of callow young men, from Morris in *Shadow Dance* onwards, who is about to have his egocentric vision of the world rudely shaken. And indeed, already patently out of his depth in a foreign culture 'where the light made movies and madness' (p. 81), he eventually ends up exactly where he should. Although he escapes the dramatic extremities of Evelyn's fate, his 'ghastly sense of incipient humiliation, or impending erotic doom' (p. 79) is nevertheless fully justified, for on realising 'how peripheral I was' (p. 85), he resolves to flee back home to London, helplessly cowed by the very illusions he began his story affecting to understand.

This narrative, therefore, is written very much with the knowledge-able reader in mind; although in the final analysis it is far more than just a playful reiteration of *The Passion of New Eve*. On the contrary, it can be viewed as a kind of revisionary commentary on the earlier novel which demonstrates the change in Carter's treatment of the relation-ship between fantasy and fact that had taken place since she wrote *The Passion of New Eve* in the seventies. While Tristessa is a being who cannot live outside the culture of simulation, for she has no sense of herself outside her self-created persona, Mannheim's case is subtly different, in that his immersion in the role of the *femme fatale* is a much more considered one. Having always had a leaning towards cross-dressing anyway, it gives him a kick to actually live publicly as a woman, with the aid of a little judicious plastic surgery and a lot of make-up. Already an expert in the art of illusion, therefore, it costs him very little effort to turn that art upon himself – but, rather like Nora and Dora, he retains a certain actorish detachment that prevents him from being completely consumed by the deception. That is why the narrator is eventually 'let in on the masquerade'; because Mannheim cannot resist letting at least one person appreciate his virtuoso performance:

> Perhaps, having constructed this masterpiece of subterfuge, Mannheim couldn't bear to die without leaving some little hint, somewhere, of how, having made her, he then *became* her, became a better she than she had ever been, and wanted to share with his last little acolyte, myself, the secret of his greatest hit. (p. 84)

The Spirit, therefore, is presented as a mask who can be occupied by anyone who is man enough for the job; indeed, the terrible constraints of iconic femininity are something that perhaps only men would wish to assume. This is emphasised by the presence in the story of Mannheim's wife, the original actress from whom the Spirit was born.

Sister, rejoicing in her freedom to simply be herself, embodies the liberating aspect of masquerade – providing, of course, that it is played out by someone else. So while the expertise of Mannheim is admirable, and the creature he creates in every way as miraculous as Tristessa, the Spirit nevertheless lacks Tristessa's terrible seductiveness, which springs from her burning conviction that she actually exists. It is a conviction which is so strong that it seeks to change reality itself in order to fit the pattern of her desire, yet it is lacking in the Spirit who, retaining a sense of existence outside simulation, is not destroyed by discovery.

Carter's changing configuration of the relationship between reality and simulation is summed up in a remark which, although it appears in another piece collected in *American Ghosts*, could well act as an acerbic comment on the conclusion of 'Merchant of Shadows': 'Things don't change because a girl puts on trousers or a chap slips on a frock, you know' (p. 109). 'In Pantoland', a piece which is half short story, half a study of popular culture, purports to be an analysis of the British pantomime tradition. It is in actuality a wonderful piece of verbal burlesque, which carries with it distinct echoes of *Wise Children* in its exploration and exposure of theatricality. Carter defines Pantoland as a place of 'illusion and transformation' (p. 99) where 'everything is excessive and gender is variable' (p. 100). If the real does intrude – in the form, say, of real dogs or horses – it is rendered so insignificant by the garish exaggeration of its fictional surroundings, that:

> 'large as life' isn't the right phrase at all, at all. 'Large as life' they might be, in the context of the auditorium, but when the proscenium arch gapes as wide as the mouth of the ogre in *Jack and the Beanstalk*, those forty white horses pulling the glass coach of the princess look as little and inconsequential as white mice. (p. 99)

The scenery may be two-dimensional and distinctly shaky, but this is carnival, which hinges on the reversal and inversion of accepted hierarchies, including that which privileges the authentic over the fake.

However, in spite of the freewheeling anarchy inherent in pantomime, the piece nevertheless ends with acquiescence to the real. It may be with a certain reluctance, but it has to be done, no question, for:

> As Umberto Eco once said, 'An everlasting carnival does not work.' You can't keep it up, you know; nobody ever could. The essence of the carnival, the festival, the Feast of Fools, is transience. It is here today and gone tomorrow, a release of tension not

a reconstitution of order, a refreshment . . . after which everything can go on again exactly as if nothing had happened. (p. 109)

There are, in other words, no new stories and no fresh starts to be had – we're stuck with what we've got. *American Ghosts* reiterates this even more openly in two stories set in the American Wild West, in which the New World, far from being a fresh start, constitutes only a different setting for the dramas of the Old World – and Carter's own favourite childhood reading – to be played out. 'John Ford's *'Tis Pity She's a Whore*' expresses this through clever linguistic play, where the Jacobean dramatist elides into the American filmmaker of the same name. In a narrative which mingles quotations from Ford's actual play of incestual tragedy with a script for an imaginary Western, both telling the same story in different forms, Carter demonstrates that there's nothing new under the sun; an opinion she reworks in a slightly different way in 'Gun for the Devil', in which a Faustian drama is played out in a Mexican border town.

However, it would be easy, but false, to convey the impression that stories such as this are imbued with an aura of resignation, even of defeatism, on Carter's part. On the contrary, novels such as *Wise Children* and the narratives collected in *American Ghosts* attest to the vitality, variety and indestructibility of story which, while on one level may only be manufactured illusion, nevertheless provides a way to negotiate with the real conditions of living.

Notes

1. Catherine Belsey, *Critical Practice* (London: Routledge, 1980), p. 75.
2. John Haffenden, 'Magical Mannerist', *The Literary Review* (November 1984), pp. 34–8 (p. 37).
3. Olga Kenyon, *The Writer's Imagination* (University of Bradford Print Unit, 1992), pp. 23–33 (p. 28).
4. Denis Porter, 'Soap Time: Thoughts on a Commodity Art Form', quoted in Tania Modleski, *Loving with a Vengeance: Mass-Produced Fantasies for Women* (London: Methuen, 1982), p. 90.
5. Angela Carter, *Wise Children* (London: Vintage, 1992). All further references in the text are from this edition.
6. In Peter Kemp, 'Magical History Tour', *The Sunday Times* (9 June 1991), Carter traced the genesis of both Fevvers and Dora Chance to the experience she gained in writing radio plays, which 'gave her "confidence in actually inventing people by what they say"'.
7. Kate Webb, 'Seriously Funny: *Wise Children*', in Lorna Sage (ed.), *Flesh*

and the Mirror: Essays on the Art of Angela Carter (London: Virago Press, 1994), pp. 279–307 (p. 295).

8. Laurence Sterne, *The Life and Opinions of Tristram Shandy* [1760–7] (Harmondsworth: Penguin, 1985), p. 41.

9. Linda Hutcheon, *Narcissistic Narrative: The Metafictional Paradox* (London: Methuen, 1984), p. 37.

10. Ann Snitow, 'Wild Thing: Conversation with a Necromancer', *Village Voice Literary Supplement* 75/4 (June 1989), pp. 14–17 (p. 14).

11. Hélène Cixous and Catherine Clément, 'The Guilty One', in *The Newly Born Woman*, trans. Betsy Wing (Manchester University Press, 1987), pp. 3–57 (p. 8).

12. Mary Russo, *The Female Grotesque: Risk, Excess and Modernity* (London: Routledge, 1994), p. 9.

13. ibid., p. 166.

14. Mary Ann Doane, 'Film and the Masquerade: Theorizing the Female Spectator', in <u>*Femmes Fatales*</u>: *Feminism, Film Theory, Psychoanalysis* (London: Routledge, 1992), pp. 17–32 (pp. 25–6).

15. ibid., p. 16.

16. Mary Ann Doane, 'Masquerade Reconsidered: Further Thoughts on the Female Spectator', in <u>*Femmes Fatales*</u>, pp. 33–43 (p. 34).

17. ibid., p. 33.

18. Lorna Sage, 'Angela Carter', in Malcom Bradbury and Judy Cooke (eds), *New Writing* (London: Minerva Press, 1992), pp. 185–93 (p. 187).

19. ibid., p. 186.

20. In Susannah Clapp, 'On Madness, Men and Fairy-Tales', *The Independent on Sunday* (9 June 1991), pp. 26–7, Clapp quotes Carter as saying that 'In the end she couldn't get them all in: there's no *Two Noble Kinsmen*, and . . . no *Titus Andronicus*' (p. 27).

21. Terence Hawkes, 'Bardbiz', in *Meaning By Shakespeare* (London: Routledge, 1992), pp. 141–53 (p. 149).

22. ibid., p. 143.

23. Carter clearly had the 1935 film of *A Midsummer Night's Dream*, directed by Erich von Stroheim, in mind when she wrote this book.

24. Andrew Ross, *No Respect: Intellectuals and Popular Culture* (London: Routledge, 1989), p. 139.

25. Susan Sontag, 'Notes on "Camp"' in *Against Interpretation* (New York: Dell Publishing, 1966), pp. 275–92 (p. 287).

26. Webb, p. 279.

27. Ross, p. 151.

28. See Lorna Sage, *Angela Carter* (Plymouth: Northcote House, 1994), p. 57.

29. Webb, p. 289.

30. Clapp, p. 26.

31. Angela Carter, *American Ghosts and Old World Wonders* (London: Chatto & Windus, 1993). All further references in the text are from this edition.

EPILOGUE

It is no accident that Angela Carter's most memorable characters are all, in one way or another, performance artists, for they echo their author's own bravura performance; poised perfectly, as well as perilously, 'on the edge' of propriety, convention and classification. But while it is easy to conceptualise marginalisation in terms of estrangement, solitude and silence, I hope that this study has demonstrated that for Carter it was nothing of the sort. Envisaged through her writing, the margins are transformed into a place of life, colour and movement, a discursive area where the writer can engage with a multiplicity of theories, ideas and fantastic notions, and feel free to mix them into often startling combinations.

Nevertheless, Carter was not blind to marginalisation's negative aspects; something which is conveyed particularly clearly in much of the fiction she wrote at the beginning of her career, where countercultural subversiveness merges almost imperceptibly into madness, death and moral exhaustion. In early novels such as *Shadow Dance* and *Several Perceptions*, the beautiful, decadent figure of the dandy demonstrates Carter's awareness of the risks she runs constructing herself as marginal subject, who must not only resist the pull towards the centre and reintegration with the mainstream, but also the risky drive to push still further outwards, until one has passed entirely beyond the boundaries of communication and meaningfulness. Embodiments of this contradictory balancing trick, Honeybuzzard retreats into mayhem and madness, while Kay Kyte brings redemption and reconciliation to his 'floating world' of misfits.

In her writings of the seventies, however, Carter reacts against an increasingly reactionary culture by moving towards a more overt anatomisation of the marginal state: a cultivation of the 'stranger's eye' which it is impossible not to read as also being linked to her own experience of being a foreigner in Japan. The central characters of such novels as *The Infernal Desire Machines of Doctor Hoffman* and *The Passion of New Eve* are much more conscious of the boundary line which divides the world of fiction from that of fact, and invention from reality, thus echoing their author's movement towards the creation of self-conscious fiction which is well aware of its own status as literary construction. In this decade, too, the twin impulses which inspired much of Carter's writing – the serious intention to challenge her audience's preconceptions linked with the mischievous desire to shock – find their apotheosis in *The Sadeian Woman*, which, while a sincere examination of power relations between the sexes, cannot help but also flaunt its provocative engagement with the pornographic text.

Outrageous as Carter's work of this period tends to be, however, the publication of *The Bloody Chamber* in 1979 signals the emergence of a new preoccupation on her part with community and connectedness. While these stories are absolutely characteristic of Carter's work in the way they strenuously work to subvert the illusory comforts offered by the traditional fairytale form, they nevertheless also assert the importance of family structures and relationships between the sexes based on a sincere exchange of affection. These are themes which assume an increasingly foregrounded role in Carter's subsequent writing where, in novels such as *Nights at the Circus* and *Wise Children*, Fevvers and the Chance sisters emphasise that the dangers involved in the commitment of self to others are as nothing compared to the isolation experienced by the subject who lives only in and for the self. Although Carter was previously fascinated with this solipsistic nightmare, represented most overtly by the glorious monstrosity of such figures as the Count and Tristessa, *Nights at the Circus* stands as a definitive break with all they represent, in its assertion that forging links with others is a key element in establishing one's existence as independent subject.

To argue that Carter ended up upholding the benefits of community does not compromise her commitment to marginality, for instead of moving from the outside into the centre, her fictional families and lovers travel in the opposite direction. Moving instead from the inside out, they traverse and delineate the societal and discursive margins, and make of illegitimacy a virtue to be shared. Communities such as this, built out of endlessly elaborated anecdotes and generous affection, shore their members up against the ever present threat of death, with which each person's narrative must inevitably end. However, if their story has become interwoven with those of other lives, it will survive for as long as there are people, like Angela Carter herself, who love to tell tales.

SELECT BIBLIOGRAPHY

Ackroyd, Peter, 'Passion Fruit', *The Spectator* (26 March 1977), pp. 23–4

Allison, Dorothy, 'Love Among the Ruins', *Village Voice Literary Supplement* 75 (June 1989), p. 15

Anwell, Maggie, 'Lolita Meets the Werewolf: *The Company of Wolves*', in Lorraine Gamman and Margaret Marshment (eds), *The Female Gaze: Women as Viewers of Popular Culture* (London: The Women's Press, 1988), pp. 76–85

Armitt, Lucie, *Theorising the Fantastic* (London: Arnold, 1996)

Armitt, Lucie, 'The Fragile Frames of *The Bloody Chamber*', unpublished manuscript, forthcoming in Treva Broughton and Joe Bristow (eds), *The Infernal Desires of Angela Carter* (London: Longman, 1997)

Bakhtin, Mikhail, *Rabelais and His World*, trans. Hélène Iswolsky (Bloomington: Indiana University Press, 1984)

Bakhtin, Mikhail, *Speech Genres and Other Late Essays*, trans. Vern W. McGee (Austin: University of Texas Press, 1986)

Barker, Paul, 'The Return of the Magic Story-Teller', *The Independent on Sunday* (8 January 1995), pp. 14, 16

Barthes, Roland, *Writing Degree Zero*, trans. Annette Lavers and Colin Smith (New York: Hill and Wang, 1968)

Barthes, Roland, *Empire of Signs*, trans. Richard Howard (London: Jonathan Cape, 1983)

Barthes, Roland, *Mythologies*, trans. Annette Lavers (London: Vintage Books, 1993)

Baudrillard, Jean, *Simulations*, trans. Paul Foss, Paul Patton and Philip Beitchman (New York: Semiotext(e), 1983)

Baudrillard, Jean, *America*, trans. Chris Turner (London: Verso, 1988)

Bedford, Les, 'Angela Carter: An Interview' (Sheffield: Sheffield University Television, February 1977)

Benjamin, Walter, *Charles Baudelaire: A Lyric Poet in the Era of High Capitalism*, trans. Harry Zohn (London: Verso, 1983)

Booker, Christopher, *The Neophiliacs: A Study of the Revolution in English Life in the Fifties and Sixties* (London: Collins, 1969)

Boston, Richard, 'Logic in a Schizophrenic's World', *New York Times Book Review* (2 March 1969), p. 42

Bradbury, Malcom and Judy Cooke (eds), *New Writing* (London: Minerva Press, 1992)

Britton, Andrew, 'For Interpretation: Notes Against Camp', in *Gay Left*, issue details unavailable

Butler, Judith, *Bodies That Matter: On the Discursive Limits of "Sex"* (London: Routledge, 1993)

Cagney Watts, Helen, 'Angela Carter: An Interview', *Bête Noir* 8 (August 1985), pp. 161–76

Carter, Angela, *Shadow Dance* [1966] (London: Virago Press, 1994)

Carter, Angela, *The Magic Toyshop* [1967] (London: Virago Press, 1981)

Carter, Angela, *Several Perceptions* [1968] (London: Virago Press, 1995)

Carter, Angela, *Heroes and Villains* [1969] (Harmondsworth: Penguin, 1981)

Carter, Angela, *Love* [1971] (London: Picador, 1988) [rev. edn]

Carter, Angela, *Fireworks* (London: Virago Press, 1974) [rev. edn.]

Carter, Angela, *The Infernal Desire Machines of Doctor Hoffman* [1972] (Harmondsworth: Penguin, 1982)

Carter, Angela, *The Passion of New Eve* (London: Virago Press, 1977)

Carter, Angela, *The Sadeian Woman: An Exercise in Cultural History* (London: Virago Press, 1979)

Carter, Angela, *The Bloody Chamber* [1979] (Harmondsworth: Penguin, 1981)

Carter, Angela, *Nothing Sacred: Selected Writings* (London: Virago Press, 1982)

Carter, Angela, *Nights at the Circus* (London: Vintage, 1984)

Carter, Angela, *Black Venus* (London: Chatto & Windus, 1985)

Carter, Angela, *Come Unto These Yellow Sands: Four Radio Plays by Angela Carter* (Newcastle upon Tyne: Bloodaxe Books, 1985)

Carter, Angela (ed.), *The Virago Book of Fairy Tales* (London: Virago Press, 1991)

Carter, Angela (ed), *The Second Virago Book of Fairy Tales* (London: Virago Press, 1992)

Carter, Angela, *Wise Children* (London: Vintage, 1992)

Carter, Angela, *American Ghosts and Old World Wonders* (London: Chatto & Windus, 1993)

Carter, Angela, *Burning Your Boats: Collected Short Stories* (London: Chatto & Windus, 1995)

Carter, Angela, *The Curious Room: Collected Dramatic Works* (London: Chatto & Windus, 1996)

Carter, Angela, 'My Maugham Award', *Author* (Winter 1970), pp. 173–5

Carter, Angela, 'Fin de Siecle', *New Society* (17 August 1972), pp. 354–5

Carter, Angela, Letter to Neil Forsyth, 26 August 1974, *The European English Messenger* V/1 (Spring 1996), pp. 11–13

Carter, Angela, 'The Power of Porn', *The Observer* (10 April 1977), p. 9

Carter, Angela, 'Masochism for the Masses', *New Statesman* (3 June 1983), pp. 8–10

Carter, Angela, 'Notes from the Front Line', in Michelene Wandor (ed), *On Gender and Writing* (London: Pandora Press, 1983), pp. 69–77

Carter, Angela, 'Sugar Daddy', in Ursula Owen (ed), *Fathers: Reflections by Daughters* (London: Virago Press, 1983), pp.20–30

Carter, Angela, 'Truly, It Felt Like Year One', in Sara Maitland (ed), *Very Heaven: Looking Back at the 1960s* (London: Virago Press, 1988), pp. 209–16

Cixous, Hélène, 'The Laugh of the Medusa', trans. Keith and Paula Cohen, *Signs* 1 (Summer 1976), pp. 875–93

Cixous, Hélène and Catherine Clément, *The Newly Born Woman*, trans. Betsy Wing (Manchester: Manchester University Press, 1987)

Clapp, Susannah, 'On Madness, Men and Fairy-Tales', *The Independent on Sunday* (9 June 1991), pp. 26–7

Clark, Robert, 'Angela Carter's Desire Machine', *Women's Studies* 14 (1987), pp. 147–61

Cronan Rose, Ellen, 'Through the Looking Glass: When Women Tell Fairy Tales', in Elizabeth Abel, Marianne Hirsch and Elizabeth Langland (eds), *The Voyage In: Fictions of Female Development* (University Press of New England, 1983), pp. 209–27

Doane, Mary Ann, <u>*Femmes Fatales*</u>: *Feminism, Film Theory, Psychoanalysis* (London: Routledge, 1992)

Duncker, Patricia, 'Re-Imagining the Fairy Tales: Angela Carter's Bloody Chambers', *Literature and History* X/1 (Spring 1984), pp. 3–14

Dworkin, Andrea, *Pornography: Men Possessing Women* (London: The Women's Press, 1981)

Evans, Kim (producer), *Omnibus: Angela Carter's Curious Room*, BBC1 (15 September 1992)

Felski, Rita, *Beyond Feminist Aesthetics: Feminist Literature and Social Change* (Cambridge, Mass.: Harvard University Press, 1989)

Foucault, Michel, 'What is Enlightenment?', in Paul Rabinow (ed), *The Foucault Reader* (Harmondsworth: Penguin, 1984), pp. 32–50

Gąsiorek, Andrzej, *Post-War British Fiction: Realism and After* (London: Edward Arnold, 1995)

Gerrard, Nicci, 'Angela Carter is Now More Popular than Virginia Woolf . . .', *The Observer Life* (9 July 1995), pp. 20, 22–3)

Gilbert, Harriet, 'Gothic Novelty', *The Guardian* (13 September 1994), p. 14

Gunew, Sneja, 'Framing Marginality: Distinguishing the Textual Politics of the Marginal Voice', *Southern Review* 18 (July 1985), pp. 142–56

Haffenden, John, 'Magical Mannerist', *The Literary Review* (November 1984), pp. 34–8

Hamilton, Alex, 'Sade and Prejudice', *The Guardian* (30 March 1979), p. 15

Harron, Mary, '"I'm a Socialist, Damn It! How Can You Expect Me to be

Interested in Fairies?"', *The Guardian* (25 September 1984), p. 10

Hay, George, 'Marionettes with Metaphysics', *Foundation: The Review of Science Fiction*, vol. 3 (1973), pp. 69–71

Hutcheon, Linda, *Narcissistic Narrative: The Metafictional Paradox* (London: Methuen, 1984)

Hutcheon, Linda, *A Poetics of Postmodernism: History, Theory, Fiction* (London: Routledge, 1988)

Jordan, Elaine, 'The Dangers of Angela Carter', in Isobel Armstrong (ed), *New Feminist Discourses: Critical Essays on Theories and Texts* (London: Routledge, 1992), pp. 119–32

Kappeler, Susanne, *The Pornography of Representation* (Cambridge: Polity Press, 1986)

Kemp, Peter, 'Magical History Tour', *The Sunday Times* (9 June 1991)

Kenyon, Olga, *The Writer's Imagination* (University of Bradford Print Unit, 1992)

Lauretis, Teresa de, *Technologies of Gender: Essays on Theory, Film and Fiction* (London: Macmillan, 1989)

Makinen, Merja, 'Angela Carter's *The Bloody Chamber* and the Decolonization of Feminine Sexuality', *Feminist Review* 42 (Autumn 1992), pp. 2–15

McEwan, Ian, 'Sweet Smell of Excess', *The Sunday Times Magazine* (9 September 1984), pp. 430–4

Melly, George, *Revolt Into Style: The Pop Arts in the 50s and 60s* (Oxford: Oxford University Press, 1989)

Palmer, Paulina, 'From Coded Mannequin to Bird Woman: Angela Carter's Magic Flight', in Sue Roe (ed), *Women Reading Women's Writing* (Brighton: Harvester Press, 1987), pp. 179–205

Paterson, Moira, 'Flights of Fancy in Balham', *The Observer Magazine* (11 November 1986), pp. 42–5

Punter, David, *The Literature of Terror: A History of Gothic Fictions from 1765 to the Present Day* (London: Longman, 1980)

Punter, David, *The Hidden Script: Writing and the Unconscious* (London: Routledge, 1985)

Rosinsky, Natalie M., *Feminist Futures: Contemporary Women's Speculative Fiction* (Ann Arbor: UMI Research Press, 1984)

Ross, Andrew, *No Respect: Intellectuals and Popular Culture* (London: Routledge, 1989)

Russo, Mary, *The Female Grotesque: Risk, Excess and Modernity* (London: Routledge, 1994)

Sage, Lorna, 'The Savage Sideshow: A Profile of Angela Carter', *New Review* 4/39–40 (July 1977), pp. 51–7

Sage, Lorna, *Women in the House of Fiction: Post-War Women Novelists* (London: Macmillan, 1992)

Sage, Lorna, 'Death of the Author', *Granta* 41 (1992), pp. 235–54

Sage, Lorna, *Angela Carter* (Plymouth: Northcote House, 1994)

Sage, Lorna (ed), *Flesh and the Mirror: Essays on the Art of Angela Carter* (London: Virago Press, 1994)

Smith, Anne, 'Myths and the Erotic', *Women's Review* 1 (November 1985), pp. 28–9

Snitow, Ann, 'Wild Thing: Conversation with a Necromancer', *Village Voice Literary Supplement* 75/4 (June 1989), pp. 14–17

Sontag, Susan, *Against Interpretation* (New York: Dell Publishing, 1966)

Warner, Marina, *Monuments and Maidens: The Allegory of the Female Form* [1985] (London: Vintage, 1996)

Warner, Marina, *From the Beast to the Blonde: On Fairytales and Their Tellers* (London: Chatto & Windus, 1994)

Waugh, Patricia, *Metafiction: The Theory and Practice of Self-Conscious Fiction* (London: Methuen, 1984)

Waugh, Patricia, *Harvest of the Sixties: English Literature and Its Background 1960–1990* (Oxford: Oxford University Press, 1995)

Wilson, Elizabeth, *Adorned in Dreams: Fashion and Modernity* (London: Virago Press, 1985)

Wisker, Gina, 'Weaving Our Own Web: Demythologising/Remythologising and Magic in the Work of Contemporary Women Writers', in Gina Wisker (ed), *It's My Party: Reading Twentieth-Century Women's Writing* (London: Pluto Press, 1994), pp. 104–28

Wood, James, 'Bewitchment', *London Review of Books* (8 December, 1984), pp. 20–1

INDEX

197